HOMESICK

HOMESICK

a memoir of family, food, and finding hope

Jenny Lauren

ATRIA BOOKS

NEW YORK · LONDON · TORONTO · SYDNEY

ATRIA BOOKS

1230 Avenue of the Americas
New York, NY 10020

ATRIA BOOKS is a trademark of Simon & Schuster, Inc.

For information regarding special discounts for bulk purchases,
please contact Simon & Schuster Special Sales at 1-800-456-6798
or business@simonandschuster.com

Library of Congress Cataloging-in-Publication Data
Lauren, Jenny.
    Homesick : a memoir of family, food, and finding hope /
Jenny Lauren.—1st Atria Books hardcover ed.
        p.   cm.
    1. Lauren, Jenny—Health.   2. Eating disorders—Patients—
Biography.   I. Title.
RC552.E18L385   2004
616.85'26'0092—dc22   2003063920
[B]

ISBN: 0-7434-5698-X

First Atria Books hardcover edition April 2004

10 9 8 7 6 5 4 3 2 1

For
Mom, Dad, Brad, and Greg

PART ONE

1. Twitch

This twitch is driving me crazy. It's 1997, I am twenty-four years old, and for a year I have been in physical discomfort. That is 365 days with my butt twitching and an inability to contract my gluteus maximus muscles. Three hundred and sixty-five days with bugs up my ass, 365 days of wanting to jump out the window, 365 days watching the entire lower half of my body turn into jelly and atrophy. This is a sick joke.

Now, understand, it is with these muscles that women often feel sexy. The tight squeeze, the swaying of hip to hip, the alignment of the pelvis and the flattened stomach are what gives a woman so much strength to conquer the day. Losing this sensation is basically losing my connection to any kind of sensuality. So it doesn't surprise me that the depression I've often suffered from has become stronger and more unbearable this past year. Of course, this darkness, *my old and dear friend,* has led to the recurrence of my bulimic symptoms and to the deterioration of my emotional self.

You might say, especially if you are a psychiatrist, that it's my emotional fears, depression, feelings about my sexuality, past disappointments, and all that crap that have caused my building to collapse. I will not deny this. My coping skills are far worse than they were, but after a year (and, yes, I am as bored with this as my world-famous neurologist suggested I ought to be), I am at my wit's end. I'm trying so hard not to lose my mind, but I'm very aware that my power to intellectualize and make any sense of this is descending rapidly.

3

I've tried to become as spiritual as possible; I've always believed in the mystical and magical journey through life, but after such pain, I need a *tangible* answer. I used to be able to heal myself from my depression. I learned how to use my body to ward it off, with vigorous runs, enlightened yoga, and techno-electric-charged race walks. Only, now I can't do any of that. And without that, my mind is not getting enough juice, and my creative soul, the one that carries the nervous depression and adrenaline out of me, is utterly blocked.

It was the same when I painted. I want to paint again, but that, too, is locked within my ailing body. I need to dance while I move the paintbrush, or simply feel the energy flowing throughout my body onto the canvas. I studied ballet for thirteen years. The mirrors, the leotards, all of it had an impact on my self-esteem. I had to stop in my last year of high school. I thought I'd never find anything as fulfilling. When I began to paint I was relieved. I was able to merge these two passions. Music or silence set the backdrop as I moved my body to the rhythm of my strokes, to the colors I saw and heard, and to the composition I was creating. I was using a freestyle improvisation. My gestures, my actions, and my inspiration came most deeply from my pelvis, deeply from my core. But now thinking about painting depresses me because I no longer have the energy to get downtown to my studio, let alone paint. Some osteopath actually said that I had no *chi*.

It's these painful twitches, though . . . they're absolutely maddening—and in the most demoralizing place. Of course the twitches are not in my eye, not in my shoulder, *but in my asshole*. And they just keep on pulsing and breathing constantly. It's quite the symphony, with a wonderful crescendo. Great large and climactic twitches fizzle into small fluttering twitches that keep me gripping my thighs for hours. It's like there is a huge monster grabbing me between my legs. I've been telling the doctors that I think this actually all began in my stomach, that it's gotta be a digestive problem. After I eat, even the tiniest of meals, a sucking candy or a rice cake, for God's sake, my stomach begins to fill up with air. I begin to choke and the food just doesn't want to go down. It stays lodged in my chest and flows back up into my throat.

Then, every sensation, especially an overwhelming sense of muscle weakness, becomes pronounced.

Ugh, and taking a shit (vulgar no matter how you put it) is like giving birth, with the baby's head getting stuck for hours. I even have to stand and massage my stomach as I go, just to make things move. But then the sensation is always there, singing its lullaby or rock music all freakin' day long. Me and my twitch.

I can't exercise at all, can't even walk comfortably. The other day I taped myself up to see if it would help me run. I thought it might make my buttocks feel stronger and help me forget the twitch a little if my cheeks were pushed tighter together. I wrapped a large piece of masking tape around my cheeks as if it were a belt that kept them squeezed together, and I ran. God, how I need to sweat and pant. But I had to keep stopping to redo the tape because it wouldn't stay stuck to my sweats. Then I just gave up because it also made my hamstrings burn and ache. I had to limp from the reservoir in Central Park to Fifth Avenue to hail a cab. I was afraid I was going to have to ask my doorman to carry me upstairs to my apartment.

All year I've begged my internist, Dr. W (for Dr. Worthless), to make this stop, to find the cause. It has taken him months to take me seriously. When I first went to see him last summer, he reasoned that I was too young to be put through a series of medical tests, and he attributed my discomfort to stress. So I carried on with my life, trying to move through the days like a machine. I painted at my studio, worked at a nonprofit art organization, and scouted for beautiful/eccentric homes for a well-known design magazine. Okay, maybe it'll go away, maybe it's nerves, I thought.

The problem, though, was that I was depressed and tired all the time, and then the physical symptoms became worse. It was getting harder and harder to leave the house. I would wake up, attempt to go to the bathroom, and then the twitch would just take over. Forget the studio. Forget work. Forget seeing friends. Forget everything.

I would panic most mornings and rush up to 87th Street and Park and sit and wait in Dr. W's office, sometimes for hours, to see him. As I sat there holding my breath and clenching my legs together to stop the twitch, I'd rummage through the pile of magazines, flipping through all the fashion ads. *Oh, there's Uncle Ralph with his two dogs in a Purple Label ad. Whadda ya know, there he is again. Not his face but a Ralph Lauren fragrance ad with a young beautiful couple wrapped in velvet and in love. The good life, huh? . . . things to aspire to.* Reminding me of everything I hated, everything I loved, everything I wished I could be . . . *but that was then. Look at me now.* By the time Dr. W called me into his office, I had finished skimming the magazines from the late eighties, with Paulina and Christie Brinkley splashed all over them, and gotten through the nineties, with enough of Crawford, Turlington, and the fashion world up my nose.

Dr. W aggravates the living shit out of me. He listens, takes notes, and then speaks to me in his calm, methodical, and patronizing style. He has been my parents' internist forever, and they have great confidence in him. Six years earlier, when my father suffered a subarachnoid hemorrhage and was lying in bed in severe pain during recovery, it was Dr. W who found the phlebitis in his lung and leg that could have killed him. My dad was rushed into surgery on Thanksgiving Day as I shoved hospital cafeteria turkey and cranberry sauce into my mouth. I know I owe him a lot for saving my dad's life, but my confidence in him helping *me* is fading. He has never been able to provide relief. Everything is always fine; he says my blood is good and I don't have hemorrhoids. He suggested I watch my diet, give up acidic and gassy sugar-free foods, and come back if I didn't feel better. *How come he can't make it stop? He's a doctor for goodness' sake!*

After six months of this, Dr. W starts to shift his position ever so slightly. He gives me a sigmoidoscopy, a test where they shove a scope up the lower part of the colon to take a picture of what's going on inside and they look for tumors or obstructions. It shows nothing, so he sends me to other gastroenterologists. Dr. D is a specialist who is known for a unique *device* he uses. It can measure the fluttering and spasms of my rectum. I've now visited him and his device five times. I have a ritual: I wait on the corner of Central Park West drinking coffee and watching the gorgeous guys go Rollerblading into the park. When the spasms get really intense, I rush to his office so he can stick this thing in my butt and see what I'm talking about. Each time he has said, "Well, they certainly exist, but I'm not sure why."

Dr. W finally gives me an esophagoscopy, which shows that I have an irritated esophagus and stomach lining (they call it a hiatal hernia), a symptom common to bulimics. But that only explains some of my discomfort, like the choking sensation and the acid reflux, and not the twitch or the overall muscle malaise. W's diagnosis doesn't stop me from continuing to vomit a few times a week even now. Sometimes I convince myself that purging will stop the twitching. *As if I could only just vomit up the alien between my legs everything would be fine.* Then, two months ago, he gave me two colonoscopies (these evaluate the entire colon) as well as a barium series (X-rays taken after digesting radioactive dye). *Took him long enough.* The barium series showed that I have a dilated small intestine, which is evidence that something else must be going on. But Dr. W can't figure out what it's from. All year he prescribed various medications . . . Propulsid, Levbid, Prilosec . . . so many meds I can't keep track, but they've warped my body even more. Now I have glycerin suppositories to stick up my ass to calm the spasms, and I use them frequently, praying they'll do something, but they don't. Even with these medications, I can feel the limpness in the lower half of my body, my tummy drooping, my thighs turning to mush. I can barely stand up. *How can this not be some major disease?*

I have questioned everything. Is this PMS, hormonal? I went to see an endocrinologist, who said that some of my fatigue and symptoms might be because I have low estrogen levels. She suggested I go on hormone-replacement pills. *No way.* I didn't believe this was the problem. Anybody with a continuous twitch in the ass would get exhausted. That in itself probably caused these severely depressed hormones. Then my kinesiologist said my adrenal glands were *definitely shot* from all the pain. So last year I tried to address the hormone issue and took progesterone to bring on my period, but I got even more whacked. I just sat in the studio for hours staring at my blank canvases.

Two months ago I went to an acupuncturist, who also suggested that my sensations might be because I never get my period. Needles were placed all over my body. I tried to do what he suggested, to focus my energy on my pelvis "smiling." I was so tense that I couldn't even enjoy this narcissistic candlelit ritual. It didn't work. I loved him, though. I mean, at least he heard me. He thought it was my spleen or liver and had me taking about twenty-four herbs a day for a month. Trust me, any bit of Jenny that was left has been washed away with those strange, crazy herbs. Since then, my eyes and the lower part of my cranium have been twitching too, and I feel spacey all the time.

My other daily ritual is hauling myself up to Barnes & Noble to read up on my symptoms. I've read about cancer, connective tissue disease, the candida yeast syndrome. I've checked for parasites and have had five tests for Lyme disease. At one point I even believed the mercury of my fillings could have been the cause. As I sit in the bookstore I wonder who else has come in that day to solve their own puzzle, who else is forced to diagnose themselves, who else is as desperate as I am for relief.

Eastern, western medicine . . . who the hell knows anymore. I've been to chiropractors, kinesiologists, massage therapists, along with doctors with Harvard MDs on the wall . . . those arrogant fucks who just take notes and stare at me like I'm nuts. Meanwhile, I keep binge-ing on chocolate. I'm like the person with lung cancer who keeps on smoking.

2. Modeling

I always wanted to be a star. The problem is, I wanted to be recognized for everything I ever did: the way I looked, my paintings, my dancing, my outfits, my humor, my sensitivity. It was a real pain in the ass to have to carry that load. Especially with the demons that made me crawl into my bed every fifth or sixth day of the week and close the blinds to the world.

My father has been head of Men's Design at Polo Ralph Lauren since 1973. He is also Ralph's older brother. I remember when I first modeled for Uncle Ralph, in this tiny showroom crowded with chairs surrounding a narrow runway aisle. It was an intimate gathering for the first little girls' fashion line. There were about forty people there, all watching, staring, and taking notes. I was seven years old, pouty and seductive. I came out from behind the mock dressing room, a small office where about six of us girls were being dressed in outfits hanging from a rack. I wore gray flannel Bermudas, a purple Shetland sweater, with the beautiful white lace collar of a blouse lighting up my face, and I walked with my hands in my pockets feeling really natural. They had swept part of my long black hair up softly with a barrette, so I would resemble Diane Lane as the young American girl living in Paris in *A Little Romance,* the *perfect* little girl. Sweet and feminine but aloof, innocent but cultured, irresistible but unapproachable, and very, very dramatic.

It was around then that my father told me that Uncle Ralph thought I was the most beautiful creature he'd ever laid eyes on. I cannot blame anyone for my own destruction, but those words were intoxicating. I craved the admiration; it felt like a prize. Now sometimes I mourn for that time, when the concept of beauty was less complicated, when I didn't have to work so hard for it. Later, as my weight went up through the years, I'd be embarrassed to see my uncle, to let him down, as if there were shame in the fact that I was no longer that "beautiful little creature" he once gazed at in awe. It was hard enough seeing my own father's look of approval and judgment.

In my senior year at college, I used to meet my parents for Sunday dinner at our favorite Italian place on Lexington Avenue. All day I'd look forward to that meal because it was the only time I felt comfortable eating. It was as if being with my parents at dinner gave me permission to enjoy a good solid meal. By the time I arrived I would be starving and cranky after working out all day. My father would immediately comment on how beautiful I was, how chiseled my face looked, or how great my jacket fit me, and I would grit my teeth. I remained silent as my father took in the rest of the room and nodded hellos to the families we knew. My mother would order her white wine immediately. I'd sit there wondering why I had even bothered joining them. *Beautiful? Dad, you think I look beautiful? Chiseled? Do you know how hard I need to work for this? Do you really know how hard?* I felt the grief and loneliness from the previous week welling up and realized that it was about to start all over again the following morning. The whole thing: getting my runs in every cold fucking morning in Central Park, then fitting in the calisthenics before I showered and left to go all the way uptown to 116th Street and Broadway for classes. Then missing my first class. Then roaming the college cafeteria looking for something without oil to eat. Then being hungry the whole rest of the day while I sat through my other classes. Then rushing to a power yoga class down on 18th Street, where I felt like I would pass out during a sun salutation. Then arriving home late and having to research and write a whole paper that I had, of course, left for the last minute. And then the vomiting. *You think I look beautiful, Dad? Great. Thanks. But for what, Dad? What really is it all for? So I can still live alone in my head? Alone with my neurosis? My fear? I'm so fucking tired, Daddy. So tired.*

Then, after my mother and I had finished our chopped salads without any dressing and my father had polished off his baked clams, we would all relax a little until our entrée was served. My mother filled me in about my brothers, my grandmother. I finally had some nutrients going to my brain, and my mother had become more chatty as she continued on to her second glass of white wine. My father would say how cozy and happy he was to have his two girls with him. Hearing him say that always made me cry. I can't count how many times I cried in front of those Italian waiters, the same ones who made me smile when I really was a little girl, when they sang "Happy Birthday" to me every year in their heavy Italian accents. By the time my mother and I had completed our dry filet of sole and my father was almost done sucking the marrow from his osso buco, I was on a roll, babbling and finding comfort in their being there to listen. And then I would let it all come out, all my insecurities, my loneliness, how tired I was, how the professor I was in love with wasn't giving me any attention, how I didn't know what the hell I was going to do with my life. I told them that most of my friends were moving to Los Angeles to try the acting thing. Not just acting for acting's sake, but to become movie stars. Part of me clearly understood that drive. *What exactly did we learn in college?* With all the time I spent working out to stay looking fit and pretty, I sometimes just didn't see the point if I wasn't going to use it. I asked my parents if they thought I ought to try acting. Or modeling again. I still recall the relief I felt when my father said in response, "You can be a beautiful painter, you know, or a beautiful writer. You don't have to be a model or an actress to feel worthy. More power to you for being beautiful, smart, and talented." And for a moment or two I really did feel better as he acknowledged my painting and my mind. But then I remembered the huge smile that came to his face when he watched me walk into the restaurant and told me how beautiful and *chiseled* I looked.

I made my second trip down the fashion runway in a purple velvet dress with a gold satin braided cord tied around my waist, wearing tiny ballet slippers and my hair hanging loose. It was exciting having all those faces smiling at me. The hushes. The whispers of "Look, there's Jerry's daughter, isn't she precious." I pretended not to notice, staying focused, doing the job, trying to fit the image of the clothes. Although I was shy, it wasn't hard for me to prance down that aisle. I had seen the older models do it before. I knew how to saunter, turn, and then flash my eyes and my smile at the audience. But in my gut, I felt uncomfortable with people staring at me. *What do they see? Why are they making such a big deal about me?*

I was at war with the focus on my looks. As a young child I think I knew that physical beauty was fleeting. Although I was excited by people telling me that I was striking or pretty or had the most beautiful blue eyes, I also felt uneasy. When I looked in the mirror, anxiety would overtake me. I just couldn't keep it up. I was going to lose it. The turning of heads and the constant attention for my looks seemed to outweigh anything else I was truly about. I started to feel uncomfortable and more self-conscious. *What are you looking at? Jesus . . . leave me alone.* I took no credit for having a pretty face or light blue eyes. It was all from my parents' DNA and a mere genetic roll of the dice. I hadn't earned the compliments. But I developed a love/hate relationship with all the intrigue. I wanted to be admired. I needed validation. After all, *maybe I was special.* Laura Ashley called my mother later that year and asked if I could do some modeling for them. Before the Ralph Lauren little girls' line came out, my mother had taken me to Laura Ashley to find dresses. I'd stare up at the huge photos in their store of girls dressed in white, running in fields with flowers or standing by the water in navy blue sailor outfits. *Maybe I could be up there.* I wanted to do it. My mother agreed.

It seemed even more natural to stare at a camera and pose. But I became upset when they dressed me in sweet "babyish" outfits. The other girl they used, four years older than I, wore a bikini. I already knew that showing flesh was sexy. And at seven years old, I wanted to be sexy. Still, I did the job, and I'll always be pleased to have those pictures. They capture an innocence I don't really remember: one of me real playful in a blue-and-white dress and long braids, holding the Madame Alexander doll Jo from *Little Women;* and another with me all regal in the most exquisite white-lace high-collared dress, standing beside my then idol, Clotilde, the famous Ralph Lauren model. Many times I've wondered who that little girl was . . . and where she has gone.

Then there were the times we let the photographer who lived in my building take photos of me roller-skating in Central Park, and in my home wearing only a black leotard, eating peaches. The photographer was a gregarious guy who seemed very taken with my looks. He oohed and aahed at every face I made. My mother let me go up to his apartment alone once, so he could take photos of just my hands for his portfolio. He said I was elegant, a photographer's dream. I really didn't mind him taking all those photos. *It was for the sake of his art and his career.* I look at those pictures now, and I can't believe how erotic they are; it's frightening to me. Little Lolita. Sometimes I wonder if the guy was a pervert, but he never once made me feel awkward. Anyhow, since my parents allowed him to photograph me, I wasn't ever scared. I felt like a professional. I had this image then that when I was older I'd be a model, tall, slim, with my dark hair falling loosely to my waist, and I'd drive a red convertible.

But more than the modeling, I wanted to dance, to be a graceful ballerina. I studied ballet and modern dance at the Harkness Ballet School three times a week. My two older brothers and I put on dance performances for my parents in our small living room. My brother Greg used a soap microphone from the shower to present me, and my other brother, Brad, chose the music. I would twirl and do splits to Donna Summer's "Hot Stuff." Then I'd move slowly and sensually to Streisand and Diamond's "You Don't Bring Me Flowers." I wanted to cry when I heard the music, and I danced as if I were releasing some great pain that lived inside me. My parents would stare at me with wonder. The more they seemed captivated by me, the more I wanted to move, sway, and leap. Afterward they'd say, "Jenny, you're so graceful. You have such a gift. You're just so beautiful to watch."

Only, as I studied dance through the years, I wasn't growing any taller, while my quads kept getting bigger and bigger. *I hate these bulging thighs. None of the models or other dancers look like this. They're straight and sleek. Bony and lanky. I'm not going to be pretty anymore.*

The first time I tried to starve myself was at ballet camp, when I was ten. For a few years following that summer I ate normally; but after ballet camp there was never again a time when I was comfortable with my body image. When I was fourteen, I started starving myself in earnest. I learned early on that images of thinness, especially a certain kind of thinness, were tied to notions of beauty. The importance of beauty was always in my face—from the next season of Ralph Lauren ads that lay in piles at home to the fashion shows we attended in spring and fall. The gorgeous models, clothing, and the adrenaline that pumped through the audience, left a powerful imprint on my young, fragile mind.

At fifteen, after a year of starving, I stood five feet four inches and weighed eighty-five pounds. I hadn't really planned to try modeling again, but everyone I knew, and even strangers, would come up to me asking if I did. "Why aren't you in your family's ads?" I fell for it. I went to the Katie Ford model agency wearing a faded forest green Fruit of the Loom T-shirt, ripped jeans, high brown Ralph Lauren boots, my hair hanging loose, and no makeup, feeling pretty damn cool. I stalled on the corner outside before I went in, chewing four Double Bubbles just to get a little energy. The woman who interviewed me was really nice, but then, as if it were just another question, she asked me if I had an eating disorder. She said they didn't like to hire girls with this problem. *Are you kidding? I'm finally skinny. Just like the rest of the models. Give me a break. I can't win.* She also told me I was a bit too short for her agency. She recommended that I try some commercial acting, and look for some jobs where they wanted dancers.

I found a commercial agent who suggested I dress more ladylike. *What did she know? It wasn't as if I was Miss America.* Still, she had me read some lines. She pronounced me a natural and gave me some tapes to take home for practice.

A few days later, she called me to go on an audition. I was very surprised. They wanted someone real boppy and young looking. She said, "So wear your hair in a ponytail and look real cute." As I pulled my hair up high into a rubber band, I was seized with anxiety. *Do my ripped jeans and Indian suede jacket work? What should I wear then? I might as well just forget about it.* I called my father and he said to go, take a shot at it, but after racing back and forth around the apartment attempting to find the perfect outfit, I chickened out. I didn't want to have to sell myself, be a product, or pretend I was something I was not. *I am not boppy looking . . . I am sophisticated.* The truth is I was too goddamn hungry and weak to deal with it.

A few months later I made myself vomit for the first time. It didn't take long to become a full-fledged bulimic. And although most girls become thinner or remain the same weight when they add vomiting to their repertoire, that's not what happened with me. I gained a lot of weight, my face was always swollen, my eyes were bloodshot, and those pretty days were over for a long time.

3. Just Do It

It's April 1997, and after eleven months of suffering, I'm now in some comatose state, spending my days in a tortured trance, living in total isolation. I don't want to see anybody. I'm embarrassed that people might think I'm in my depressed, eating-again, fat mode. This is grandiose and paranoid of me, yes, but even my neighbors have always commented on my weight. "Gosh, you're half the size you used to be." *I'm really glad you thought the Lauren girl was such a hippo.* And when I've put the weight back on, they never fail to comment too. "Um . . . uh, you look, uh, different." Why say anything at all? I know that these people have watched me grow up in this building, seen me in all different shapes and sizes. I know that I show my emotions through the size of my body, and that the constant fluctuation of my weight makes me a target for curiosity. I know that I should let it bounce off me, but has anyone heard of a thing called tact?

So at this point, I don't want to see anyone or, rather, don't want anyone to see me. The other day, one of my neighbors called my parents to ask if they knew what kind of a state I was in, that they hear me crying and that I look sick. My parents keep telling me to get it together, I'm scaring people. They think I'm "a little off." *No shit.*

Even I have to wonder if this is all a crock, a cliché type of hypochondria. Am I fixated on my bodily sensations and functions because I'm finally, you know, completely off my rocker? There is no doubt that this is possible, that finally the madness of this eating disorder, my sadness, my anxiety, my craving to be loved has manifested itself in these awful physical symptoms. Perhaps this twitch in my butt is because I'm so utterly depressed. Sure. It's possible. A twenty-four-year-old female trying to leave the nest, be mature, paint so-called masterpieces, have a relationship with a man that isn't just in her head, leave her wildly overprotective parents. Yes, it's a hard time. Yeah, maybe I'm panicking. Maybe it is what that asshole neurologist said: somatization.

It's last fall, and Dr. F (I'll call him Dr. F for Dr. Fuckhead) has just finished one of his fabulous rectal exams. I am finally reclothed, with my ass no longer bare, and I am sitting up on the examining table waiting for his comments, perhaps a possible explanation for my twitch.

Dr. F inquires, "Are you sure these twitches are not little orgasms?" It is very hard for me to believe he is world-renowned.

Dr. F prescribes Depakote, a medication most often given to epileptics, in case these are little seizures in my butt. After a few days, my face blows up and I am feeling relatively awful. He's not winning points.

At the end of the second unsuccessful visit, Dr. F says, "I really don't know what these are," and then asks, "How's your mental state these days, my love." *Well, Doc, I'd really like to kill you.* He gives me Xanax.

Over the next few months, I'm still complaining, so my parents suggest that I go see Dr. F yet again. *Doctors do know best, Jenny darling, and after all, he is the best, honey.*

Dr. F takes some tests for MS, Parkinson's, Lou Gehrig's, all the major diseases. There is a strange result in my peroneal ser test, and one of the nerves in my leg is showing a delayed response, so he finally takes me seriously and asks me to come back to see him.

On the fourth visit, the test is repeated and Dr. F announces that it was just a fluke. "There really is nothing wrong with you," he says. "Wish I could find something for you, but I can't. Listen, kiddo, I think you should find a good shrink."

The doctors, my parents, they all have got to be kidding. What an insult. First of all, I've been seeing shrinks since I was ten. I changed therapists last year, and I now go kvetch to a nice old guy on 84th and Madison who has no clue. Why can't anyone of them understand that I am an athlete, a dancer? Can't they see that someone who is literally obsessed with her body, and has been for years, knows if something is wrong inside her? My father always said that I had major antennae, that nothing could get past me. *So Daddy, why can't you trust me now?*

Is it my mental phobia about eating that has caused this? Have my anorexic fears—the ones that caused me to shake my legs purposefully after a meal to burn calories, the ones that couldn't allow me to think straight after I ate, the ones that forced me to run six to ten miles a day and extra if I had binged, the ones that would lead me to devour thousands of calories and then ingest poisonous ipecac—caused this? Have the constant fears of feeling full and of growing fat come to life? The extended stomach, the saddlebags, and an inability to exercise . . . have my worst nightmares come true? My phobias have caused my phobias to come alive. And that is why I wonder if I am going insane.

A few months later my mom, dad, and I sit in the surgeon's office staring at a set of X-rays that show my small intestines resting in the middle of my rectum and vagina. Yes, that's right, my small intestines are sitting in the space between my rectum and vagina. They are dumbfounded. My dad, who has finally been able to take a break from work and is dressed in an impeccable tweed suit, laughs and says, "Jesus Christ. She's not crazy. It's like everything she described from day one was true. We're lucky to finally find it." For a whole year I'd been telling everyone there was a monster living between my legs, breathing, pulsating and alive. I sit there in the surgeon's office barely able to think from my rectum twitching, having eaten nothing all day for fear the monster would really come alive, and I think, *Fuck you, Dad. Fuck you all.* So I say to the surgeon, "Can you do it now? Can you do the surgery on me right now?" *Okay, on with the show . . . knew it . . . want my life back . . . now!*

He says, "It's a four-hour procedure, Jenny. We have to arrange it, maybe within the month."

So close, but oh so far. I'm thinking I can't make it. I just can't take it. It's like trying to hold in pee when you know you have ten more miles to go until the next rest stop.

The surgeon then explains that he will have to do the procedure through my abdomen. Otherwise, it would be easy to mess up. The surgery is extremely complicated.

And I ask, "So, um, there'll be a big scar?"

He nods sadly, "Yeah, pretty large," and I wince, thinking *there go bikinis.*

My dad consoles me, "Jenny, scars are sexy." Sadly enough, I'm a bit relieved by my father's *great insight.*

The surgeon is supposedly an expert in the colon/rectal field. He shows us an article written by a woman he helped, called "The Painful Silence." She credits him with saving her after many screwed-up surgeries because she was incorrectly cut while giving birth. She had been leaking feces for months and didn't want to tell anyone. The surgeon then reveals to me that women are never taken seriously for this kind of problem and are often sent to the loony bin instead because no one understands their weird symptoms. *No, really?*

I ask the surgeon if I have caused this.

He says, "Well, you may have had a congenital weakness," then hesitates and says softly, "but it's more likely a result of the straining from your eating disorder."

Just for curiosity's sake, I ask the surgeon what happens if I don't have the surgery. He raises his eyebrows and says, "You will probably become incontinent."

I am aghast. I can't even look at my parents. I laugh to myself matter-of-factly. *So, Jenny, this is your fate.*

4. The Pact

I was ten years old the first time I made a pact with myself to starve. I was at ballet camp in the Berkshires, staring at myself in the mirror of the dance studio. As I pointed my toe, an intensely lonely feeling traveled up my leg into the pit of my stomach. I thought of my mother. I longed for her. I missed her blond hair and the way it caressed my cheek as she hugged me. I missed the smell of her freshly cleaned skin. I missed hearing her whisper in my ear, "I love you, Monkey Face," as she cupped my chin in her palm. In that same minute I vowed to myself: *I'm not going to eat at all this summer.*

That past spring I had started to watch my weight. I would stare down at my thighs when they were tucked under my school desk and cringe because I was uncomfortable with how far they spread across the seat. I would sit there in the fourth grade at the Dalton School and try to read while concentrating on trying to keep my legs moving, and fixating on a position that might make them look less big.

After school I would rush off to catch the 79th Street crosstown bus that would take me to my ballet class. I wouldn't linger with my friends. I didn't want to share in an after-school feast of Doritos and candy bars. I decided that I would eat "well" like my mother. Which meant that I would eat my meals only, nothing in between, and skip the bread. My mother was always trying to do this.

In addition to taking four afternoons of ballet, on the weekends I started attending aerobics classes with my mother. I would take back-to-back classes, just like she did. I liked the feeling of dancing and hopping to the music. I liked the adrenaline pumping through me. I always had to be in the front line, right there in sync with the instructor's intensity. Later in the dressing room, we'd be half naked and my mom's friends would come up to my mother, look at me, and say, "Your daughter moves so well. I just follow her." I felt pressure at every class to be up there leading the troops. I knew I was being watched.

Afterward my mom and I would refuel ourselves with huge bran muffins. *We deserved them.* We'd sit and discuss which aerobics teachers we preferred and plan which classes to take on Sunday morning, if Dad didn't mind us going. He'd usually let us, because he knew my mother needed it to feel good the rest of the day. Some days we'd also shop at Capezio for bright leotards and fluffy leg warmers. I couldn't wait for the next class, where I'd display my new purchase.

That spring I watched an after-school television drama called *The Best Little Girl in the World,* where a young teenage girl starves herself. I'd never heard of such a thing. *Is that possible? Can a person really not eat? Wow. Maybe if I didn't eat, my thighs wouldn't be so big. Maybe I would look as skinny as all the girls in my ballet class. . . . Maybe like the models too. Hmm.* Only it wasn't the girl's body that appealed to me so much. There was a drama to it all that captivated me. There was a scene where she steals diet pills in a pharmacy and then passes out. I was intrigued.

Every day at camp I focused on going to all the activities that were offered in addition to ballet class: gymnastics, aerobics, hiking. I hated going to the dining room in between. My friends and the staff would urge me to eat, maybe a little cottage cheese, maybe a little fruit, and at times I had to take a few bites to get them off my back, but I didn't even want the food to touch my lips. I liked the gnawing pangs in my ribs because it made me feel strong. It was a signal of success. I watched all the girls rush to the dining room after a full day of dancing to take gigantic bites of juicy hamburgers soaked in ketchup and eat greasy fry after greasy fry. Not eating made me feel superior. Even on the very first day of camp I was ecstatic in the nurse's office during my medical checkup because I weighed less than my friend K.T., a redhead from the School of American Ballet who was ahead of me in line. When she and C.B., a very petite dark-haired girl who had performed in the *Nutcracker* at Lincoln Center and seemed half my size, and I were picked to do a dance together, I vowed to be thinnest of all by visiting day, when we would present it.

Following my rules and holding true to my pact also helped distract me from missing my mother. Daily I would find some quiet place outside on the green lawn or under a huge veranda to sit and write a letter home describing everything to my parents. I couldn't skip a day. I was afraid my parents would feel bad if I did. I covered the letters with drawings and hearts and "I love you" and "miss you" all over. I wrote about my activities, the trip to Saratoga and to a Lena Horne concert, and about all the books I was reading in my free time. I wrote about how much I missed their beautiful faces. How I missed my two older brothers too. I asked them if next summer we could all stay together and rent a house in the Hamptons. I never told them I wasn't eating. I wrote only to my brother Greg at his tennis camp about my fear of food and of using toothpaste because it had calories. He sent me postcards back telling me I should eat because I needed the nutrients to grow healthy and strong.

At the beginning of camp I was well liked. I initiated the pillow fights. I giggled and leaped around like a jovial kid. Suddenly I turned quiet and stopped engaging. The second week there, K.T. called me an "anorexic snob."

My bunk went to Friendly's one night. I had anticipated the outing for days. *Would I have to eat anything? What about all that ice cream? What if I ate it? Could I have a little?* My bunk mates were giggling, screaming, and dancing all over the shop, excited as anything just about the *silly ice cream.* I felt left out. *What was happening to me? Did everybody hate me now?* I decided to order three scoops of Heath Bar Crunch ice cream just to show them that I was still cool. *I could still be a fun girl.* When it was served in front of my face, I became queasy. *Was I really gonna eat all that?* I brought a tiny spoonful to my lips. The sweet and creamy flavor melted in my mouth. I took another spoonful. And another. Another and another. I looked up and caught all the girls at my table staring. Some of them were cheering me on, "Yeah! Yeah! Jenny's eating. Go, Jenny!" I stopped. I realized what I had done. My whole body began to shake and I started to panic. I started crying. My counselor took me outside to console me. I told her how much I missed my mother and begged her to let me call home. When we returned to campus, I wasn't allowed to make that call. I swam one hundred laps in the pool.

A few days later the camp director began to sit me at my ballet teacher's table during meals. She was blond and stunning and looked like Michelle Pfeiffer. She wore her hair in a bun and her neck was long and beautiful. I was totally intimidated by her. I'd watch her and what she ate. She'd dig into her breakfast. Three huge bagel halves with globs of cream cheese would be lined up on her plate with eggs, bacon, fruit, and a side of oatmeal. *How can she be so thin and pretty and still eat that way?* She smiled at me during the first few meals, but I quickly averted my eyes. She suggested in front of the rest of the girls that I eat a little something. At lunch one day she urged me to eat a slice of roast beef, just one, she begged. I just couldn't, wouldn't. The more people focused their attention on my not eating, the more stubborn I became. A few days later, at dinner, my ballet teacher began to cry. Then she sobbed hard and loud. She removed herself from the table. *What's going on here? This is too weird. Why is my ballet teacher crying?*

That night after the meal she came to see me in my bunk. I couldn't believe she came to see *me*. I felt awful that I made her cry. She put her arm around my shoulder as we sat on my bed and she told me that it was a horrible thing not to eat. She said that she had had this problem when she was younger and it was very dangerous. She told me she had performed for the American Ballet Theatre (*Wow! That's Baryshnikov's company!*) but was forced to stop performing. She said it wasn't worth the pain. She said I had too much talent to waste and that I wasn't dancing with the same energy I once had. After that, she never mentioned my eating again.

But a few weeks later, the director rushed into my ballet class, pulled me from the bar during our grand pliés, and dragged me across the wooden floor of the studio into the corner. Beethoven stopped abruptly, and the only sound was my shrieking. She said, "You're losing too much weight." Then she manually forced my mouth open and poured pineapple juice down my throat while the rest of the little girls dressed in pink stared at me in horror. I kicked, screamed, and spit the

liquid in her face and ran all the way across campus and hid myself behind a tree.

When I was retrieved by my counselor, I was informed that my parents had been called and that they were driving up the next day to take
me home. I lay awake under my covers the whole night, imagining the
warm safe feeling of being held by my mother.

It started with a banana, and then some ice cream at the end of the
four-hour ride home from ballet camp, and just like that, I was eating
again. In the car I told my parents I wanted a Pralines and Cream cone.
My dad raced over the 65 mph speed limit to get his starving ten-year-
old daughter to the Swenson's Ice Cream shop right down the block
from our apartment. My dad had been deeply affected by my not eating
that summer. When my parents had greeted me, he stared at me with a
look of shock, then took my mother's arm and looked away as he broke
down crying. I had never seen my father or any grown man cry before
that. He says I was emaciated, but I can't remember what I looked like.
We took no pictures that summer. As I licked my ice cream cone, my
parents watched me gleefully. The following day, after a good night's
rest, I said I was in the mood for a veal chop at Ginos, our Italian place.
We went for lunch and I devoured the large piece of meat down to the
bone. Somehow being with my parents made me feel safe again. It was
as if they gave me permission to eat.

For the rest of the summer, dancing and physical activity were ban-
ished from my schedule by my pediatrician. My parents took me to the
bookstore and chatted patiently with a salesperson while I took my time
reading the back flap of every novel in the young adult section. I must
have flung at least twenty books into the basket to buy. My parents had
no qualms with this obsession of mine; it was obviously much healthier
than exercising all day. I would go home and lie in one of my brother's
bunk beds and read. I always stayed in my brothers' room when they
were away because it was bigger and I could shut the door. My room
was a measly closetlike area that had been carved out of our living room

when I was born. There was just enough space for my desk with its overhead bookshelves and a narrow bed that was lined with pillows and dolls. I was claustrophobic in there, and I had no privacy because my doors were only flimsy shutters. My room was next to the tiny kitchen, where my mom usually stood preparing meals, cleaning up, or talking on the phone. When the boys were home there was around-the-clock traffic in and out of that kitchen, and a TV was always on in the living room. There was constant noise. I also shared a bathroom with the boys, and half the time I sat on the toilet while one of them was showering or brushing his teeth. I took advantage of their room when they were gone, and made myself quite at home.

I was incessantly hungry and obsessed with thoughts of what great meal my mother might be making next, her delicious warm tuna casserole with the big shells, or maybe her London broil, which I would soak in lots of ketchup. At the end of lunch, I would ask my mother what was for dinner and count the hours until it would be served. I figured I could finish the last few hundred pages of my novel, start the next one, and then the meal would be ready. The books were markers for my meals, and they gave me a sense of structure, otherwise I would go crazy dreaming about food.

But it was not that simple. After a few days of so-called normal eating, I panicked. I could tell I was putting weight back on, and started feeling scared and lazy. I just lay in my brothers' bunk beds crying and ignoring my mother when she stated that dinner was ready. I ate a tomato one night, and that was it for seven days. I was forced to see my pediatrician once a week for a weigh-in. He said if I didn't start eating I'd have to go to the hospital. He prescribed Sustacal pudding. My mother bought stacks of the chocolate-flavored kind, and I was supposed to eat one can every day in addition to meals. But I wouldn't eat those things; they were too delicious.

My brothers came home from their individual camps and we went to the Hamptons for the month of August. My father traveled back and forth for work. Friday nights were a big deal. The boys and I would get excited to greet him at the station, where we'd throw pennies onto the track and wait for the train to come in and flatten them. Then we would all go out to dinner. With my brothers' coming home, the new environment, and returning to more physical activity, like swimming and playing kickball with the boys, I began to eat again. It was mostly controlled, though, and I allowed myself no snacks in between. We'd go to Gosman Seafood House in Montauk and I would order a steak like my father did and finish the whole thing. Other times I would look at the plate placed before me and just cry, debating whether to eat or not. Many times the evening activity was about getting Jenny her one dessert, and I usually opted for a Häagen-Dazs strawberry ice cream cone from town. Because everyone was worried that I might starve myself again at any given moment, I almost always dictated my family's meals, nights, and moods. I didn't realize then how much I made my family walk on eggshells. It's not so simple to say that I enjoyed the attention, or that I used it as a source of power. At least it definitely wasn't a conscious thing. I mostly remember being consumed and plagued by the fear, the joy, and then the inevitable guilt from eating.

Some doctors say that I was the one who manifested my family's dysfunction. That there is always one child who takes on the problems of the family. I didn't yet know what my family's dysfunction was, but I do know that my brothers were affected too. That summer, one of them was having intense nightmares and difficulty sleeping at night, and the other was feeling depressed. With my problem at the forefront, my therapist recommended that the whole family try therapy. We did family sessions, and then, in addition, my brothers went to see their own doctors. The brother with the nightmares was willing, but the other went reluctantly. My parents weren't necessarily advocates of therapy, but they were the kind of parents who would do anything and everything for their kids. They wanted to make all our problems go away. And they always wanted to *fix things fast*. And they also put a lot of trust in authorities. Since therapy was recommended, that was the route they would take. From what I know, my brothers went to therapy only for a month or so, and their immediate issues were resolved quickly. I, on the other hand, remained in therapy for quite a while.

5. The Diagnosis

I'm panicking before I sit on the commode for this test called a defecogram. If this doesn't show something, then I will go to Santa Fe and find a spot in the desert and shoot myself in the head.

My mom gives me a hopeful smile as she leaves the room. The radiologist explains that I am to sit down on the commode and bear down as if I am going to make a bowel movement. A camera will take an X-ray of what happens as I do this. Even though he's really handsome, I'm not even embarrassed—I'm too desperate. As I perform this exciting act, I begin to cry because it is so painful.

I yelp to the radiologist, "I can't . . . I can't . . . I can't push. This is what I'm talking about." I can't push at all. For nearly six months I haven't been able to make a bowel movement without standing and massaging my stomach.

He is in the other room looking at a television screen of me trying to take a shit, and he says, "Just try . . . okay, that's it . . . okay . . . okay . . . WOW . . . Wow . . . uh-huh . . . uh . . . just a few more minutes while . . . I . . . wow . . . Jesus . . . all right."

Did he find something? *Please, God, please.*

He comes out and I lunge at him. "Did you find something? Please tell me you did."

He says, "I found something, all right, but we need to do a second part."

"What . . . what"—*if he thinks I can wait any longer now that I'm this close*—"what is it?"

My mother comes in and he points to the indecipherable films. He explains to both of us that what I have is very rare.

Still gaping and shaking his head in awe, he says, "Everyone has a space under the perineum between the rectum and vagina about this size." He uses both his hands and distances them from one another as if he is holding a small grape. Then he opens his hands to the width of a basketball and says, "This is the size of your space."

Huh? My mother and I look at each other in confusion and then back at him.

He explains further, "It's like somehow gravity has stretched this space. It's like a muscle herniated and is causing an obstruction when you try to move your bowels." I will find out later that it is a huge balloon-like thing called an enterocele, or cul-de-sac, that has stretched, fallen, and has been resting on my anal sphincter for God knows how long; maybe more than a year. Still, I don't really get it.

He continues, "But I need to do another part of the test to find out more. You need to drink barium first."

This nurse comes out with a cup the size of those jumbo Diet Cokes you get at the movies. *Shit, if I drink that, how's it gonna come out?*

It turns out I have to drink six of these cups, and my mom curls her lips down and grips her jaws, a face she makes when she sees the three Sweet'N Lows my father and I empty into our coffee. I try to walk around the hallway for forty-five minutes to let the barium digest. Then I sit on the commode again and repeat trying to poop. It simulates what happens inside me after I eat a meal.

Back in the waiting room, I ask my mother if she noticed whether the radiologist had a wedding band. She laughs and says she thinks so. I'm not past dreaming. Girls will be girls even at the worst of times. I am feeling rather hyper about finding a possible diagnosis. So I keep walking in circles, kind of in a rhythmic prayer, or trance, letting this energetic hopefulness give me enough momentum to hold my doubled-over torso up and move forward. I debate whether to call my best friends Nikki and Stella, or wait until there is more info. During a few loops, I take a break to phone them and anxiously wait to hear their responses on the other end of the receiver, but neither one is home. I make a list in my head of all the people I am going to tell, all the people who might be curious to know I just may not have been bullshitting all year.

I keep walking and praying. It reminds me of the day I waited to see if I had made it into School of American Ballet, walking back and forth down the hallway after my audition with all the other little girls, hoping and wanting. It was a moment in time that I knew could impact my future immensely. It was a time, similar to this, that I was being judged by how my body performed.

The Great Commode . . . Starring J. Lauren . . . Academy Award winner for her magnificent toilet scene.

It's hard to fathom the results of the next X-rays. They are so utterly bizarre. I am in shock when the radiologist explains to us what he thinks might be the case. Somehow, after digesting the barium, part of my bowel—well, my small intestine—has actually fallen into that space he was describing. It has literally sunk, and there it is, resting in the balloon-like sack. As it was trying to digest the barium (just as I have noticed with any piece of food), I began to feel the twitch. My small intestine is the monster!! Oh, my God!

This is how I understand it in laymen's terms. My perineum, which is the space between my vagina and rectum, has overstretched (*to the size of a basketball? Yikes . . . no wonder I had trouble walking sexily for a few years, especially in heels*). And because this is the very area that helps support the pelvic floor, the laxity of the muscle and gravity probably caused my small intestine to drop, where it made itself quite at home on my anal sphincter, creating an obstruction and a bearing-down kind of sensation. This is a mind trip, especially if you think about how the body works not only physically, but also energetically and spiritually. It's as if my very own root chakra has fallen apart. It's like pulling out the foundation of a building . . . it can only collapse. I think about the connotations a lot. Perhaps I destroyed my very own foundation by not respecting my body, *my temple*. Or maybe it's the other way around; my very root and sense of core has been so weak that I have been working most of my life to hold myself up, literally and metaphorically.

What is there to say to this diagnosis? Hurrah! Hurrah! Cool! Neato! I'm not stunned. I just remain silent, feeling relief, anger, happiness, fear, a bit of everything. *I will just get it fixed. Hope it won't be too painful. I'm sure it's a piece of cake.* I see a montage of Jenny all better, jogging around the reservoir, doing yoga poses, and painting a huge mural for some film festival like I did just a year ago. I see myself dressed in a black turtleneck, short black skirt, high black boots. I am a toned, slender, and sexy figure, back and better than ever, glowing with triumph.

My mom gets down to business immediately and inquires, "So what do we do, Doctor?"

The radiologist, my handsome savior, says that he is not the one to decide or really give an opinion, but that in the few cases he has seen like this, they sometimes do surgery; but in older women, where this is more common, they don't necessarily do anything.

What? Do nothing? Are you kidding? I'll die . . . no way . . . please . . . please help me . . . somebody, please! He says that he will get the films to my internist as soon as possible.

The montage of my future glory begins to fade, my great dream merges into a nightmare from which I can't seem to wake. I imagine myself back at home, lying contorted and folded on my bed with legs clenching together to try to comfort the twitch up my ass, my hands tightly squeezing the rails of the black modern headboard of my bed, my eyes fluttering so I can barely focus, my neck spasming as if I have swallowed a frog. I try to fixate on the blank vanilla walls of my bedroom; I roll my head in the other direction toward the window and count and recount the windows of the gray skyscraper that faces me. I watch the television, wondering what it feels like to have an upright body, a clavicle. *Where did all of these beautiful women on TV come from? Am I still a woman?*

In my nightmare, an old man in a white coat with two devil's horns appears by my side and says, "We cannot help you. Good luck." I am weeping and smelling the stink of my fear, agitation, and loneliness. But now I have gray straggly hair, my body is mushy and atrophied, I have drool rolling out of my mouth, and my eyes are glazed over. And I'm on a cot in a padded white cell of a mental institution. Every so often I mutter, "My ass, my ass." Day after day, night after night, minute to minute, second to second I try to bear it. Time is not a luxury. I'm not sure this is a dream. This may be my life.

6. Chocolate Chip Cookies

When I was fifteen, my father went on his yearly business trip to Europe for two full weeks. The evening before he was to return, my mom baked chocolate chip cookies for him. At midnight, after smelling them from my bedroom all night, I went into the kitchen, lifted up the tinfoil as quietly as I could, looked at the dreamy sweet treats, and tried to let myself taste one. But then I couldn't stop. I just wanted to keep on eating. I ate until I was shaking from all the sugar and the nausea and the fear. I went into the living room and sat on the couch and found myself fifteen minutes later in a statue-like pose, panicked and petrified. What would these cookies do to my body? I was going to be fat again in the morning. And if not fat, I would no longer be underweight like everybody said I was. I had to vomit.

I knew I couldn't use my bathroom because my mother would hear. So I took a large brown paper bag and a roll of toilet paper and snuck out of the apartment. I went into the stairwell at the other end of the hallway, hoping the sounds wouldn't wake up my neighbors, and spent an hour trying to vomit into the paper bag. I wanted everything to come up, to make sure the calories wouldn't invade my body. I needed to get the poison, the sugar out. I couldn't get fat. I felt like such an idiot for giving in. I was so tired. So, so tired. I just wished I could go to sleep. But I was afraid Daddy would come home the next day and think I got fat. I knew I had to keep trying. Keep trying until I was free again. Nothing was coming up. I eventually gave up and sat on the fluorescent lime green cement stairwell and started sobbing quietly. I went back to the apartment, tucked myself way down under the covers at the bottom of my bed, curled up like a baby, and cried myself to sleep.

I couldn't move the next day from all the sugar. I had a hangover from chocolate chip cookies. My mother kept telling me to get up for school, but I kept ignoring her and hid under the covers. I wanted to die. She started to get angry at me. I lay there as the tears kept rolling. I told her about the cookies. She was very surprised and asked why I didn't go to her before I ate them. Uggh. That kind of question is annoying. Bulimic episodes involve a compulsion, a compulsion to binge and purge, and if I could stop and get myself to tell my mother or someone first, then it wouldn't really be a compulsion, would it? And then I wouldn't really have bulimia. And then everything would be dandy, but that's not the point, *Mom*.

There was no way I was going to school that day. My mother stopped fighting me. Instead I put on lots of layers of sweats and went running in the park. I jogged slowly so that I would have enough stamina to run a long distance. I ran until my legs were numb and cold from sweat. After seventeen miles I stopped and just walked. It was like moving against a pool of lead. When I got home I had diarrhea from all the cookies and running, and I slept until seven at night. My dad came home that evening, and I heard my mother's worried whispers to him when she greeted him at the door. He immediately came into my bedroom and made some remark about how upset he was to see me looking so pale. I looked in the mirror. I *was* pretty pale, almost as white as my bed linens. I loved the way I looked. I finally felt better about eating all those cookies.

After that week, I stopped going to school. All I did was exercise, starve, or binge. I was not functioning normally. It was time to say goodbye to the therapist who I had been seeing since I was ten, who treated me like her granddaughter. When my parents had sent me to her the month after I left ballet camp, I liked her instantly. When she gave me psychological testing, she would listen to me wide-eyed and eager while I interpreted her Rorschach images. She told me I was extremely creative. I felt smart and, most of all, understood by her. For the first year, most afternoons we'd just play Connect Four and Battleship. She really was more of a playmate to me than a doctor. And through the years, she became another person for whom I lived to please. I would draw pictures for her in my spare time and bring her little gifts. The more she complimented me and seemed to like me, the more I wanted to impress her. Sometimes I even sensed that she was a lonely person, and I wanted to make her laugh.

I've been called a perfectionist, and perfectionists don't just strive to satisfy their parents. They strive to please everyone, even the cabdriver or the person behind the cash register, and God forbid I'm not nice enough to the phone operator. My relationship with my first therapist wasn't professional enough. I needed a psychologist who would be stricter and save me from the depression that was threatening to engulf me.

My parents had to literally drag me out of bed to go see Dr. Bowen, a psychiatrist who specialized in eating disorders. It wasn't that I didn't want to go; it was more that I didn't feel skinny enough to go. I felt like my problems had no validity because I weighed ninety-five pounds and not a drastically low weight like seventy. But when I got there and cried through the whole session, the psychiatrist did diagnose me as suffering from depression, anorexia, and bulimia nervosa. He suggested that I try antidepressants. I resisted at first because I surmised that there would be a possible weight gain. By the end of my next session both my parents and I consented for me to try the antidepressant Pamelor.

Dr. Bowen warned me of the possible side effects, but I had no idea how intense they'd be. After the first night I awoke with a very dry mouth, and when I stood up I got a violent head rush. That only lasted a few seconds, but I realized that I would have to get up slowly from now on. In my mind I had entered the real sicko zone. I was taking medication for my brain, and I thought that was proof that I was truly crazy.

I made plans with Dr. Bowen and my parents and the headmaster at Dalton to switch to a small private school where the classes consisted of eight students at the most, and where the schedule was more flexible. Housed in a little brownstone in midtown, it was attended by kids with all kinds of problems, including drug addicts, manic-depressives, and those who had failed or gotten kicked out of another school. When my mom and brother went to look at it, my brother relayed that my mother cried. It must have been difficult to accept that her sick daughter was going to be in this shithole after having been a top student at one of the most distinguished private schools in the city. But we all agreed it would be temporary. Dr. H, the headmaster, and my homeroom teacher, who had been caring and compassionate since the beginning of the year (he was one of the first to tell me I was getting too thin), told me that as soon as I felt better I could return to Dalton. But I didn't care if I ever went back to high school at all. I was numb, as if all my worrying and fear and starving just made me brain-dead.

But before the winter term started, there were the holidays to get through. My family was going to St. Martin that Christmas. I prepared by working out constantly, shopping, and spending my afternoons seeing Dr. Bowen. My mom and I went to Barneys and I bought these wild bright bikinis, Norma Kamali, Agnes B., size petite. I tried to buy bras but I no longer filled them out. I had mosquito bites for breasts. I wasn't sure how much I liked them. My mother couldn't look at me in the dressing room, and I saw that she was teary-eyed. I was upset that I couldn't fill out the corsets I wanted to wear with jeans, like the models did. I was so confused. Why weren't the clothes looking good on me? How could they be big? I would get so weak shopping. But I wouldn't stop for lunch with my mom. Instead, I would work out or sleep. I didn't speak to any of my friends. I received tons of concerned phone calls and cards but I didn't respond. I didn't think anybody really cared; I thought their effort was just obligatory. Although I have to admit I was touched when I received a huge packet of handmade monoprints from the students in my former printmaking class at Dalton. It had been my favorite course. One guy I had always worked next to had even beaded a necklace for me. I never really got to know him, but I wore the necklace every day.

When we were away at St. Martin, I enjoyed showing off my new clothing purchases. My favorite was a Betsey Johnson purple-and-black rubber dress I had bought from Antique Boutique the week before with Greg, after he had come home from Princeton. I had modeled it for him. He had urged me to buy that dress and a shimmery orange one. I had also bought tons of short colorful tank tops to wear with my ripped jean shorts. On the beach, when we mingled with all the families we knew from the year before and with the new ones, I was a star. *Sure.*

The first afternoon, when I was running a vigorous ten miles in a bikini, I saw a car driving up to me on the concrete streets near the casitas, and it was Timmy, the first love of my life from Dalton. I had been totally infatuated with him and used to watch him play basketball in the gym after school. We always liked each other, and even though he gave me his varsity jacket when I was in the eighth grade, our age difference made a realistic relationship difficult. He was in college already. A tanned Timmy stuck his head out the window and said, "Well, Ms. Lauren, whadda ya know?" I hadn't seen him in a year, but I didn't want to stop. I needed to get my run in. I never stopped during my runs, never, otherwise it would cancel it out. I wouldn't get the same aerobic benefit. He looked at me a bit oddly when I slowed down and asked what he was doing there. There were many Dalton families who went to St. Martin for vacation, and he had joined the club. He didn't comment on my weight. For the entire trip he didn't say anything regarding my foreign skeletal figure, except to make antagonistic remarks to me at the disco like, "Your skirt short enough?" On one hand, he seemed jealous because I was flaunting my new form in front of other guys, yet on the other, he seemed sad sometimes when he looked at me, like he knew something was wrong.

But I wasn't thinking of Timmy that first night when we all went to the casino and I met a guy named Pete Mitch through other New York friends. I immediately got feedback that he was interested in me, and what did I think about him? He was dark-haired, tan, short, and pumped up like an iron man. He walked around the place with a subtle smirk, and appeared quite confident. His interest didn't really faze me. The next night when all the Dalton, Horace Mann, and Riverdale private school kids were hanging out at the casino, tan and dressed in polo knits and short dresses, it was a real party. A real scene. *Half glamorous, half ugly.* Pete and his posse kept looking over at me. I sat next to my dad for safety, cheering him on while he played blackjack and trying to avoid Pete's gaze. My mother stood nearby talking to other mothers while my brothers played the slots with their girlfriends they had brought along. Pete finally came over, took sips of his alcoholic beverage, said hello to my father, and tried to make small talk with me. He was polite, friendly, charming. There was nothing not to like about him. I smiled back at him but didn't have much to say. I remember feeling flattered that he was attracted to me but also thinking: *He doesn't even know me. How can he like me?*

The following night at the disco I didn't even go to dance. I was exhausted from my daily run, the sun, and fixating on how full I was from dinner, the one meal I had eaten. I just wanted to go back to the room. I noticed men looking at me a lot, and I peered at the surrounding discotheque mirrors to see what they might be seeing. I viewed a vision of a thin, lithe, sexy girl in a purple-and-black rubber dress, but I didn't see Jenny. I didn't know where or who she was.

And then Pete came over, and just like that, grabbed my hand and started caressing it. I just let my fingers sit in his while I watched all the kids hanging out, dancing, drinking, laughing. I can do this, I thought. But I was scared. Timmy was sitting there too, and I felt sad, guilty. I was choosing the guy who couldn't see, the guy who didn't know what I was about, the guy who didn't really care about me. It was easier. I looked away from Timmy and went to dance with Pete. I remained distant, cold, aloof. Later that evening when I had freed up my hand and sat waiting for Greg and his girlfriend to take me home, Pete approached my brother and asked permission to drive me home. I stood behind Pete, frantically mouthing "No" to Greg, but he must have been so impressed by Pete's manners that he responded, "Go ahead. Have a good time."

I acted very blasé about joining Pete. I didn't really care either way. But now I was trapped. Pete and I walked, and he led me by the hand to the beach. We sat there looking out at the ocean, listening to the soft sound of the waves, and suddenly I started to cry. I cried because I was nervous. I cried because I didn't want anything or anybody to get in, to touch me or awaken me. I cried because his hand felt foreign and comforting at the same time. It had been a tough year. I was about to start a new school. I was hungry. I was lonely. He wiped away my tears and cupped my chin in his palm and started to kiss me. I responded and we rolled around the beach getting sand in our hair, teeth, and underwear for over an hour. Even though it felt good, I had butterflies in my stomach the whole time, experiencing moments of nausea, and enjoyment. I also felt an urgency to pee as he rubbed up against me. And very tingly. I finally put two and two together. *Okay, now I get it. Boy, do I get it.* With all those romance and Judy Blume books I had devoured, I still hadn't learned much. After getting up and excusing myself from Pete to try and pee for fifteen minutes in the cabana bathroom, Pete called in, "Hey, are you okay in there?"

I yelled out, "Just fine. Uh, sorry . . . I'll be out in a second." I gave up on peeing, but I didn't want to come back out and face him.

When I did finally exit, he grabbed me, kissed me some more, and then I asked him to take me home and he kindly obliged. I had to get back to do my nightly calisthenics by my cot in the living room before I went to sleep.

The next morning I stretched near the pool by my room for two hours. I was avoiding going to the beach where everyone hung out. I was embarrassed to see Pete. When I finally gathered up the courage to go, I saw him at the beach bar, drinking a banana daiquiri with some guys. He gave me a big smile. All of his friends did too. Then he exclaimed to them, "Doesn't she have great abs!"

That night I saw him at the casino, and we sat at the bar talking. He was smooth, Mr. Confident. He had his number down pat. He was talking to all the other girls who came up to him while I just sat there. But I talked to the other guys. I could play the game too. Or maybe I couldn't, and deep down I knew that. But the night ended up being a memorable one. Pete convinced me to come back with him to his villa. He had his own separate casita away from his parent's. It was beautiful in there, very romantic, like a Ralph Lauren home-furnishings ad set in Africa. It was dimly lit, and the bed had a veil of transparent cloth hanging over it. He lit cream-colored candles that smelled of vanilla and turned the radio on low. He walked over to me and picked me up and put me on the bed and kissed me tenderly. Then he slipped my silk shimmering orange dress over my head. It felt so intimate and intense, relaxing and soothing. It was three hours of motion, all softness and caresses. Then we lay there and he said, "You're anorexic, aren't you?"

I was a bit bewildered. "I don't know. I guess so."

He said, "I used to be. All this past year. Now I eat but I work out a lot." Oh. Okay. *Weird.* I had never heard of a male anorexic. *What, did he think it was cool or something sharing that information with me? What, were we bonding or something?* It actually pissed me off, this subject becoming a focus.

Then he said, "You're so little. You're so beautiful. How much do you weigh? I bet less than ninety pounds." I told him I didn't want to talk about it. He smiled a lot at me. I don't remember smiling. I was ready to go. He drove me home, kissed me by my door, and left. I never got a chance to say good-bye to him because he went back to New York City the following morning.

I spent the eight days left running ten miles a day, tanning, and going to sleep early. I was starting to really feel the effects of my antidepressant and an extreme tiredness would take me over at 9 P.M. during dinner, after I had finished my first and only meal. My parents were upset that I wouldn't eat anything during the day. One morning on the beach, in front of all the private-school families whose beach chairs were lined up as if they were a members-only club, my father called me over to him. He told me to take a sip from his large bottle of orange juice. I stared at the rich orange liquid, thirsting for a taste, but I was too stubborn. I wouldn't touch it. I couldn't break my rules. My dad started yelling at me in front of everybody about how ridiculous it was for me to wait all day until 8 P.M. to take my first bite of energy. He threatened to force the juice down my throat. Why was he doing this? Embarrassing me like this. I looked around at all the families and people we knew who were gawking and then pretending to look away like they weren't interested. Then I got up, gave my dad an evil look, and I walked along the beach away from the danger and cried.

Later in the afternoon, when I came back, a little girl came over to me as I was lying there suntanning and said, "My mommy says you can't go back to school until you gain some weight. Why don't you just eat?" Humiliation and confusion overtook me. What a nosy little brat. Is that what the gossip was? Did all the private-school parents spend their vacations gossiping about Jerry and Susan's anorexic daughter who couldn't handle Dalton while their children were thriving? I said to the brat that she had no idea what she was talking about.

In St. Martin I reached eighty-six pounds. My mother had weighed me there at Dr. Bowen's request. Ironically, I had thought I gained weight since starting to see Dr. Bowen, but I had been ninety-eight pounds at the start of our sessions. The twelve pounds had come off so quickly. My mother called him from the resort and he told her to warn me to stop right where I was, otherwise I would be hospitalized when I got back to New York.

7. My Choice of Medicine

On a cold snowy morning in January 1988, my mother woke me up for my first day at my new school. I resisted her every bit of the way. I threw a tantrum and stubbornly announced that I was not going. I planned to lie in bed all day instead. But somehow she got me out the door. I walked the long twenty blocks stiffly wrapped in the bundles of clothes she had forced me to wear. My wet tears were blending with the snowflakes that stuck to my chin. All I wanted to do was turn back.

When I entered the small brownstone I saw only a few kids. I was early. I went into the dean's office to meet the headmaster. A woman with a dirty blond mane hanging to her butt and thick eyeglasses sat surrounded by a cloud of smoke as she puffed on her cigarette and yapped on the phone. She saw my tear-stained face, gave me a big smile, and motioned to me to come in and sit down. She finished her call and got up to shut the door. She said, "I'm glad you're here, Jenny. I'm Linda. I know it's been hard, but this school will be good for you. You're seeing Dr. Andrew Bowen, right? He's a wonderful man. There's some nice kids here. Come, I'll introduce you."

Two shy girls from Staten Island showed me the garden where students were smoking and hanging out. Then they took me upstairs so I could see the tiny classrooms that were separated by flimsy dividers. I caught glimpses of the kids and heard a snide bit of a conversation that included the really polite language of, "Yo, suck my dick," and "Your ass is grass" between two big guys with big gold chains who looked old enough to be married and have children already. *No wonder my mother cried.*

I was supposed to look for a girl named Tory, who was friendly with my best friend Nikki's sister and was bulimic. Nikki and her sister's friends had eating disorders; meanwhile, both of them were skinny, with A-1 bodies, and ate what they wanted. My eyes were drawn to a beautiful girl with golden hair and bright blue eyes who was dressed in sleek black pants and a tight black turtleneck sweater. She had the skinniest legs I'd ever seen. She looked like a string bean, so I asked her if she was Tory. She laughed and said that Tory was a good friend of hers but that she wasn't here today. *Too much bingeing and vomiting, hmm?*

My first class was math, and the teacher resembled Igor. The girls clued me in that he was perverted. I did notice that when he spoke he stared at our chests. Still, I thought the girls were being ridiculous—he was probably just shy. I wanted to hate everybody. I sat in my chair with a snarl on my face.

But I immediately bonded with Graham, the English and history professor. He was six foot five and British. With his red hair and a red mustache that wiggled up at the ends, he reminded me of a cross between Sherlock Holmes and Donald Sutherland. He was witty and engaging and started his class off by apologizing for his sharp accent. He warned us that he used some strange British words and that what he called rubbers were erasers. We laughed. There was something about him that welcomed and inspired me. I could tell he was a good teacher because when we answered his first few questions he made warm eye contact with each student and encouraged us to continue speaking. In class I noticed a skinny boy with dark hair and blue eyes sitting in the corner and looking at me. We were both dressed *rather floating* in blue Oshkosh overalls. We looked kind of alike. His wrist was so skinny. I wondered if he was anorexic too. After class he said his name was Sam and asked if I wanted to go to lunch with him. We walked out of the brownstone and around the corner, where he took me to a vegan place. He ate a huge salad while I drank an iced tea. We were instant pals; we didn't even have to talk.

I met Tory the next day. She was in my math class and sat next to me chewing her gum really hard and popping it. She was slim, not that thin, though. She sent me a note that read, "Do you vomit?" I wrote back, "Not really. I can't." She wrote back, "Use ipecac."

After class she told me, "It's really cool, like you can eat anything and then, like, puke it all up, like chocolate and cookies. It's great." At the time, I didn't know that Karen Carpenter had had a heart attack and died from repetitively using ipecac. But even when I found out, in those moments of panic I didn't care. My insides were strong, I thought.

The very same day that I learned of ipecac, at ninety pounds, I ate some chocolate and some ice cream. Then, like a robot, I went into a pharmacy and found it sitting on the shelf with all the other first aid equipment. I buried it between a box of tissues and Tylenol, hoping the salesperson wouldn't wonder why a fifteen-year-old was buying a bottle of something to rid herself of poison. She just rang it up, probably didn't even know what the stuff was. I raced home with fear and excitement. *Let's see if this shit really works, otherwise what a run I'll have to take.* I took two tablespoons of the sweet syrup and a large glass of water. I waited a bit.

Within ten minutes I thought I was going to die. I began to tremble, to salivate, my ribs began to pull and heave. My dad happened to come home early from work to find me lying in my brother's bottom bunk bed sweating and as green as a lime. And then I threw up over the side of the bed and kept throwing up even after there was nothing left inside me.

"What did you do?!!" he yelled. "What did you do?"

I told him, and he kept yelling.

His exact words were "I oughta put you through the roof! How could you do that? Do you want to kill yourself? Are you crazy?"

And I remembered his tears when he picked me up from ballet camp and saw his baby at ten years old half starved. But this time he was angry. And all I wanted was for him to hold me tight and protect me from myself. Eventually he calmed down, and I slept the experience off as if I had the flu.

But I still continued to use the ipecac, sometimes with fear, sometimes without. I swear I know every pharmacy in New York where you can buy it. One warm spring day while walking along Second Avenue, I ate everything in sight: pizza, doughnuts, ice cream, *you name it*. When I was finally nauseated beyond belief, I panicked and thought ipecac was the only way out *this time*. I picked up a bottle and went to St. Catherine's Park on First Avenue and 68th Street, the park I grew up roller-skating, flirting, and eating ice cream cones without guilt in when I went to public school, the park that later turned into a drug zone. How perfect. I took my drug and waited, scared to death that it wouldn't work. Waited and waited in the corner of the park. And then it began. I started to walk home, stopping to throw up every two steps. Like a bum on the street, I gagged, heaved, and missed the garbage cans. There I was, dressed in a tiny white French Connection blouse and khaki cut-offs and little brown loafers. *And they were getting very dirty.* I tried to stop and sit on the steps of a public library to rest. I watched little girls holding their mothers' hands, leaving with a pile of books. I saw people exit after giving blood to the blood drive at the center next door. I looked toward the park and saw bare-chested male athletes throwing basket-balls into hoops. There I was, still slim but sick. I was jealous of every-one else's peace. What was happening to me? Why was I so ravenous and out of control? How had I become addicted?

I called my oldest brother, Brad. "Brad, I don't feel so well. Threw up all over the street."

He started to laugh nervously, then asked, "What do you mean? Why?" He had this image of me puking uncontrollably on the street. I started to laugh. There was a little humor to this. "Go home and rest," he suggested. "Don't do it again."

I always had to tell somebody after I took that shit, usually my mother. In the recent years when I was staying in my apartment, I'd curl up in a ball under my covers, sick and nauseated, and I'd reach for the phone. I'd call her up and beat around the bush. In a raspy, strained and monotone voice I'd tell her that I wasn't feeling well, just wasn't feeling myself. She'd know instantly and say, "Did you slip? You didn't take that stuff, though, did you? Did you take that stuff? Oh God, Jenny. Oh God." I'd start crying heavily and admit it to her. I had to confess my sin, and I had to ask for help.

I got through the rest of the spring without bingeing or using ipecac too frequently. I would go work out at Body by Jake and Tina in the early morning and then grab myself a huge cup of coffee to bring to Graham's first class. I looked forward to his course. We read lots of poetry, and somehow I managed to write papers for him that earned me As. I felt like I could break the rules in my essays for him. I wrote freely, and I designed big bright covers for my papers. There was something sophisticated about his top-floor discussions. He was the best teacher I'd ever had, and he made me feel smart.

Sometimes I would stay late after school just to chat about life with him and Linda. I also loved my Buddhism class. I taught *myself* how to smoke. I hung out with club kids who wore motorcycle jackets. I was inspired to wear creative outfits at school, like all black one day, with tons of colorful beaded necklaces around my neck, two leather belts lying on the hip, and red sneakers. Then, on the next day, maybe it would be a lace camisole, a tiny cardigan tucked into huge men's long johns with striped suspenders, and big faded brown hiking boots. I was hyper from the Prozac, so I giggled and flirted a lot. I sat outside in the garden writing in my journal. When the kids played the boom box I danced and was in with the hip-hoppers. I was also in with the Mafia gang and with the bisexual coke addicts. There was a little bit of everything at this small school. I was learning about people. It was refreshing. I felt comfortable, like I could be myself. I was thankful that a place like this existed. It was cool. In many ways, cooler than Dalton.

My parents took me on spring break to Santa Fe. I had requested we go to that place where there was beautiful beadwork. *You know, like where Aunt Ricky and Uncle Ralph get all that gorgeous southwestern art.* I had seen all the stuff floating around their homes: the exotic blankets, the woven basketry, the Fritz Sholder abstract painting of an Indian/cowboy on a horse. I also had become obsessed with beads earlier that year because they were so colorful. We stayed in Tesuque, New Mexico, in a rugged and quiet casita. The air smelled so fresh, and the sky was so big and blue. I loved everything about it, especially running in the dirt roads during early morning. After all the chaos of that year, getting a new doctor, starting an antidepressant, St. Martin, changing schools, I finally felt at peace. The shops were filled with colorful beadwork by the American Indians and bright paintings. There were crafts and art all over, and the place overflowed with creativity and magic. I walked along the roads in my suede-fringed jacket, ripped jeans, and cowboy boots, and I felt empowered. I fell in love.

I actually ate on this trip, wonderful flavorful meals. The smells of green chili and salsa and fresh guacamole and earthy cozy adobe restaurants soothed me and made me feel comfortable. Still, I did force myself to run six to ten miles before our long days of sightseeing, gallery hopping, and hiking. Each afternoon I looked forward to going back to our casita and doing yoga in my piñon-scented room and then dressing up all western for dinner. I loved sipping my father's margaritas.

My mom and I bought tons of beads, colorful seed beads, and heshi shell and turquoise and all the right findings so I could make lots of jewelry. The beads were like candy to me, so many colors and sizes and textures. They were absolutely delicious. I was inspired.

When we returned to New York, I convinced my parents to let me redo my brothers' room, which I was going to inherit now that they were both gone, in Santa Fe style. It was a project I became obsessed with. My parents called this rugged guy from creative services at the office to come over, and I showed him pictures of a loft bed made of logs and pictures I had taken in Santa Fe. We discussed plastering the walls to look like adobe and tiling the floor and ordering fresh twigs for shutters. They ordered logs for the bed and ceiling. We planned to start work over the summer. I don't know if my parents let me do this to express my creative spirit, or rather just to indulge me. Years later when they were trying to sell the apartment, it was my crazy room that kept most people from purchasing it.

I finished the term at the Tutoring School of New York. I had made it. I had even been voted the sexiest girl and the girl with the prettiest eyes. I really felt good there. I planned to return the following year.

On my sixteenth birthday, in June, I invited my four close friends from Dalton to dinner with my family. It was great to see everybody. We were all wearing short, tight dresses, and we admired one another's outfits. I ate. I saw my friends watching me. My friend Jane said, "It's so good to see you eating again." Forget it. That made me self-conscious. I stopped. Then we went to MK's, a nightclub, and we hung out by the pool table checking out guys. It felt strange to be with them. I felt like things had changed so much, like I had changed so much.

That night before I went to sleep I felt aroused. I remembered when Dr. Bowen had asked me, "Do you ever masturbate?" I had giggled and been embarrassed and said, "God, no."

He said, "It's nothing to be ashamed of; it might be good for you to get in touch with your sexuality." So that night I took his suggestion. It was great. It made me hungry. I went to the kitchen, yeah, only a few feet away, and took a box of Frosted Flakes out of the cabinet and brought it to my bed. I ate the entire box.

A few days later, my brother Greg and I were play boxing in the garage while waiting for my parents to get the car to drive to our Connecticut country house that they had purchased a few years earlier.

Greg had one of his cute friends with him, so I was showing off, kicking my leg high and trying to karate-chop Greg with it. I was in my hyper-giddy Prozac mode. Greg caught my leg and I tried to flip away from him, causing me to go flying through the air like Superwoman, and then *crunch* . . . landed on my left wrist. I broke it.

The doctor told me not to jog or exercise for at least a month, and I was a bit relieved, actually, to rest. That summer I kept beading necklaces and earrings as well as I could with the use of only my right arm, and I ate. A lot.

I began to binge more often, and I was afraid to use ipecac all the time. So I would strain and force my hands down my throat and my body would resist me. Then I'd be stuck with the calories, the torment, the growing fear that I was out of control, and my growing body. Put on twenty pounds just like that over the summer. My face was always swollen and puffy but I didn't even care that I was destroying my beauty. I really just couldn't help it.

When we were at our Connecticut country house, I began to sneak entire cereal boxes up to my bedroom, homemade muffins . . . cookies . . . potato chips. All of a sudden I just couldn't stop, couldn't get enough food, especially sweets. I would eat, try to vomit, playing dumb when the old 1785 toilets got clogged, fall asleep, then eat more, and try to vomit again. I didn't change my clothes often or come downstairs to be with everyone.

When my parents found me at 3 A.M. vomiting into an empty carton in the attic, things were at their worst. My mom started hyperventilating so intensely that we thought she was having a heart attack. I can still see her ghostly white face. It looked as if she were going to die. But it was me they sent to a hospital in White Plains.

8. Hospital Time

The door was locked. It was large and heavy. I used to stare at it from inside, eagerly awaiting the social worker who would open it up for the visitors and doctors, just to catch a glimpse of life beyond. Freedom was supposedly on the other side. Which side did I belong on?

I had no clue where I was going on September 26, 1988, the day I surrendered to my parents' and my doctor's request to admit myself to the hospital in White Plains, New York. Suddenly, at sixteen, I found myself locked up and being treated as a person who had committed a crime. The crime, of course, I had done to myself.

The social worker met us in the lobby and then escorted my parents and me upstairs, then down a long hallway, and finally to the door I would come to know well, where she jingled her big mound of keys. I peered inside and looked all the way down a long fluorescent-lit corridor. There were chairs and sofas and people scattered about. I heard whispers and rustles and noticed various girls looking up at me, transfixed. "She must be a bulimic," someone said, and "Shit, is that Courteney Cox?" "Whose bed is she taking?" I didn't want to stare, but I got a glimpse of one ghostlike skeleton sitting alone away from the others with an IV in her arm. She smiled at me.

I was brought to the nurses' office first for a medical exam while my parents waited outside. I slipped into the blue gown quickly because I couldn't bear to look at my body and see all the fat flesh I had gained over the summer. I didn't want to be weighed. The nurse asked, "Why are you here?"

I said, "Uh . . . well, I've been making myself vomit. I put on a lot of weight this summer. Before, I guess I wasn't eating."

She asked, "How many times do you vomit a day?"

I wasn't sure. It was always different. "Well, uh . . . about three to four times a day." She stared at me blankly. She continued taking my measurements, my pulse, my blood pressure, my weight. I weighed 117 pounds. I cried. I knew I had gained weight, but that was a lot since the last time I stepped on the scale at 95 pounds. All those times alone in the house, stuffing my face, followed by numerous hours struggling to rid myself of what I'd eaten. It hadn't done shit for me. I wasn't even a good vomiter. I asked the nurse why I had gained so much weight. The nurse explained that starving and vomiting wrecks a person's metabolism. After periods of starvation your metabolism tries to adjust to the introduction of food but has significantly slowed down, which accounts for the rapid weight gain. The body is overcompensating in fear of future starvation. Vomiting is not only hazardous because nutrients don't get metabolized, but it also doesn't work as a weight-loss technique because most of the calories still get absorbed as soon as the salivary glands, the fat cells, and the amino acids start breaking the food down. She explained all this like a math teacher solving an equation at the board. To her it was all simple mathematics. I was pissed. Pissed at myself, pissed at the doctors, pissed at my parents. They all told me I couldn't go on with my earlier behavior, when I was running and eating *my* way. Then they gave me those damn antidepressants and that progesterone, which screwed with my discipline. I had been thin. And I couldn't believe I fell for it, the vomiting thing. I never thought I was the type to take the easy way out. No wonder it didn't work.

At the end of the checkup, the nurse said, "You're fortunate your health is pretty good. But you have swollen glands. You're lucky your teeth are okay." Part of me was relieved. Part of me wanted to be really sick. I wanted to have a heart problem, an arrhythmia like a girl at school. Something at least to validate the mess I had made. And something to prove how good a bulimic I was.

I wouldn't sign the admittance papers until I was convinced that I could leave if I didn't like it. They said since I was under twenty-one my parents would have to sign me out. My parents smiled and told me that it was for the best for now and we would see what happened. The average stay was two months. That seemed rather long. I knew there was nowhere else to go. I knew I needed help.

I didn't cry when my parents left. I was numb. The nurse told me to make myself comfortable and sit near the other girls until they gave me a room. The girls all acknowledged me immediately, as if they were hungry for conversation, for fresh meat, for my story. One tiny boppy twelve-year-old said, "Don't worry. You'll get used to it. Are you bulimic?" I began telling them my situation. They were really friendly. Some of them were so skinny, and some were very overweight. And they all were anorexic and bulimic or both. It scared me that the heavier girls were once anorexic. I was told that the doctors really plumped everyone up. Everyone asked me, "Do you have to gain? What's your ideal weight?" Shit, I was hoping they'd help me lose. I was fat.

I was okay sitting there until some bald creature came up the hallway from the kitchen zipping all over the place like Woody Woodpecker. The creature hopped up the corridor, then sped back down and then spun back up until she found a spot in the corner, where she remained running in place. A girl who was sitting next to me said, "Don't mind her. That's Kate. She's been in eight hospitals where she was strapped down and nose-fed. She can't sit down." I felt so bad for her. *But I wasn't like her. I wasn't a total loony, was I?*

In general, most of the girls were nice (at that early period there weren't any men on the unit), some befriended me with I-know-how-you-feel smiles, while others just sat in their chairs staring out like zombies. One thirteen-year-old gum-chewing girl from Long Island who was of average weight and wore a huge Adidas sweatsuit seemed to take the role of ringleader. She came over, told the girl who was in a chair next to me to move, sat down, and explained the deal to me. She didn't forget to mention right away that they had made her gain thirty pounds, she was leaving the following week, and that she just couldn't wait to get out so she could lose it all over again. She said the first three weeks I would have to remain stationary and inside. There was no exercise, no free time outside, no TV room. I was to stay in the restricted area and could only get up from my chair to go to meals or doctor sessions. Eventually I would have to go to school there and to the main house for aerobics. They wanted us to learn how to eat and exercise in moderation. I was mostly upset that I couldn't hang out in my room, which would be locked. I thought I was going to be able to stay in bed and sleep. Take a vacation. Uh-huh. Right.

I was fidgeting in my chair when another nurse came out of her office and yelled, "Commodes!" The girls rushed out of their seats and stood outside their rooms waiting for their doors to be unlocked. One girl chuckled and said, "You'll love this. Did they give you a tin?" I asked what she meant and she explained that we had to go to the bathroom in it. "Have fun." What? Is she kidding? Then I was taken to my room, where I found my bag, which had been opened and searched, on a tiny cot. There was a mint green plastic container that I was supposed to pee in. I was going to pee in cat litter. It took me ten minutes to relax enough to go, and then I was led to the bathroom, where the girls were in a long line; it smelled of urine and poop. We had to measure the urine and dump it for the nurse, and then wash the container and return it to our rooms and then come back out to our seats. We had to do this six times a day.

I gathered they couldn't trust us, but it was so degrading. Some of the nurses were nice about it, but some were downright hostile. There were a few who just seemed as though they were following the drill, but others made a big to-do out of it, looking at us suspiciously or making us beg to use the bathroom when it wasn't commode time. To some of them we were lab animals. Then there was the showering routine: two girls at a time in one stall with no curtain in between for privacy, while a nurse stood by. No razors unless it was an earned privilege. I expected warmth at this place, some understanding. I guess it was that thing they call tough love.

There was no p.c., physical contact, allowed. That was difficult because as we bonded, we were unable to show one another any affection. As we convulsed in tears after group meetings, we were unable to pat each other on the back or give a hug. When I was later put in a room with three other girls, we got away with braiding each other's hair in our rooms at night before we went to bed. We took turns crying each other to sleep. The doctors believed we were all too vulnerable to be touched.

Eventually I would discover that many of the girls had been sexually abused.

The first meals were intense. There were three tables. In one corner Kate and the severely underweight girls sat and drank liquids and Sustacal shakes. At the other two tables, girls sat picking and playing with the food on their trays. Everyone had a different number of items because there were different goal weights and the calories precisely calculated for every girl. I didn't have to gain, just had to remain somewhere between 116 and 123 and consume about 1,600 to 1,800 calories a day. I was disgusted by the reality that my weight had escalated that past summer from all the bingeing and unsuccessful attempts at vomiting. There was a lot of crying in the room. I ate everything the first night. I knew they would record everything you did or didn't eat; I wanted to be a good girl. But hell, I was also hungry. Some girls stuffed everything down so they could get the torture over with. Others sat and stared at their trays. One girl chewed food, spit it out, and kept rechewing it, and finally spat it out, leaving it on the rim of her plate. Some girls moaned as they tried to swallow their food. Afterward we all had to sit together where we were watched over. No chance to vomit.

If we smoked, which I had started to do that past spring at the Tutoring School, we were allowed four cigarettes a day, one after each meal and one after our night snack. I savored those cigarettes. They were holy cigarettes. The way the girls looked at their cigarettes while they sucked at them and sighed after their first puff was enough to make anyone want to start smoking. There was such passion. After cigarette time came meds. Our names were called out individually to report to the office and get our candy. My meds were Prozac and eventually Colace and prunes. Half the girls were constipated like me. I could never shit in that place. All the bingeing and purging had already started to mess up my bowels. Saved a lot of embarrassment for me during the commode thing at least.

The first night I was in my room I twisted and turned on the uncomfortable cot. I just wanted to sleep, but I couldn't. I was exhausted from all the bulimic episodes and the crying from the week before. I felt some relief to be there. It wasn't a cozy, warm, safe relief. It was as though the noise in my head had been abruptly turned down, but the silence was blank and ominous. I lay there on that cot feeling like a foreigner in my own country. Half scared, half excited to be away from home. Away from the last year. Away from my parents. I didn't miss them that much yet. After twenty minutes of staring into the darkness, I became startled and jumped up when I saw a flashlight beam in on me through the little window of my door. I saw a black man's face staring at me. I was mortified. I learned that they did rounds, peeking in six times a night to make sure we weren't exercising or doing something illegal. There was no privacy. That and the fear of remaining fat, of eating, of never getting out of there, was the worst part of all.

The following day a man with a chestnut brown beard and bright blue eyes came onto the unit. The girls whispered, "There he is. Ooh. Ooh." They stared. One girl said, "That's Dr. Shark [I will call him], he's so cute. Is he your doctor? You're so lucky if you get him." I didn't think he was anything that great. I hated beards. It seems that all male psychiatrists have beards. What is it, a dress code? Dr. Shark was my doctor. He came over to me and introduced himself as the other girls batted their eyelashes at him. He asked me to follow him. We were going out of the locked door. Yeah! We were going upstairs to his office.

I sat on the couch facing him at his chair. He asked, "Do you mind if we record or videotape these sessions?"

Of course I minded. This guinea-pig, lab-animal bullshit was too much. I said, "I'd prefer not." Most of the session was wasted on arguing about being videotaped. I couldn't believe it. I didn't like Dr. Shark. I didn't like this whole thing. He was arrogant, and I assumed that he got off on how much the girls fawned all over him. Well, I was not one of *those girls*. I felt feisty with him, ready to attack. Occasionally I tried to imagine what it would be like to sleep with him, to see what the others saw in him. He was a flirt, no doubt about it, and I think he did it on purpose to rile all of us up. He really seemed like a male chauvinist. It was that smirk he always had on his face. It made me uncomfortable.

I couldn't understand how he could be a doctor at an eating disorder unit that consisted of all females when he was such a jerk.

After he finally dropped the recording business, I flat out said, "Listen, I wasn't sexually abused, my parents aren't divorced, and I've been loved to death, so I don't know where we're gonna go here."

He said, "Tell me about being loved to death."

9. Fashion and Family

At twenty-four years old and physically ill, I can't look at a fashion magazine now, let alone a beautiful Polo/Ralph Lauren ad. In fact, I don't even want to hear my father speak of how great the line opening went or ask me if I like the "look" he has on for the evening, charcoal pinstripe suit over charcoal cashmere turtleneck, or if he can get away with the navy sport sweats with the navy Shetland sweater. And then I check out my mom, now in her fifties, still lean and sleek in her brown suede leggings or jodhpurs, and as blond and elegant as Grace Kelly in her navy or black sleeveless high-necked evening gown, and although proud, I cringe with jealousy. Right now I feel confined to being a total slob, wouldn't even try to force on the size 4 tweed skirts I so happily used to wear when they hung off my hips.

Growing up in the family of a celebrity fashion designer, Ralph Lauren, yeah, *the Ralph Lauren,* has been a peculiar existence. It gets even more complicated because my father, Ralph's older brother, is also extremely talented and supervises the design of the menswear line with the utmost devotion and passion. I will not speak for him, but I imagine it's a hard position to be in. So I spent my childhood trying to give respect to my own father. I don't like being referred to as Ralph Lauren's niece. When asked over and over again if I am related (and I'm sure it will continue until I change my name), I say, "I am the daughter of JERRY LAUREN, THE HEAD OF MENSWEAR DESIGN." It's not that I felt defensive or angry, it's just that people often didn't know exactly how close it all was to me, in the sense that designing clothes is my father's life and soul. It didn't matter that I was Ralph's niece because my experience, my excitement or conflict with it all, was directly related to my father's take on appearance, image, fashion, detail. I always wanted people to know who my father was, not just for me but for him—a man who is brilliant and creative and has devoted his energy, heart, and gifts to that empire. I took great pride in my father's work, because I knew how much he thrived on designing, on guiding his team, and how he used his sense of humor to break the ice in a second. I also knew how much he respected his brother Ralph, and I think because of that, he often downplayed his own talents. Never wanting to take away anything from his brother. My uncle relies on him. They rely on each other. But being a "Lauren," for me, is mostly about being my father's daughter.

In the beginning, almost thirty years ago, when the design team was just forming, there was this tiny office space; you'd enter and you would instantly see everyone who worked there, some busily sketching, some buried by swatches of fabric, maybe a famous model or two being fitted; it was like this tiny creative factory of elves. Then there were those few with their own separate offices, and I felt proud to walk into my father's, with its own window. With fascination I would peer up at the patterned swatches tacked up to the wall or at sample clothing lying on chairs (hoping I could take something home with me). Color galore, everywhere. I'd come to visit and my father would hold up a bunch of ties, or, with this huge, childlike grin, show me a pile of knits. "Whadda ya think about these, eh? . . . Great, eh? Look at these kelly greens, these paisleys? Great, eh?" He was on fire in there, creating. He'd say, "Look at this herringbone, look at this houndstooth; oh, and what about this silk tie, isn't it fabulous?" It took me a long time to know the names of the tweeds, or remember the face that went with a name that I had heard before, because I was so self-conscious and dizzy every time I went there. I loved taking a peek into my dad's world. It was then I realized that he had a whole other life that his family was not really a part of.

Sometimes I was jealous. I was even jealous of my dad's relationship with his brother. They've always had a bond, a private kind of kinship that included a language all their own. I think they grew up dreaming and looking at the world in a similar way, taking everything and anything in for all its worth, with a sensitivity to the details, the mood, the feeling evoked by people, things, places. Their language is based on a shared understanding and appreciation for style, fashion, ambiance, image, art. And then, of course, their mutual upbringing.

When I was a young girl, my uncle Ralph was always the mysterious, cool gray-haired man that my father would point at in the office and say, "Come, Jenny, I want Uncle Ralph to see you. I want you to say hello. Don't forget to give him a kiss." When I would say hello to my uncle, I was shy and intimidated. There was something about the way he looked at me, the intensity of his gaze, that made me feel beautiful, special, and like crumbling into pieces all at once. At a young age I could feel the power he emanated even in his silence. My father would ask if I enjoyed seeing Uncle Ralph. "He just adores you. He couldn't take his eyes off you."

"Yes, Dad, he's very nice."

My dad would baby talk, "But who do you think is more handsome?"

"Daddy, of course you're more handsome."

I did have a crush on my uncle when I was young. He looked like a real cowboy, a Redford type, the electric horseman, to me. The faded blue of the denim jackets and dungarees he wore and his gray, weathered hair did wonders for his light blue eyes; there was no getting around the fact that my uncle was rugged and cool. But I considered my dad dreamy . . . tall, muscular, dark, handsome, with green eyes that glowed. He was the navy cashmere turtleneck type, totally "deadly" looking (a word frequently used in my family), but he was also the preppy, pink oxford type. (My mom recalls meeting my dad for the first time in the elevator of the place they worked in the garment center and says, "And he was wearing a yellow oxford. I couldn't believe it. Handsome, preppy, and cool. A yellow oxford!" My dad says, "She was wearing a short skirt, and I got a look at her legs and tiny ankles and that was it, I was in love.")

I had a crush on my father too. I think I still do.

Vanity played a role in my father's household. My dad was one of four siblings, three very handsome males and one attractive older sister. They lived in the Bronx, and the ongoing discussion around the dinner table was probably about who was the most handsome of the brothers or rating one another from a scale of one to ten. I've felt a kinship and empathy to their sister, Thelma, being forced, in a sense, to live among handsome, dominating, and opinionated men. I'm not kidding, the three brothers were gorgeous, and they knew they resembled the likes of Cary Grant and Gregory Peck, and they knew the power that comes from that. I always wonder what a typical Friday Sabbath dinner could have been like. Conversation floating freely from talk of James Dean's great red jacket, Grant's houndstooth blazer, the blond bombshell who worked in the delicatessen wearing the soft pink Shetland sweater and pearls . . . *Baruch a ta adonai,* Marlon Brando's motorcycle jacket, and . . . pass the gefilte fish, please.

I feel guilty calling my dad's family vain. Mostly because I am at war with the concept of vanity. What's the difference between the vanity that comes from feeling mediocre, or unattractive, that causes people to become obsessed with face-lifts, breast implants, hair rugs, and nose jobs, and the kind of vanity that comes from being naturally attractive. Either way, vanity to some extent is forced upon us, and grows within us.

They had the goods in every way. They were incredibly talented in the arts, in drawing, painting, and in athletics. My grandfather was one of those semi-brilliant types, an Albert Einstein look-alike who taught himself to paint and play the violin and organ. Unfortunately, his career as a house painter never really took off, but he was warm and gentle and fostered in his children a great love and respect for the humanities. Supposedly he painted murals in the lobbies of some New York apartment buildings and synagogues, but my father claims they've been painted over. One of my art teachers from college who uses Jewish biblical themes in his work flipped when I told him this. He was on a mission to find them, but nothing turned up.

The kids were all on the neighborhood and school sports teams, and they played that legendary stickball in the schoolyard. I hear about it every time my dad throws a ball in Connecticut with my brothers and me. The boys, of course, were competitive about sports too. They all were artistic, especially Thelma. In fact, she later married an archaeologist and led a bohemian lifestyle, painting and drawing in her upstate New York home. When I was in college, she gave me an amazing piece of her work, a drawing on corrugated cardboard of an exotic dark-haired voluptuous girl with huge thighs hidden in a transparent blue veil. I thought it resembled me. *The thighs.* Her children are about fifteen years older than I; her daughter is an illustrator whose rapidograph pen is her magic wand, and her son is a mathematics professor who is married and lives on a kibbutz in Israel. Now *that* is cool.

My other uncle, Lenny, the eldest boy, now lives in New Rochelle and was in the jewelry display business. Every time we used to visit his family I looked forward to spending time with his two daughters, who were drop-dead gorgeous. I always wished they were my older sisters (the youngest was twelve years older). They both are extremely creative and work for Polo/Ralph Lauren now. My uncle Lenny always had to find a gift for me. He'd go down in his basement and come up with some cool pin or relic for me to take home. In recent years he'd flash his gleaming smile and exclaim, "Jenny, you look gorgeous. When are you coming to the club? You should come play tennis with me. Have lunch. I know a great young lawyer you should meet."

My grandmother was a very short, stout, buxomy woman—the epitome of the Jewish mother. She held down the fort, feeding, nourishing her kids, literally and metaphorically. She made a great matzo brei, and loaded on the heavy cream. A meal was not a meal without the cream, the butter, the salt. My father didn't grow up with much money, but life on Mosholu Parkway in the Bronx was rich in love, intellect, artistic passion, and starry-eyed dreams. I always felt bad, though, *that my fa-*

ther never got that bike he wanted for his bar mitzvah, something he has told us kids over and over when tears form in his eyes as he talks about how hard his parents worked.

But the Lauren family has always been overly dramatic, overly sensitive, and complex. I could read the worry on my grandmother Freda's face as she whined, "Yus Yus, when will you come visit next, why are you leaving so soon? . . . Why is Jenny not eating? . . . Here, Yus, make her eat some Mandel bread. Yus, are you sure Susan is really Jewish?" (Years after they were married I think they still didn't believe him . . . they thought most pretty blondes must be WASPs.) There were constant phone calls from my grandmother, pleading with my father to go visit, or bring us over, that made him feel guilty. I'd watch him on the phone, his face showing utter agony, "Ma . . . Maaaa. Give me a break. I'll come over tomorrow. Susan's busy. The kids have homework. And I worked hard today. Maaa. Did you hear me?" He'd hang up and frown all night anyhow. It was a no-win situation. He couldn't please them enough. When my dad lay in a hospital bed after almost dying from a hemorrhage in his brain, he made sure his parents never knew. All those weeks, no one told them because my father was afraid they couldn't handle it. *Were they really that fragile?*

My grandparents were Russian immigrants who came over to America before World War II. I always liken them to the suitcases they must have carried. Old, weathered, strong enough to have endured long travels and strife, but just about to rip. Even though there was great humor during our visits, and my grandfather cracked jokes constantly, there was still an intense somberness. Everyone always seemed plagued by something. My grandmother kept trying to nurture, her kids always felt nagged and uneasy, and then I had my problems too. It displeased them that I didn't want the *mandel* bread, and that I went to ballet school four days a week instead of attending Hebrew school like the boys. *Of course, they didn't hear the faux pas I made about having had the shrimp in lobster Cantonese sauce at the Chinese restaurant on Sunday night.* Maybe there was a solemnity built into the family mood because they were orthodox Jews and followed their rules pretty strictly. *Or maybe it was just me*. My father went to Yeshiva University, although he didn't become a rabbi like they wanted him to. Eventually I think they were very impressed by his career. At a Passover seder, amid the seriousness, my father would look at my uncle Ralph while attempting to say the Hebrew prayer perfectly and they would both lose it, giggling, unable to stop. Then I would look at one of my cousins, another one of them would look at the next, and there was a huge domino effect. Laughter befell us. It was really extreme if we had too much of the Manishewitz wine. Perhaps this actually was all quite normal, like any family. No doubt about it, though, there was still a sadness on my grandfather Frank's face, in his music, even in his smile. Worry, anguish, struggle, doubt . . . fear. I picked it up.

I always could see tension on my uncle Ralph's face too. I would misread it when I was younger. My dad would explain, "Jenny, he's not aloof, he's just distracted." Now I recognize that same expression on a lot of older working men, that distracted but important look. *Beauty catches their attention, though, for a little while.*

It was complex with my uncle and my father; they'd stare at me and fuss over me, tell me I was a beautiful creature, and play me up to be a princess. But then my uncle would ask me a question out of the blue about an article of clothing or an ad as if my opinion was the most significant thing in the world. He'd ask what I thought of the cologne ads or the new Lauren model. I was, like, eight years old and he'd be waiting for an answer as if I was a marketing executive. My feedback? *Little ol' me?* I felt important; and I needed to *say* something important, but every time he asked me my opinion through the years, I always became discombobulated. "Um . . . uh, um, they're great, yeah, uh . . . really beautiful."

My dad and Ralph both married their pretty blond wives within the same year. There was an instant bond between my aunt Ricky and my mother, who looked and acted like sisters in their own right. And ironically, after that, both couples each had three kids in the same order, two boys, then a girl, all close in age. There are many old photographs of them pushing baby carriages side by side, both looking lean, fresh-faced, and naturally stylish. They would wear similar outfits, jeans with their mahogany leather, pony-skin, tweed, or bomber jackets with Jackie O or Ray•Ban sunglasses. There are also tons of pictures of my father and my uncle in their rugged Carhartt jackets or navy toggle coats, with a glint of their huge matching Rolex, Porsche, or Swiss Army watches shining on their wrists. The photos of them all in Central Park and on the streets of New York are like scenes from a movie.

Most of my early childhood memories consist of the camaraderie that developed between our two families. We spent many weekends and summers in Amagansett, Long Island, at my uncle and aunt's country house on the beach with their three kids. These were my favorite times, times when we all were these goofy kids just running around all over the place. We'd all go to the beach, hanging out barefoot in ripped dungaree shorts and faded T-shirts. We'd scout for shells or play Marco Polo in the pool, or ride bikes. Everyone would look for the adventure . . . lots of drives in my uncle's new Porsche (he had a huge garage of beautiful sports cars, one lush shiny-colored great car after another in rows) and the go-cart or the motorcycle rides with the boys. I always wanted to ride with David, my cousin who was a year older than me, because he was comforting. I'd clasp my arms around his back and he'd scream "Just HOLD ON . . . Whoopee! You'll be fine!" But sometimes I just let those crazy outings be the guys' thing. I wouldn't want to ruin the fun for them by being too scared, and I'd opt to stay around the house with my younger cousin, Dylan, the other girl. She would busy herself with little projects or her rabbits, while I covered myself with beacon blankets and sat on the wooden window seat in the children's playroom reading.

At night we'd often freshen up for dinner, capturing a collective mood with what we wore. On the gals . . . maybe a little sundress, a faded jean jacket, or a fresh white button-down tied at the waist. Shoes mattered too, either espadrilles, guaraches, or ballet slippers; something light, simple, and feminine. The guys . . . in khaki chinos cut ruggedly at the calf, or faded dungarees, a polo knit or chambray shirt, a simple white tee, maybe even a blue-and-white-striped Picasso-looking shirt. On their feet, faded and weathered loafers or sandals or Stan Smiths. My uncle could really get away with cool leather sandals and even a sarong, especially if he was tan. He looked like a Grecian king, master of his island domain. My father couldn't wear that look, he was too big and too dominating. If it was fall, we'd probably all have on our own vintage brown leather jackets and cowboy boots and exude an essence as cool as James Dean's as we trooped into the green army jeeps to go to Gosman's for seafood on the water, or Sam's in town for pizza.

How we looked, what we wore, was always a big to-do. First I'd have to consult with my mother, and then I'd have to check in with my dad, let him look me down and up to make sure I was wearing the right thing. Then we'd all have to run our outfits by each other and make sure we looked great individually and as a group, especially for my uncle. I wasn't even conscious that we were not necessarily a normal family just getting ready for an evening. We were more like a tableau of American style with a large audience. To me, it actually felt more like a game, a game of play and dress-up. But later on it wasn't that fun anymore—especially when I was busting out of the clothes.

There was constant activity among the Lauren household during those weekends. The night never ended young. We'd drive home and pile into the cozy living room with glass doors that looked out toward the ocean. I'd lie on a Navajo blanket on top of the white ottoman chair, waiting for the film that Uncle Ralph was putting in an old-fashioned projector. There would always be a problem with the reel; it was either tangled or needing to be rewound, and we'd wait anxiously to see a movie about image and inspiration, whether it was Marlon Brando's *On the Waterfront, Rocky,* a James Bond movie, a Redford and Newman collaboration like *Butch Cassidy and the Sundance Kid,* a Woody Allen with Diane Keaton clad in Polo, or one as stylized as *Chariots of Fire,* very white, peaceful . . . *elegant.* As we watched, some of us would drift into sleep, and others would gasp and comment on how great a line was or on an outfit or on a scene. We were always learning about taste, but for me it began feeling more and more like pressure to always remain beautiful. To have style.

Early on I figured out that style wasn't about the polo player label or even wearing clothes that had a label. Fashion should be like makeup: one shouldn't know a woman is wearing it; the more natural-looking, the more she sparkles. The essence of my family's clothing was about creating a mood, and it could be attained by simply wearing a weathered Fruit of the Loom T-shirt and Levi's, or a black leotard and floral sarong from the Caribbean, or an old thrift-shop pinstriped man's vest. I always tried to be creative with my attire, to go out of the bounds of wearing Ralph Lauren. It was about the search for something that spoke to me personally, that was pertinent to me. Similar to anyone who loves to collect antiques, the quest is often about finding an item that says something about who you are, what you are attracted to. It could be old atlases, toy cars, cigar boxes, top hats . . . anything that makes you tick. I never liked to dress up. I wanted to feel like I was born wearing the clothing on my back.

We all got the message that clothes defined your image. I hunted around with my brothers for thrift-shop goodies, vests, bandannas, blazers, jeans, jodhpurs, lace corsets, gabardine shirts, army fatigues, old knapsacks, you name it. I always felt the most comfortable in my old jean jacket or my faded burgundy Harvard sweatshirt, soft, light, and pliable to sweat and my body. I cringed when the whole Double RL line came out. The line that was inspired by old weathered vintage clothing. The secret was out. Everyone would now understand the value of worn, lived-in clothing, and the prices would be jacked up. Tourists would come to America and pay a few grand for an old beat-up jean jacket. It killed me, because I felt my favorite way to dress had been usurped. There was no longer anything unique about it now that the world dressed that way. But it was also tied up to my past, a sweet past, a sweet time.

I wonder sometimes how much being in my family contributed to my disease. I always denied it to shrinks because my parents were so loving, and I thought I had developed my own sense of style. Only when did I have a chance?

In my early teens, the weekends in Long Island became less frequent. My uncle's family began to go away on weekends to their house in Jamaica or their ranch in the Southwest, and my parents bought their own country house in Connecticut. When we did go visit in Jamaica, the same lifestyle, the activities, the dressing, the fun still continued. We kids got in trouble from the parents for swimming past the coral reef, or getting too giddy, or obnoxious, and we were grounded and all forced to go to bed early at times. But there was less intimacy at these gatherings. Meals were more formal, there was a lot more hired help, and we were required to have a change of clothes for dinner. I guess it was inevitable that a self-consciousness would come with that formality.

In high school I purposely rebelled against wearing Ralph Lauren clothes. I used to get pissed off when my parents would say, "We're going to Jamaica, so get all your whites together." I'd cry and stamp my feet and tell them I was going to wear all red. The funny thing is, I might actually wear red and Uncle Ralph would say, "That's really cool, Jenny. I like your look." He was always open to new ideas, new moods. He demanded perfection and would notice if my sleeves needed to be altered, but he was still interested in understanding what made someone choose to wear something, even if it was entirely out of the ordinary. He's always looking for something fresh and new to express amid his respect for the classic and the traditional. I remember a show of mine in college where I had a painting on the wall that I did in a hideous yellow ochre. Most people thought it wasn't quite up to par. Too strange a color. Uncle Ralph saw it and loved it. Yet even the desire to be the one to find some clothing article or outfit that was unique or hip was exhausting. And if I had found something great like a new vintage piece, my uncle would say in his baby talk, "Hey, that's great. Can I have it?" That was his stamp of approval.

It wasn't until my early teens that I felt the distance between our two families. I think it's because during those years the little company basically evolved into an empire, the 72nd Street mansion opened up, the offices moved, and RL became an adjective.

But it also had to do with me. I had been at Dalton with all my cousins, running into them constantly in the hallways. My cousin Andrew was in Greg's grade and I would see them palling around. I was in biology class in the seventh grade with David, who was in the eighth grade. We used to go to dances, goof off, be silly. We went to tennis camp. All of us cousins had the same sense of humor, so I enjoyed spending time with them. Then I got sick, left Dalton, and switched schools. Went into the hospital. They probably didn't know what to make of it at the time. And then there were dinners and birthday get-togethers that I didn't show up for *"because I just wasn't myself,"* my parents would explain. My uncle used to tease me and tell me I reminded him of Greta Garbo. He would say, "She vants to be alone." It wasn't really true. But he chose to see me as dramatic, like he always had. I didn't mind. I guess I seemed more interesting that way. My aunt Ricky always tried to understand me. She was a teacher, studied psychology, and has been on what you might call her own spiritual quest for years. She gave me the book *Women Who Run with the Wolves* when I was in college. Once at a dinner *I made it to* the year before my diagnosis, she saw my pained expression and came to sit by me. She took my hand and stated emphatically, "One day, you're going to do something important. One day you'll go beyond all of this."

For years, basically since college, I have avoided visiting my father at the new office, the forest-green-and-mahogany palace that resembles the moody mansion of the Polo store on 72nd Street and Madison. *(Especially because they keep gigantic bowls of peanut M&Ms in every room.)* I get overwhelmed. Feel too displaced. I used to walk by 72nd Street on my way to Central Park for a run, and I'd cringe, and I wouldn't want to stop to look at the windows. Every time I pass the store I think, *What happened? When did this happen? When did this Lauren thing turn into such an empire? Was I here? Who am I? Jenny Lauren, who the hell is that?* Then I try to look at the windows as I hold my breath. I get anxious *. . . life is moving too fast . . . a new line already . . . what happened to*

Cruise, Fall already? Oh, it's so fuckin' gorgeous, though . . . look at that mannequin . . . that blazer, those alligator shoes . . . shit, I want that, and I want that and that and that and that too. Too much candy, too much pleasure, too much desire, and *anyway my Levi's are even cooler, so fuck it. As long as I am thin and look good in those jeans, it doesn't matter what I wear. But I think I'll ask my mom if she can find out about those suede pants.*

Walking by those 72nd Street windows induced the same kind of panic I had at the fashion shows. They were overstimulating. They were sensuous and erotic experiences, and I just sat there stunned with feelings I didn't understand. As one began, the most provocative and moody music traveled through the air, the audience's attention drawn to the perfect, elegantly dressed woman who strode down the runway aisle as if she were born into the clothes—and the royal family. She'd reach the end of the runway, lean into a one-legged stance, pause for a moment, and then gracefully pirouette, leaning into her other one-legged stance. She'd head back up the runway while our eyes focused on the next beautiful woman strutting toward her. As model after model walked out, creating a hypnotic rhythm, there were gasps, claps, and cameras flashing and clicking in the air as everyone tried to grasp as many details as they could. It was so easy for me to be overwhelmed by the newest line—perhaps luxurious camel overcoats, navy suits, black-beaded evening gowns, the velvet or crocodile shoes—and by the models' chiseled faces and outrageous bodies. Electrifying chills went down my spine every time, no matter what season's collection it was. And at the end I would always cry as the models formed a line and my uncle came walking down the aisle, usually in his weathered jean jacket cowboy look, and kissed my aunt and my cousins while everyone stood and applauded voraciously. Then we waited to congratulate my uncle and I'd panic all over again about having the right thing to say. Afterward I would rush off to school and try to feel like my day was normal. But I'd stay alone in a trance and think, *I will one day be thin enough to wear that stuff* or *Am I related to that man?* Or *How can women that stunning exist? How can we not worship women that beautiful?* And then I would vow to never go to another fashion show in my life.

Since I've been ill for the past year I've kind of missed what's going on in that world. Now I wish I could just take back time, be close with my cousins and be innocent again like the days in the Hamptons. But I could care less about any of the hoopla. It all feels intangible to me anyhow. The joke of it all for me is that when people have found out I'm related to the Lauren family they think I have God knows what: money, luxuries, fortune. Usually I get reverse discrimination; guys become intimidated. That's more common than being used (I get that too, though). I remember once calling up an older artist I was very intrigued with. I asked him about the Broadway show he had just seen the night before and his response was, "It was no big deal. I'm sure it isn't anything as exciting as what you do and get to see." I wanted to say, "You mean like the toilet bowl I stare at so often?"

I don't know if the "Do you get all your clothes free?" or "Do you think you could get me some shirts?" will ever stop. Or the "Hey, weren't you a Lipshitz?" and "Ha ha . . . your lip shits, my ass stinks." I then explain how my grandparents were given that name when they came over as immigrants and that, yes, it was my father and Ralph's decision to change their name in their early twenties after my father's experience in the army being mocked for it, and the name's Lauren, not Loren, and we're not French, okay . . . *and you're not that funny.* I could never understand how certain people could be so tactless, or shall I say "tacky." First of all, why do they care so much, and second of all, who taught them their manners? But the interest that people have in my *Laurenness* never ceases to amaze me.

It might be easy to blame my disease on fashion, and my family. I can't. I will not deny that it played a huge role in affecting my psyche. I did feel that I had to be not only beautiful and thin, but honest, funny, sincere, dramatic, *and* productive. Now, that already leaves a lot of room for insanity. But maybe there was something in my own makeup to account for the extremes I've driven myself to. My own sensitivity.

My own demons. *Maybe it was birth trauma. Maybe it's a past life thing. Maybe it's a missing synapse in my brain.* There had to be something inside me, lurking there, and in my core. My disease is a result of a combination of many factors. It was never just about wanting to look good in those suede pants.

10. Waiting

Turning twenty-five soon, and I feel like a fifty-year-old woman. Right before my eyes, I am watching myself age and lose beauty. I want to pray for help and I realize that I have no religion. Last night, I spoke with my friend Stella from college about this and we discussed how food and our behaviors were our religion. Who and what do I pray to? When the pain happens I pray to God to make it stop, but it is just a desperate plea for help. Do I really believe there is a God? Am I truly in touch with any belief system, anyhow?

I've always had faith in the mystical collisions of people's lives and their ability to communicate on some deeper level of consciousness, and so then I wonder, *Do I really think that there is a higher power guiding us all?* It's hard to fathom that it is that *power* that stops or prevents pain. Maybe it's just supposed to guide us in a direction.

Unless this is truly happening to save me? Unless there really is a so-called master plan for me and for all of us. I usually cringe at that New Age mumbo jumbo. But I realize my thinking is similar to accounts I've read of extremely ill patients who have an epiphany and believe their disease happened for a reason and that the life they led before was the real hell. Maybe I will be lucky and this will only be a glimpse of pain, which came to me to show me that the life I led was being wasted on a disease and loneliness. I kind of believe that, and yet I still can't bear looking at my flabby thighs. I wish these ideas weren't in such violent opposition. Still I must think positively today. *Aah bull-*

shit, the demon wants to say, *you don't know how. What's the use?* But there is a romantic Jenny still there, not yet demolished—maybe a bit less desperate—who wants to see her world transformed. How can I sculpt a new one for myself?

It has been days since Dr. W, my internist, first got the films, and he says he needs to study them before sending me to a surgeon. I understand that there are ten million patients dying with some disease and that I am only one little case, but Dr. W has witnessed me in all this discomfort and he still moves like a goddamn turtle. My life is on hold, so yesterday I worked through the agony of waiting with writing and watercolors. I did a lot of little watercolors that kind of look like puke. I enjoyed letting the colors get all muddy.

Color, glorious color, used to pull me out from the depths of my gloom. I couldn't ever really draw very well, but as my parents and my art teachers used to say, I sure had a great color sense. When I was a little girl I found pure delight in playing with it. With anything I created—paintings, cards, or beaded jewelry—I would revel in using an array of bright whimsical hues. I always chose reds, pinks, royal blues, fuchsias, shades that reminded me of exotic fruits and of happy things. I would draw big bold black outlines and shapes that resembled crowds of flowers, or crowds of people, and design coloring books for myself. It was all about creating a great huge color field. Then I could just celebrate in my picture, charming myself with all the flavors as I filled the regions inside the lines with so many colors. No space could remain blank. The task was to make the colors work like a puzzle, the finished product pleasantly vibrant to my eye.

I remember vividly that at the age of fifteen—my brothers were both at college—my parents went away for the weekend and decided to let me stay by myself for the first time. The freedom and aloneness were quite uncomfortable for me. I walked around the house, I flicked the TV stations, I kept going to the refrigerator. Eventually I binged on halvah, cheese, and God knows what else and tried to vomit, an activity that was becoming more frequent for me around that year. By midnight Saturday, I was sitting on the floor outside the door of the bathroom and staring at the door of my bedroom in a trance of both disgust and relief from my great destructive act. I felt a wonderful impulse of creativity flow right through me. The door was the greatest blank space I had ever seen, and I was going to fill it in. I gathered my big thick Magic Markers, blasted Fleetwood Mac on my stereo, and all over the door I began drawing a huge face of an American Indian girl with enormous eyes, wearing braids with gems adorning her neck. Then I began to color and remained awake all night until I had covered the door completely. When I was finished I stood back and stared in awe. It made me happy. It definitely made up for my actions earlier in the night . . . no more loneliness either. Surprisingly, when my parents returned and saw my masterpiece, they weren't the least bit angry. So I asked them if I could do the bathroom door. Right after coloring the doors with Magic Marker, I bought paint to make them permanent. With a door, paint, and paintbrushes I had found my calling, and my relief. My parents knew that when I was doing something with my mind or making something with my hands that I would enter a calm place. A place far away from all my worries. Before they really understood how much trouble I was in, they knew that my creative drive was the only thing that could save me.

When I studied fine arts in college, I painted at least sixty of these colorful coloring-book-type paintings of crowds, of women, or of funky tribal clans. Junior year, one of my professors suggested that the technique I used was too flat, and that I ought to explore the paint medium, my style as well as my palette. I had become obsessed with my formula. The exercise turned out to be an exciting adventure. I found the varying textures and brush strokes tantalizing. I still found inspiration from bright colors and based most of my work on the American folk art my parents collected—old painted game boards, weather vanes, mill weights with remnants of chipped paint and faded patina, American Indian beadwork, and my favorite, the Buddy L bright red toy trucks from the 1920s. I understood why those objects made my parents so happy, they were candy to the eye. But I began to free up my gestures, drawing fluidly with the paintbrush and expanding my relationship with paint as well as color. I began letting go. I based my senior art show on images of the bright bold wheels from the Buddy L toy. I was lured to the circular shape, firm and solid. They became circles floating amid a landscape. Wheels moving in time.

I am still trying to paint the wheel in space, only now the colors are muddy. They're an account of the gloomy days of this period in my life. Another phase, *my blue phase.* Either I'll keep 'em or burn the mother-fuckers. I have so much anger this morning as I wait for the torture chamber. I'm taking advantage of this small window of time before I eat or go to the bathroom to get my emotions down on paper. Within the next hour the infamous twitch in my butt will begin to do its dance, and I will become preoccupied by it all weekend until there is some respite. No more watercolors, no more writing. I will be a prisoner.

Last night Dr. W said over the telephone, "Just take a Xanax and call me in the morning." *Well, I don't wanna take a fuckin' Xanax, you egotistical old-school shit.* But I did, and it helped a little. However, today I'm too anxious to take the goddamn pill because I'm afraid if I don't stay fully awake and vigilant, the doctors will get nothing done. They go on with their own lives (last weekend my dad was afraid to disturb Dr. Worthless while he was playing golf at his country club in Westchester) as I sit in my parents' house hysterically crying from the agony. God, I sound like a real pisser. I know they care somewhat but, shit man, make this stop, pull up the intestine, push the space together, and be a bit snappier about it, thank you.

When I finally fall asleep, I dream Dr. F, my neurologist, invites me to the hospital pool. I am shocked to see his huge belly overflowing out of his shorts. It grosses me out. There are lots of kids swimming. He proclaims that he just wants a little exercise. But it is a scam, the truth is he just wants to watch me swim to see how my muscles are working neurologically. But then it seems like some romantically sick dream where all of a sudden my body appears perfect in a red bathing suit and he is just watching me and grinning. I swim like a beautiful mermaid. He can't take his eyes off me.

Thinking about the dream, I connect it to the fact that he took a phone call in the examining room in the middle of giving me a rectal and left me with my gown up and my bare ass staring at him for five minutes. The *fucker*. I wish I didn't think he had nice blue eyes. I want my revenge on Dr. F. I can't wait to tell him what the radiologist found on the results. There is indeed something wrong with me. I race over to his office with the films, the proof, and wave them before him like a victory flag. I sit there hungry for his reaction, for some satisfaction. Some acknowledgment of my pain.

But all Dr. F says is, "Good girl. Good for you for persisting."

11. Anger and Hysterics

Another week goes by and Dr. W still hasn't sent the films over to the surgeon. Every day this week I call my mother from my bed, crying. I'm worrying there's more to all of this. She thinks it might be a good idea for her to go with me to see him. When my mother gets involved, Dr. W moves. I think he has a crush on her, which wouldn't surprise me. He seems to like blondes. All his secretaries and nurses are fair, and he has a picture of his thirty-something blond girlfriend on his desk. When we walk into his office, he greets us politely but he seems to be engaging more in a conversation with my mother. My mother tries to alter the conversation so that I, the patient, am the star. She says, "Jenny sweetie, tell Dr. W what's on your mind."

I am afraid he is going to tangle up my words so I try to communicate as clearly as I can and say, "Well, Dr. W, I'm wondering what you think about the films? But I need to tell you that I have all these bizarre symptoms and I just want to know if you think they are caused by this diagnosis? Because it doesn't totally make sense. I'm worried it's part of a larger picture."

He already seems frustrated and says, "Well, Jenny, I can't tell you for sure. But would you like to keep searching for another problem or do you think this might do? No, it doesn't necessarily explain all your symptoms, but it's something." Then he gets out his pad and says, "Susan, why don't you describe Jenny's symptoms."

My mother looks at me with sympathy. She knows he's being a complete asshole and second-guessing me.

My mom says, "I think it's best if Jenny describes them."

I tell him about the spasms in my neck muscles, and that I can feel fluttering and pulsing sensations all throughout my body and in my veins. I tell him my hands are too weak to open, and that I am having trouble picking anything up. I tell him my toes twitch. I tell him my eyes can't focus. I want to tell him he's a cocksucking loser.

He just stares at me with his famous *you are fucking crazy* expression.

My mom interjects, "Doctor, do you think that surgery will help Jenny?"

He says, "I think surgery must be done. I can't promise it will take away these other symptoms but it will cover something."

I begin to sob. *I can't live like this. I need relief.*

He then continues, "Jenny, I'm beginning to think that you're not in an emotional state to have surgery."

You condescending fuck.

My mom looks helplessly but sympathetically at me like *shh, baby, shh. Don't worry. Just get through it.* It's the same expression she makes after my dad has made an upsetting comment to me about fixing my hair, or my sleeves being too long, or that he wants to burn the skirt I've been wearing because it does nothing for my figure. I want her to defend me and tell off Dr. W, but my mother is always too polite, so she remains silent. She only seems to get riled by cab drivers taking the wrong route and by phone solicitors calling at dinner hour. Then I get embarrassed and try to calm her down when she lets them have it. She's like this sweet thing and then she explodes. My father, on the other hand, has no qualms about getting angry and saying exactly what's on his mind. My dad once had a heated argument with a painter who did a shitty paint job on our Connecticut country house. My dad complained about his work and the painter said, "Well, Jerry, I didn't know you were such a perfectionist." My dad raised his voice and nearly took a swing at him. "You bet your ass I'm a perfectionist. Whadda ya expect? Now you do the job right or get the hell out of here." All of Connecticut must have heard him. My dad doesn't get angry often, but when he does, he goes full out. Just a few weeks ago we both had a tantrum and yelled and screamed.

He had said, "Jenny, they can't find anything. You don't have anything wrong. Maybe you are crazy. Susan, is she losing her mind?"

I started stomping my feet and howling in the middle of my mother's perfectly white and slick den. I could feel the woven sisal floor beneath me shredding up my feet. I yelled for dear life, "There *is* something wrong! Fuck you! I hate you! I hate you! Why can't you help me?"

My dad began to get a look of fury in his eyes. He started screaming over me, "You stop your screaming! The neighbors can hear you!"

Wah wah wahh. I was almost hyperventilating. From my gut I yelped, "I hate you. I hate you!" Years ago my dad kicked a chair across the living room during an argument with my mother and broke his own toe. And he tells *me* to lower *my* voice. He lunged toward me, "Don't you talk to me like that, you brat. I ought . . . I ought to . . . I ought to hit you. Susan, I'm gonna slap her if she doesn't shut up and lower her voice." My dad always could be scary. He's big and broad and his head is almost square shaped, so when I was a child sometimes he reminded me of Frankenstein. And he could get passionately upset. But I wasn't scared of him that afternoon. I was angry.

I threw myself on the floor and started kicking all about, tugging on my hair violently and trying to punch myself. "Why don't you hit me. Come on! Knock me out. Save me from my misery. Kill me. I'd rather be dead than live like this. Come on, kill me!"

That shut him up. He looked at my mother with a defeated expression.

Later, after my sobs had died down, as I lay huddled on the couch staring out into space with glassy-eyed terror, my father, with my mother accompanying him for protection, came to talk to me.

"Jenny, I don't know what to do. I just don't. I'm going to give Dr. W a call, maybe he can do something. Don't you think you ought to call your therapist too?"

"Daddy," I whispered, "Please help me."

Later, after Dr. W sent over some Valium and I had calmed down even more, my dad held me. Our emotions are almost entwined.

My fire is finally ignited after a year of this bullshit torture and, yes, I'm having frequent tantrums. I yell at Dr. W so loudly the entire office and people in the waiting room can hear, "FUCK YOU! FUCK YOU! How dare you? My emotional state was fine when I first came to you. Morning after morning I have sat like an idiot waiting and begging for you to listen to me. You haven't heard me once. You try living with a twitch in your ass twenty-four hours a day, and we'll see how your emotional state is. Now you get those films to a surgeon pronto!" There is only so much a person can take.

I don't think Dr. W knew I had such gall in me. He says it would be faster if I take the films myself to radiology at St. Roosevelt's Hospital.

So my mother kisses me good-bye, puts me in a cab, and I drag my sinking ass and the films to the fifth floor of the hospital. I wander the white sterile hallways over and over like a lab rat that can't find the way out of a maze. *Where the fuck is the radiology room? Why do they make it so hard in these hospitals?* I keep asking people in lab coats to point me in the right direction. Finally I find the counter, where I leave my films and X-rays for evaluation. I dread leaving the hospital. I really just want to be checked into a room and tended to. At this point getting drugged and knocked out would be the answers to my prayers.

12. Summer of Glory

My fifteenth summer, the summer of '87, was my summer of glory. I went with my extremely hyper and intelligent friend Zeda to the Deadhead and artsy realm of Vermont to study dance at the Bennington July Program. That was the summer I wore a temporary flower tattoo on my cheek, danced my best, and dove right back into an isolated frenzy to perfect my body.

I was in a small advanced dance class that was just purely modern; no ballet, no jazz, no rigid rules, just total creative expression. I had always found ballet confining, while modern dance, with its constant arching and contracting from the gut, was emotional and liberating. During improvisational classes I based my movements on themes from my dreams, like being trapped and running within a tunnel that had no beginning or end, or grasping for something with all my strength and not being able to hold on to it, and feelings of being lost. My teacher, Livvy, who was stout and muscular and wore a long braid, big floppy pajama bottoms, and tank tops to class, encouraged us to be as creative as we could with our movements so that eventually we would use this work to choreograph our own pieces. I liked her instantly. She was a refreshing change from the strict, graceful, and domineering ballet teachers that I wanted to impress. She was a total bohemian, laid-back, friendly, and believed in the freedom of movement. She also was not skinny. The very first week she told me I was a strong dancer and that I expressed a lot of emotion when I moved.

Although there was a freedom to the dancing, choreographing my own work seemed pretty serious. I saw that dance could be an intellectual discipline, and that made the idea of studying it and pursuing it as a possible career even more appealing. I finally felt that I had found my niche, and I desired to become, in every sense of the word, a modern dancer. With my fondness for this particular medium, and the acceptance that I didn't have to be a ballet dancer, I became more and more excited and goal oriented. And with my dancing ability growing more advanced came the lust for a better dancer's physique. My body was extremely muscular from all my years of ballet and exercising compulsively, but I was not lean. I had known already, before I even left for the program, that this was going to be the summer I finally developed a lithe and sinuous dancer's figure. In the ninth grade I had too many nights of

bingeing, with my weight fluctuating constantly, and enough time feeling bad about myself. I also had a crush on a guy named Jack, and I
thought maybe he wasn't interested because I wasn't thin enough.

And so I began my vigorous path to perfection. Only this time, I
promised myself that I would not get exhausted and I would not leave
early. I wanted to change my body forever. I was on a quest for a thinner
body, a tighter body, a sensuous body, and I was not going to let anything
or anyone create an obstacle. By the end of the first week I developed a
daily routine and did not alter it once throughout the following six
weeks. I awoke early to run five miles each morning through the green
rural roads of Bennington. I loved getting up before Zeda, or anybody
else, and knowing I was ahead of the game. As I jogged I felt my endorphins releasing and felt as if I could go forever in the fresh country air.
Then I would rush back, change into my dance clothes, and wake Zeda
for breakfast. She would sleep right through the alarm clock if I didn't
rile her. She'd lift up her head, with eyes squinting, with an annoyed expression on her face, and exclaim, "You've already been up and running?
You're absolutely nuts. I'm going back to sleep." She was not a morning
person.

Then I'd eat a balanced breakfast, cereal and a banana, and rush off
to my three-hour dance class early, so I could stretch before it started.
The fatigue from all my physical activity would hit me halfway through.
I would be starving for lunch. After I ate something healthy again, like a
huge salad with hard-boiled eggs, or tuna on whole wheat, I had a drawing class that I could barely keep my eyes open for. But then I would
change into my bathing suit and walk a mile to the lake so I could swim
for my afternoon activity. Later I would shower, eat dinner, and then go
back to the studio to spot tone every area of my body.

The more physical I became, the more my button got pressed to become a machine, to run, to tone, to lift, to strengthen, and to melt my
fat into nothing. Exercise was always a drug for me, based on some
drive that lived deep in my core and inside my susceptible brain. The
process always happened quickly. A week could jump-start my system
physically, as well as emotionally. My mind-set changed too, so I was

never living in the moment, and instead I was always planning, structuring, rationalizing. . . . I could get a lot done within six weeks in terms of changing my body, as well as fucking up my head, especially at the young age of fifteen.

But after two weeks of maniacal activity I felt bulkier. One day, as I was about to go running, I ran into Livvy while she was walking her two huge white shepherd dogs. She asked, "Do you run a lot?" I said, "Yep, every day." She said, "You know, Jenny, you ought to give your body a rest. All that running can make your muscles tight. You also might want to try alternating your strides with skipping to help elongate your muscles. Some days you should just skip around the field instead." After that I could be found many days skipping like a lunatic into town (and, for years after that, on the bridle path of Central Park).

I felt toned, healthy, and invigorated by the beginning of the third week. But as I saw progress and small changes in my body, my fear of eating returned. I started to calculate my life in terms of food and exercise. I looked at food as fuel that needed to be burned off by exercise in order to keep up the progress. The less I ate the less I'd have to worry about burning it off. The less I'd have to worry. It was warped thinking, but it always came with the territory. The contents of my meals were slowly diminishing, leaving me with constant hunger pangs. Soon the sensations of emptiness and "a job well done" manipulated and coerced me into skipping meals completely sometimes and challenging my body past stages of fatigue. When I felt hungry I felt lighter, and I felt drugged. I liked feeling that way to dance. I liked waking up like that. I liked going to bed like that. I also began to really like what I saw. Each time I looked in the mirror I thought to myself, *Okay. You look better, so don't eat or else you'll ruin it.*

Once again I isolated myself from friends and fun. Zeda and I had planned to have an exciting summer together, but I barely spent time with her. The tattoos we had put on the first day were fading, and I had no desire to put on another one. Zeda was studying dance too (a different class) as well as journalism, and hanging out a lot with the other kids, getting to know them. I was afraid to get to know anyone. I felt closed off, and I didn't want to pursue friendships that ended within a summer's time. Why invest the energy? I remember thinking that I didn't need relationships. I started seeing them as obstacles to my daily regimen. I did feel bad that I wasn't my usual kooky self with Zeda. We had known each other since the sixth grade, and laughed and goofed around constantly. We had a similar sense of humor, a hyper silliness, and we were both into physical activity. Zeda was a natural athlete, a brain, and full of creativity and style. She was also tiny, muscular, and lucky because she didn't need to worry about her weight. In my dance classes at Dalton she was actually quite good for someone who never really took lessons, so she decided she wanted to study dance that summer. She seemed disappointed that I didn't join her very often to socialize with the other kids, but we still got to spend time together when we choreographed our dance piece together for the final summer performance.

Zeda, another dancer, and I rehearsed and rehearsed. I finally felt less shame when we tried on our silver unitard costumes, although I still felt like my quads were huge. Zeda commented, "You look different. You look really great." We performed on the last day of the program when our families all came up to see our summer's work and take us home. Our piece was based on the concept of nightmares, and we danced in the dark so the audience could see only our silhouettes. We used a gigantic prop, a giant transparent construction that had three large movable pieces, and used tiny flashlights to create illusions of little fireflies on the gauze material. During most of it I ran and twirled across the stage frantically, imagining I was inside a tunnel with no end.

My parents and brothers had been there to watch. I could see the expressions on their faces, how they exchanged glances, noticing my newly toned physique. I could feel the approval. Afterward, when I went to kiss them all hello, and they gave me flowers, I heard what I wanted to hear. My brothers stared in awe at me, and Greg told me he couldn't believe how great my dancing had become, and how my body had become a real dancer's body. I was pretty psyched by their comments but I remember being scared too. What now? What will I do now, at home the rest of the summer, with no dance classes, no structure? How will I keep it up?

13. Attachment

Every night during our evening call, I update my mother with news of my awful day filled with frustration and the typical routine I have of eating things that exacerbate my hiatal hernia. Usually she's sympathetic, but tonight she got really tough with me and said that I was being "childish." She, who is just as deeply attached to me, who babies me, who—mark my words—calls me as soon as I don't call her, who used to walk me down the hallway every day to the elevator for school with more separation anxiety than I had, calls *me* childish. It's so funny, because I know her like a book, and this "childish" is not a word of hers. She went to therapy with my father yesterday and this must be an adjective that the shrink used.

I keep hearing bits of my mother's comments as I recall our conversation, maybe out of context and maybe distorted, as I sit with food lodged in the middle of my back and with the most tremendous urge to throw up. How badly do I wish to stick my hand down my throat? I used to feel like I wanted to purge myself because I was depressed or filled with hatred or anger. Now I want to purge myself for those same reasons but also because I physically can't get the choking or the pulling on my neck muscles to stop and the food to go down.

She told me I was acting childish, and said I had promised to fight the pain and declared that I was not being successful at it. She said I dwelled in the pain and everyone has pain and this is not life threatening. I could tell it was all the therapist's tape loop repeating through my mother, but as I replayed the conversation I felt myself choking. I felt like pulling my hair out, like throwing up my guts, and then, more important, like running.

God, how I wish I could run hard right now. Aah, I used to run off the anger, the anxiety, the fear, the excitement, the ache of loneliness, the urge to induce vomiting, the rage at my parents for being them-selves, for feeling trapped by them; and after I flew and breathed and sweated and felt the endorphins steaming off my body and in my chest, I could love them again instead of feeling stifled. Then I could walk down Fifth Avenue on the barren gray streets set against the green of the towering trees of Central Park, and I would be in a peaceful place, clear and able to fantasize in silence or flick my Walkman dial in search of that sexy inspirational song. Then the thought of going back to my apartment, the one that my parents had provided for me, didn't feel so confining. I would return home and stay up all night straightening up. Finally I would gather all the papers and clothes and dirty plates and candy wrappers that I had left everywhere with disregard. At times, hav-ing a pigsty cancelled out the privilege of having it too good, a free apartment that wasn't really mine.

I always felt like a woman kept by my parents. The apartment was originally furnished for my two older brothers after college, who now—fortunately for them—lead their own lives. My older brother, Brad, the protective one, the one who at times seemed overly concerned and at times just annoyed by his little sister's neurosis, lives quite contentedly on the West Side of Manhattan with his wife, Amy. Even when my par-ents claimed that six months' dating wasn't enough time to decide to get married, and that her not being Jewish was an undesirable situation, Brad went forth with his love and proposed anyway. And, of course, they adore her *now*.

My other brother, Greg, was my companion through grade and high school, and, although he was three years ahead of me, we were a bit like TV's *90210*'s Brenda and Brandon socializing together. He too has flown the coop, gone cross-country to California. He is an aspiring actor, blessed with amazing good looks, charisma, and charm.

I get so angry because two years ago I was living in Santa Fe and was much closer to freedom, yet every day I felt like I had to go back home to New York. I kept hearing my parents' words in my head that being there was *just an escape, that it was a bunch of misfits and, personally, my dad preferred green to the desert.* That affinity with the beauty of the desert, the smell of the piñon, and the quirky people were all mine. It felt just as natural a part of my life as my warring days wasting away in New York City. Why should it matter whether they like it there or not?

And yet, when my ass is spasming and I can't feel my muscles, I feel helpless and needy of love. I still avoid my friends and I search for compassion from my parents. And they can't fix the pain. Only now my mother tells me I'm dwelling in it, and I, in turn, resent her and feel no love, just trapped. And I know that if I moved away she would call and send packages with her little smiling face on the envelope. And it would hurt, and I would spend days self-destructing and thinking my life was invalid because they couldn't see or feel it. This was my routine with her when I was living in Santa Fe two summers ago: I would report back to my mother in this negative way, telling her of my depression, my food intake, my nausea. As we would talk, I would cry to her and realize that she could do nothing for me, that I do the damage and I must get out of the rut once again and run free. Then I would wake up the next morning and run and fly, ridding myself of all the toxins and undoing the self-inflicted harm, and I could call—or not call—but once again I was free to have a life. This was before the twitch.

I've known for ages that I need to separate from my parents and gain more self-esteem; it's so apparent to me and yet I cannot seem to deprogram myself. And now, when I've reached this catastrophic level, when my life is hanging in the balance, it's as if I were literally on some life-support system. I have to wait for doctors to tell me if I need surgery or not. I fear I won't need surgery. I will just have to work on it all alone, trying not to upset my system with too much raw food or bingeing on fat-free bullshit, and probably do physical therapy to get my buttocks muscles back. And to think I needed to work damn hard before all this. I had legs that couldn't decide which way to run first; now I need to build them up so I can walk a city block.

Feeling sorry for myself, yeah. I can't help it. Every fucking day the cycle begins: the fear, the anger, the boredom, the loss of fantasy and independence; and then the eating, the choking, the spasms, the call to the parents. The New York rhythm of too many people and diets, and floral dresses, platform shoes, vinyl shirts, frozen yogurt, honking horns, leering construction workers, and Korean delis. Fake sushi, men in suits rushing to work, bums lying like garbage on the street, and me never feeling any sense of self or that I own my body on this earth.

Am I a spoiled brat? How can I complain? Don't I have everything? Most people think I do, imagine I'm jetting around in a Ferrari, having the time of my life.

They say, "You must have a trust fund and a date every night and you must get all these beautiful clothes for free."

I say, "Uh, um, well, I usually prefer to just wear my brother's beat-up hand-me-downs."

They think what they want. They have no clue that I could care less. I just want peace inside my head and, now, inside my body. I will never go hungry, God knows, but I feel as if I have nothing to my name. I am a kept woman suffocating on guilt, lacking a sense of identity, wondering if that's why I'm sick. Power. Money. It's been sung once before. And what is the destiny? Where are we all going? A new design here, inspiration there, yesterday's old news, today's new gold shoes. An endless cycle and I can't even fucking mount the horse. What do I have that is so bitter that I need to purge? Some kind of shame, I guess. I just don't know where it comes from.

PART TWO

PART TWO

1. The Surgery:
June 12, 1997

It's 6 A.M. the morning of my surgery. After ten months of running around New York, a frightened little girl who people deemed was just "crying wolf," I'm now about to face the consequences of finally being heard. I can't comprehend what the surgeon has to do at this point to fix me, but he says it's too late for laparoscopic means. This adds greatly to my remorse, because if I had been correctly diagnosed earlier they could have done this far less invasive surgery requiring only the insertion of a tiny hole into the abdominal muscles. Now, instead, he says he has to cut right through my belly to pull things up, and then reattach me. *Whatever that means.* His language is nauseatingly vague. But at this point, I don't really want to know his plan, or the particulars. I just want him to make the torture end. Use his magic scalpel and just do it. Give me my life back. Basically I'm handing over my body to this man with the few ounces of hope that I have left.

Unfortunately, I have little confidence that he can truly heal me. After all this time, my system is pretty shot. I really hope it isn't too late to make amends. This morning, frustration and helplessness reside in my bloated and uncomfortable body, emotions from the year, my past abuse of my body, and my very present future. But in this exhausted state I couldn't be more ready for change, and more ready for relief.

I go into this today half willingly, half reticent. I'm terrified of being put to sleep. Where will I go? What if I wake up during the middle of it? What if I don't wake up at all?

I'm even more frightened that I will wake up and it will be the same. That I will still feel the pulling and tension all over my body, the veins of my neck and arms still throbbing hard, and the twitch still doing its dance. Please God, let me be okay. I know I obsessed about my growing saddlebags and stretch marks on my legs. I realize now that I have been sick to care so much about what my exterior looks like, to worry about controlling my weight. What I want is to feel comfortable once again and to have a body that functions properly. To have one that exists in peace, without all the clenching, gripping, and the immense effort to try to hold myself up. I took my health for granted for years, and this is the price.

In the waiting room, I hug my mom and whisper in her ear, "Mom, if I don't make it through or I don't wake up, you know I love you, right? So much." She starts to cry and I hug her again hard and long. All of a sudden, I feel brave. I don't have any choice. The truth is I also feel a sense of excitement, and minutes later when the anesthesiologist puts the needle in my vein, I know that it is time to drift away from this hell, to just shut my eyes. To surrender, finally.

The wheels are squeaking beneath me as a hospital attendant rolls me into the recovery room. There seems to be a lot of activity that sounds like buzzing and humming. I open my eyes and everything looks all foggy until I see my older brother zooming in on me as he passes other bodies lying on stretchers to get to me. Relieved to see his face, I try to smile. It's like when he was in high school and I'd wake up and see him taking his lenses out in the kitchen after a late night out. I'd say, still in dreamland, "Hi, Brad, I love you. Good night."

I mutter to Brad as he towers over the bed smiling, "It's over? Wow. They just put me out . . . thirsty . . . I'm so . . ." and lights go dark.

I wake up in another room. Nurses are there. They tell me to try and sit up. I can't. I can't move at all. I start to speak with any breath I can muster but it's kind of difficult with the vertical tube shoved down my throat. "Mommy, Mommy."

A blond, sweet angel says, "Hi, honey. Hi, sweetie. How are you?"

I tremble and say, "I can't move. Momm . . ."

A nurse says, "Yes, you can try . . ."

"Mommmm," I try to howl. My mother explains to them that I had an epidural.

I remember, and I realize my legs are numb. *Oh, my God.*

I am wheeled out of the room. I feel dizzy as my stretcher bangs into the walls along the corridors. I am being jerked all over the place. I keep looking to make sure my mom and my brother are still there with me. I hear an elevator open and they push me in. There are other people in it and I wonder what they think as they see me lying there. When we finally arrive at my private room, there is a crowd: friends, cousins, aunt, uncle, one big blur of people who move out of my way. A large man goes to lift me up off the stretcher onto the bed. *Aggh, uggh, stop.* I cry in pain.

"Mom . . . rough, too rough . . . Mommm . . ." I am feeling hysterical and scared to death of this big man touching me.

"Sweetie, it's okay. Brad will help."

Brad and the scary man count one, two, three, and lift me like an offering. Brad has tears in his eyes. The crowd outside is all hush-hush, and I can make out my best friend Nikki's sympathetic grimace of pain. They all enter. I lie there amazed at the thought of this dramatic, horrific sight of poor Jenny that they get to see. What happened to her, I think?

There are flowers and stuffed animals and people chatting. What are we celebrating? There's Daddy. *Hi, Daddy.* I am amazed at all the people who have come to support me. *Do they all love me this much? Or is this what usually happens when someone gets sick?* It doesn't matter. I feel a moment of such profound warmth, I want it to last forever.

Pain Management comes. "Do you want us to take out the epidural?"

I look to my mother. *Um, yeah.*

It's okay at first . . . only then, *Oh my God . . . holy shit! Give me drugs!*

The doctor says, "Just press the button when you need it" and "Sorry, no water yet."

Uhhhg, awwh, awwh God, please help. What has happened to me, God? Am I alive? Oh yeah, I'm alive. Pain assures me I'm alive.

I'm fixed, right? All better.

Who am I? Where am I? Can't breathe. Can't move. Press the button. *Ahh, okay. Why is this happening to me?* There are still spasms all over my body. *Don't worry, Jenny. Just go back to sleep.*

Nighttime comes. My throat hurts and my shoulders ache. Pain Management returns. They finally take the breathing tube out of my mouth and get me a heating pad for my pinched nerves. There is not a part of my body I can define.

In the morning, the surgeon comes to see me, kisses my forehead. "Mighty big fan club you have," he says. *Yeah.*

I try to look at my belly. I see a scar and staples. *That's pretty big.*

"Um, did you have to take some colon out?"

"Yes, we did. But everything is fine."

"Um, should my ribs hurt?"

The surgeon says, "Oh, I did that to you. Had to use retractors to hold them open so the scar wouldn't be larger."

Oh, thank you.

Nice nurses. Except the night one falls asleep and I yell for her. I get her in trouble.

I try to walk in the hallway with an IV attached to me. *My legs, they're different. They're shorter, I know it.* My feet twitch. They do weird things; they don't touch the ground easily. They say it's muscle atrophy. *No, they're my legs and they're different.* Don't want to think about it. *Oh God, what have I done to myself? This is hellish. I need drugs.*

Television. Magazines. Friends. Everyone is phoning me. What to say? *Just had some colon removed. Probably due to all my years bingeing and purging. I'm going to sleep now. Thanks for calling.*

I press the button all the time.

Constant nausea. Get lots of Compazine shots.

Hi, Mommy. Hi, Daddy. They come every day. Mom stays all day. She walks with me in circles.

A big team of male interns arrives early one morning, four days after the procedure. I have a crush on one.

They ask, "Have you passed gas, yet?"

I stare at them, mortified. Six men asking me if I have farted. Is this my life, for real? I have to laugh to deal with the humiliation. "Uh, not that I know of," I say, "but if you hang around I'll try."

They say they'll give me liquids as soon as I do. I guess I'm not exactly date material.

Eventually I get grape juice. *Ecch, gross.*

Eventually food. I want pancakes. They don't have pancakes. I settle for angel food cake. *Ohhh, did I eat too much? Too fattening. Shouldn't have had cake. Uggh, nauseous, nauseous.* Compazine, NOW.

My friend Mel calls from Santa Fe. I hear her voice and my eyes water. I tell her I can't open my hands. Can't stop gripping them. I get sentimental. I'm supposed to be out there under the big blue sky with her and Max, her eleven-year-old son. At nineteen, when I rented a room in their adobe home, they became my second family. I want to be sitting on their front steps analyzing life while watching the pink sunsets, or dancing with Mel and random guys to flamenco music at a rustic Santa Fe bar, or dispensing Dunkin' Donuts to a bunch of kids for Max's summer birthday party.

Mel is with her masseuse friend, who tells her in the background that my hands are clenched from fear and it will go away. I need to breathe. I tell Mel that they've given me this plastic toy that contains two colorful balls inside. I am supposed to inhale hard at the opening so that the balls rise up to the top in order to exercise my lungs. But the balls don't move.

I can see Mel's familiar expression, that gentle, kind, soulful one she always makes that shows how much she can identify with other people's pain. She tries to comfort me. Tells me everyone misses me, wants to see me. "Yeah, I ran into that musician guy you used to date, what was his name, Zele or something? He's sooooo handsome. Well, he wanted to know when you'd be back here. Asked for your number but I didn't give it to him. I told him we hope you'll get your butt out soon. Oh, and Kathy says hello too. Everybody's always asking about you, Jenny. Why don't you come this summer and stay with us? You can rest and recuperate here. I think that's a perfect idea. We can get you tons of bodywork from Deanna, and it will be quiet and peaceful, yeah, why don't you come?"

I hang up with grief and longing. It hurts more than my body.

The nurses bring me huge bags of potassium. They say I am depleted. They stick a needle in my vein and my arm feels like one big cramp. I can't stop moaning as my friend Zeda watches. She tries to distract me. Tells my mom and me about her boyfriend. And about how Prozac is destroying her sex drive. I know she hates seeing this. *I wonder why this IV is so painful.* One of the nurses looks at me sympathetically and explains that unfortunately, potassium drips burn. I try not to think about it.

My brother Greg calls me one morning from L.A. I am chipper, happy, better than the past few days. I feel the usual tinge of excitement hearing from him.

"Schvest? Schvestyl," he says, using the affectionate nickname he has for me, from the Yiddish word for sister, *schvester.* "Is it you?"

"Hey, Greggie."

"Hey there, Schvestyl. How ya feeling?"

"I guess I'm okay today. This Percocet stuff really does the job. A lot of people keep coming to see me but I'm not the greatest company. How you doing?"

Greg says, "Not bad. Not bad. I can't really complain. I know it's pretty rough for you now but you sound good. So everybody's comin', huh? All the aunts and uncles? Nikki? Stella?"

"Most of 'em. Uncle Lenny's been great. Sat a long time with me and Mom. Keeps offering to go get me milk shakes. Oh, and Aunt Madeline comes a lot. She brought me that Madeline doll who has that appendix scar. And all the friends came, even Zeda, who I haven't seen in, like, two years."

"Oh, that's great. And you're feeling okay?"

"Well, I don't know what's gonna happen, Greg. I still feel a lot of the other symptoms. A lot of spasming still. I'm kind of freaked."

"Just hang in there. Okay? Hey, guess what! You'll be proud of me, *Schvest,* I've been painting." I hear the familiar adrenaline in Greg's voice, from the excited rush of one of his new creative endeavors. He continues, "Let me know if it bothers you to talk about this subject, but those oil sticks you sent me for my birthday are amazing. No wonder you kept pushing me to start painting again. They're so cool, it's like drawing with paint. I have a bunch of questions for you about them when and if you feel like getting into it."

I feel queasy. I remember going to the art store in Little Italy last January to send him a huge package of art supplies. A day at the studio when I just couldn't work, too distracted by the twitch.

"That's great, Greg." I hear my voice getting hoarse, cracking.

I am grateful for my brother's attempt to be positive, to inspire me, to entice me with visions of myself painting again. Reminds me of the usual morning pep talks he'd give me after I'd complain to him that I was too blah to go to the studio *or feeling fat or rejected by some guy.* But now I'm lying here in a hospital bed feeling half paralyzed. I can't imagine lifting a brush to paint.

·   ·   ·

I've been here a week when a nurse helps me shower and do my hair. I want to surprise my mother. Look pretty for her. I can't hold the blow-dryer. Can barely lift my arms away from my center. *Wherever that is.* I am stiff. Weak. Can't stand long. My body is not doing a good job keeping me up. I begin to panic a little. I look in the mirror at myself in my blue robe. *Not bad.* I actually find my face pretty, kind of thin, dramatic. But my legs are changed. I can't feel my buttocks either. *Don't think about it.* My mom comes in and says, "Honey, you look beautiful." I wince at her applause for my efforts. She must think it's a good sign that I'm trying to tend to myself. But I cringe inside, knowing that my beauty will decline from here. Something is inherently wrong. *I am ruined.* And even if I begin to complain, my mother will probably remain in denial. The fatigue obliterates the obsession. I get into bed, beautiful fragile princess that I am for the moment, and fall asleep.

On the eighth day in the hospital I have a tiny bowel movement one afternoon. The surgeon says I can leave the next day. He also tells me that we can celebrate at his apartment when he gets done remodeling it. I think that is a very strange idea. He explains that it's been a rough few weeks for him. He's exhausted because he's been sleeping on his roof nightly. *You what? The roof, you say? Did I hear that correctly?* And then I think if I really do get better, with my twitch gone and all, then, absolutely, we can celebrate at his apartment. Then maybe I'll even marry him.

On the ninth day I am suddenly not looking forward to leaving. The surgeon comes to say good-bye. He whispers to me, "Jenny, we have to pray," and then cups my chin in his hand and kisses me on the lips. *What? Huh?* I think as he walks out. I don't know if it's his words or his behavior that startles me. I'm annoyed that he who had license to be the director of my body for four hours, may think he's still entitled to it. Truthfully, I wouldn't mind it so much if it had been the seal of success, but with his little message, it feels more like a mercy kiss.

I eat breakfast and am severely nauseous. A Compazine shot helps but makes me drowsy. I sleep all day. Mom picks me up in the afternoon and I still keep falling asleep. She packs up my things. I ask her if I should take the light blue gown. I have grown attached to it. She shakes her head no. I kiss the nurse good-bye. Tell her I'll take her to the movies sometime. She giggles, then says she wants to hear when I run the New York marathon. *Yeah, sure, okay.*

Mom holds me up and helps me stumble out of the hospital. The light outside is bright. I can't walk. My feet are falling out from underneath me. My mom hails a taxi and I can barely bend my legs to get in. I look around at all the people. I wish I were anyone but me. I sleep in the taxi. When I get to my parents' apartment, there is an awful silence.

2 . *L a x a t i v e s , M e d i c a t i o n , a n d S h i t L i k e T h a t*

*I*t's three weeks after the surgery, July Fourth weekend. It's an absolutely gorgeous sunny day at our country house in Connecticut. My whole family is there; my brother Greg has come in from LA with his girlfriend. It's the first time I've seen him since the surgery, although he sent me a teddy bear with an ace bandage wrapped around its tummy and called me almost every day. He walks in the door of our yellow country kitchen and says how great I look. "Like the days of the famous Häagen-Dazs picture," he says, referring to a photo of me with my long dark hair, staring sullen and pensive, wearing a simple blue T-shirt and a white hat that has red letters on it reading *Häagen-Dazs*. The picture that sits large and framed in my parents' home and in my father's office. *Gee thanks, Greg, but ya know what, it's unfortunately not those days and I can't fuckin' move.*

The day is shifting into afternoon. I'm resting on the forest green lounge chair, enjoying the soothing and cradling rays from the sun's warmth and nicely drugged by the painkillers and Xanax that the neurologist has given me for muscle spasms. I joyfully watch the kids (all in their late twenties)—Greg, his girlfriend, Karen, Brad, and his wife, Amy—laugh and swim in the pool. I'm reading and trading British magazines with my mother as we tear out all the cool places and stores we want to visit if we actually join my dad the following week on his business trip to London. I've never been there and I'm thinking I'm strong enough to go. *Yeah, I can do it as long as I've got my painkillers.* Besides, the surgeon says that it's fine.

But I keep calling the surgeon from the house. I tell him I haven't had a bowel movement since I left the hospital. He says, "Don't worry, maybe ease up on the painkillers. They're slowing it down."

My surgeon insists I can eat anything, but I'm concerned that my system can't handle everything I've been eating: chicken, cream of wheat, ice cream—real food.

He says, "Really, don't worry, maybe increase your fiber intake. Have you tried coffee?"

I hang up and tell my parents that he says not to worry.

That evening we pile into our army green Defender and ride to the quaint town of Riverton to eat dinner at the inn there. Everyone's talking about whether they're going to have lobster and how excited they are about that basket of homemade muffins and corn bread. I'm starting to feel a bit anxious thinking about food.

We're laughing, ordering wine; everyone's happy to be together. Meanwhile, I'm wondering whether I should eat any of the muffins because I'm not very hungry and they are in fact pretty fattening. But I decide *what the hell,* if the doctor says eat, then let's dig in. The salad comes; it has blue cheese dressing all over it. I eat it anyhow. I am completely away from the family now, consumed by the shooting sharp pains I'm getting in the concave of my ribs. I stop eating. I start sweating. My head is throbbing. My chest is pounding. "Ugh, you guys excuse me for a second. I need some fresh air."

I struggle to walk out the door. In the parking lot, I try to walk in circles, but I can't straighten up at all. I am so frightened. The pain is getting worse. What should I do? I don't want to ruin everyone's evening; we were having so much fun. I try to breathe. I know this is bad.

Greg comes outside to see if I'm all right.

"No," I yell loudly. "Something's very wrong. What should I do? Oh, the pain. Greg, help me."

He runs in to get Mom and Dad. They come outside. *Help me, please.* I tell them I think I'm dying.

My mom says, "Jerry, she's green."

My dad says, "I know, Susan, and she's sweating all over."

"Jerry, what should we do? I think we have to go call the surgeon. We have to leave."

No, just take me to the fucking hospital. Help me. Help me. And in the car ride back to the house, I'm sitting between my brothers while they hold me and I am howling and sobbing in pain, never felt anything worse, think I am having a heart attack. I keep apologizing to everyone for messing up the night.

Back at the house we can't contact the surgeon, so we call our savior, my mom's cousin Steven, a podiatrist who lives nearby in Hartford. He has rescued us before, when my father had the subarachnoid hemorrhage at the house years ago and he rushed over to help my mother get the cover on the jeep and drive him to the hospital. He tells us where to go and that he'll meet us in the emergency room. In the car with my parents, I feel delirious. "Nauseous. Nauseous," I mutter and then we decide I should take a painkiller. "Aggghh. Pain. Pain. Such pain." I mutter more, holding the concave of my chest.

My parents are wondering if something's gone wrong with the surgery, if it's an adhesion, an infection. *I don't care what it is, I just want it to end. I want relief.*

Steven is there to greet us. It is quiet then in the emergency room. They put me on a hospital bed in a small cubicle with a showerlike curtain divider and we all wait for a doctor. The doctor arrives and then he tries to reach the surgeon. He has to call back. The doctor tells me that I'm probably just impacted, but he'll order an X-ray to see for sure. We wait. Steven is already making me laugh but I tell him, "Don't, it hurts."

Steven is one of my favorite relatives and has the best sense of humor. Every time he comes to the house with his wife and kids for barbecues he keeps me laughing all day. And he's a runner too, so we compare notes on our running status. Sometimes he brings his medical bag and he fixes my dead toenails and blisters. I always feel like everything is going to be okay when he's around.

Finally, they take the X-ray. We wait and wait. The doctor eventually returns with the results. "Well, you are completely impacted. And considering your surgery you must be in a hell of a lot of pain. We'll try to relieve you."

They want to reach the surgeon to find out how to go about dealing with this. *Fuck my surgeon. No one ever listens to me.* I had made those phone calls telling him I hadn't shat for three goddamn weeks. Even asked him if it could get stuck and not move. He chuckled when I had asked him that, telling me it doesn't work that way. Oh, really?

We wait and wait for the surgeon to return the call. In the meantime, the pain has subsided a bit, but I am so afraid of what's to come. Meanwhile my dad says to my mom, "Snooze, I'm kind of hungry."

Steven says, "Me, too. Come on, Jer, let's go to the vending machine."

My mom says, "Get me licorice."

They come back with pretzels, Devil Dogs, licorice, and soda. I'm watching them eat, and I'm absolutely dumbfounded. I start laughing. I tell them that I cannot wait to tell my grandchildren about this.

The doctor comes back, and he has finally reached the surgeon and they decide an enema will be best. Bye, Mom, Dad, Steven.

"Don't worry, honey, we'll be right outside. You'll do fine," my mom assures me.

I love you, Mommy. I'm scared, Mommy.

A nurse comes in and places a cover over the commode at the side of the bed. She says, "Don't worry, I'll be gentle. Now try to hold it in as long as you can."

But I anxiously tell her I don't know if I can, that I don't have any sense of that muscle. So she sticks it in, and I feel like she is trying to put a piece of clothing in a suitcase that is already too full. I feel like there is no opening, but somehow the liquid gets in and I cry as the liquid rolls right out. "Mom?" I cry, and she comes in and the nurse says I couldn't hold it. "Mom, I'm gonna be incontinent!! Mom, why can't I hold it?"

"Shhhh, baby. It's gonna be all right. You're just nervous." I know she's panicked.

They get the doctor; he seems a bit worried. "Well, let's try some phosphate soda. It's pretty strong, though. I don't want to irritate your stomach; let me check with your surgeon."

Waiting again . . . The nurse says, "It's all right . . . go ahead. Drink the salt down." Yuck. Nauseating. Waiting. Nothing happens. So we try another enema. "Now try hard to hold it. Really, really try—I bet you can do it," the nurse urges.

This time I hold it longer. "Good girl," she says. "You see your muscle is working."

It becomes unbearable . . . no strength, burning sensation. She leaves me alone. I sit on the plastic toilet. A little comes out, tiny minuscule pieces. I push, I strain . . . no more. I get up, my swollen stomach is in agony, stiff, barely moving, I cannot even find my colon to massage to help it move. I attempt to walk around the little cubicle, my feet gripping and doing that weird spasming thing they do now. I feel no distinction between groin, legs, stomach, and ass . . . a numbness tinged with pain throughout. I still try to move to stimulate things. I feel a slight pressure in the rectum, which is a signal that I should sit down on the commode. I strain and squeeze. *Gosh, is this what it's like to have a baby?* I get up again. They're all sitting outside. Steven says, "I see your little feet, Jen, Jen."

"How's it going?" my mom and dad ask.

I'm so sick. "Mom, please come here." She rushes in. "Mom, it hurts, Mom, I can't bear it. I can't do it. I have to force. I'm so tired."

She looks in the commode, "Honey, that's good, that's good work. Just try a little more." She leaves.

I'm alone again. *God, I know you're making me suffer for a reason, right, because I'm gonna be okay in a few months, right, and resume my life and paint and meet my prince and go back to New Mexico, right?* And I hold those thoughts with me while I get up and go back and forth waiting for that little sign that it is time to strain again. And in the background all this exciting action begins taking place. Some drug addict comes in, cops are there. I hear yelling and the words: "You have the right to remain silent."

I am missing all the entertainment. At a certain point, I reach my limit. I call them all in. Delirious, I say, "No more. Can't do more, tired, real tired."

My parents get the doctor, and he becomes God as he injects me with Demerol. I throw up and begin to fall into a peaceful hazelike heaven, hoping it will last forever. I start to laugh. I say to them, "Guys, I'm jealous. What's happening out there?"

Steven says, "Oh, the usual, some nut, drugs, someone getting arrested."

"Oh," I murmur. "Funny. Just don't go getting shot on me." It is six o'clock in the morning and I drift off to sleep.

I awake at nine in the morning. Most of the Demerol has worn off. I am cold, stiff, my rectum and legs hurt, and I am so, so tired. My parents and Steven are still awake, especially Steven, hyper as ever. I feel so bad for them, having had no sleep. My mom will probably get an ulcer. The doctor from the night before is preparing to leave, and he suggests that I go home and contact my surgeon to find out what to do next. I thank him graciously. Nice doctor. Steven leaves us and I tell him he'd better get some rest, but he jokes that he'll probably go running.

When we return home, everyone is up having breakfast. I am happy to see all of them. We immediately phone my surgeon, who is pretty quick to return our call. Tell him of the night, tell him I barely went to the bathroom and that it was the worst experience ever. He blames it on all the painkillers and tells me to cut down on them and take a whole gallon of the extremely salty Go-Lightly laxative through the course of the weekend.

In all my years with an eating disorder I never abused laxatives. Once, at thirteen, I can't quite remember if it was a bottle of magnesium citrate or chocolate Ex-Lax, but I had taken some kind of laxative, found myself bent and doubling over in so much pain that my parents had to rush me to the emergency room, and I sat there sweating and trembling, shifting into all kinds of positions until I eventually was able to evacuate. I learned my lesson, then, that the laxative route was not the way for me to go.

So I try to drink that awful stuff and each sip is making me sicker and sicker. "Come on, Jenny, you can do it," everyone urges.

I sit outside, resting back in the old wooden armchair, trying to relieve the nausea as I watch Greg dance and do all these silly moves to some funky music Brad has blasting on the stereo. We are all laughing because Greg is so good at imitating every dance style, from John Travolta's to Michael Jackson's, and can do every hip-hop move around.

My dad yells in the background, "Ooh, what is that horrible music?" and comes out, trying to imitate Greg.

I keep laughing, and then I cry.

Greg stops and tries to console me, saying, "What? Are you afraid that you'll never be able to dance again? Trust me, you'll be the old dancing Jenny in no time."

That late afternoon we sit under the huge overhanging tree at the big round picnic table covered in Polo country table settings, a vase of wildflowers my mother has handpicked, wine, fresh salads, shrimp, barbecued chicken, and steaks. My mother has a way of setting the table, of preparing her food, so that everything looks so fresh, so appetizing, so pleasing to the eye. Informal, yet like an ad from *House and Garden*; food in old blue-and-white spongeware bowls, and apples sitting in old green Shaker baskets. She loves making it pretty even when it is just for her and my father. Meanwhile, my father is the man of power, loving his barbecue, totally in charge, turning the meat from side to side, and downing a hot dog or burger before he even sits down to eat. That means he is real relaxed. I always like watching him at the grill with his teddy bear belly filling out his big plaid shirt. Away from the office. Enjoying his house, his green land, his barn, his collection of folk art, and his own family.

Brad is in charge of the music, but he always puts on Pavarotti when Dad wants Streisand. Mom always thinks it is too loud, so he has to get up and change it no matter what. He also takes care of the wine and the beer or other alcoholic concoctions. Greg is the designated getter-upper for refills of diet cream soda for Dad. And me, I don't know, I guess I used to help set the table, eating twenty carrots or raw peppers as I went back and forth to the kitchen through the swinging screen door. The whole process of the meal made me nervous. *What would I eat? Would I restrict or give in?* Either way, I'd load up on raw veggies until I couldn't breathe. Sometimes sneak an extra dessert afterward.

But tonight I sit there watching everyone eat, clinking glasses to July 4th, mine filled with Go-Lightly. And in a way I feel safe because I am tiny and thin and weak from the surgery and I don't have to worry about eating.

After the barbecue and drinking most of the Go-Lightly, I begin to get that sensation in the rectum, and I rush to the bathroom. What did the surgeon do to me? From that afternoon until 4 P.M. the next afternoon, I remain upstairs, going from my bed to the bathroom just trying to squeeze out breadcrumbs. The pain between my legs is becoming unbearable. My mother stays by my side through the night and runs baths for me. I lie in there staring at the beautiful blue glass bottles and rosewaters that line the inner ledge of the tub. They line the blue-rimmed windows in my bedroom too. In fact, the whole inside of the house except for the yellow kitchen has been painted white with blue-rimmed windowpanes. Like anything my parents do, they made it cohesive, and *perfect*.

My mother leaves me in the bathtub, and I keep getting myself up and out to go to the toilet. I keep seeing my reflection in the glass door of the shower facing the toilet. I turn and sit sideways to avoid viewing myself. Then I get right back into the tub, freezing and tired.

"Jenny, sweetie, don't you think it's time to come out?" my mom asks empathetically from outside.

"Uh, just a little longer, okay?"

Then she comes in and washes my back with a washcloth. When I get back into bed, I hear her scrubbing the toilet. Oh, the guilt.

It continues and continues, and we call the surgeon to ask him if all this straining will hinder the healing process. He says no. I'm sure it will. And then my dad goes to the store and buys me Charms lollipops to suck on. As I lie in bed, I savor these in my mouth, the sweet cherry, grape, and lime flavors. In the past, I'd bite them down in less than a minute; but in this sick and tired state, I want to keep the taste there and stare at the beautiful bright color of the lollipop to distract myself. I look around the room that has been preserved as the "little girl's room," the room that holds all of Jenny's childhood. I see the blue pegs where an old white lace dress, a tiny blue-and-white-striped pinafore that I used to wear, and tiny hats and wreaths of flowers hang. I peer at all those blue shelves filled with all my old novels, *Secret Garden, Little Women, Are You There, God? It's Me, Margaret,* and the beautifully illus-trated fairy tales, *Snow White, Thumbelina.* On the upper shelves are all the classics and children's Japanese poetry and Madeline L'Engle and Shel Silverstein and my favorite book, *Eloise.* I remember going to the Plaza hotel on Christmas Eve with my older neighbor, a Dutch woman who I adored, just to see the picture of Eloise hanging on the lobby wall. *How cool,* I always thought, *for a little girl to live in a hotel and for a character from a book to become that famous.* Another favorite was *The Mixed-up Files of Mrs. Basil E. Frankweiler,* a story about a girl and a boy who get locked in the Metropolitan Museum of Art overnight. What a dream to be surrounded by all that beautiful art and lay in the bed of a real emperor. So many wonderful stories.

Then I look at all my old stuffed animals, some on the blue country shelves and some packed into an antique weathered gray wooden wagon with big red wheels. My Pekingese Mushy dog, and my Fluffy bear and all the hordes of Steiff teddy bears. My mother loves teddy bears, so she buys me one almost every year, even now. And then I look curiously at all my dolls: Rub-A-Dub, dressed in a baby-pink gown I once wore with the uneven haircut I gave her, my Madame Alexanders, a Scottish girl, a Japanese girl, Little Miss Moffit. Then I stare at all my antique Raggedy Anns sitting on my turquoise blue pie safe backed up against old game boards. I notice the lovely red hair, the brightness of their cheeks, and their floral outfits and aprons. And then I take the beautiful porcelain baby doll dressed in white lace, turn the screw, and hear the lullaby.

For years I was embarrassed by this room; it was so unlike me anymore, I thought.

In my New York apartment the only dolls I keep are Skookum or Native American ones that I have on a shelf and like to stare at as if they are part of my tribe, especially when I was doing my yoga and listening to Yanni. I have a mixture of flea market antiques, like an old green traffic light, old trunks, Native American shields, parfleches, baskets, bags, a cactus, cowboy hats, things I picked up along the way in junkyards. Most of these items are stored in an open metal Metro shelving system along with art books on Matisse or Picasso or books on interior design, the Southwest style, the Japanese style, tons of CDs and videos, art deco bottles, ashtrays, Lucky Strike cigarette holders, and crocodile lighters. Photos of friends and family from long ago and living in Santa Fe are taped up to the walls. Beacon blankets are piled up on my old blue armoire. I have old chairs, modern Knoll chairs, my paintings scattered about. The apartment originally belonged to my brothers, so even though I inherited all their dark black modern stuff and hated the huge forest green Polo couch, I did everything to make it feel like my own. When I'd go to Santa Fe, I'd take a lot of my stuff with me just to make it feel like home, and I'd acquire even more there for my collection.

Now, as I fight off the pain, the country room filled with my childhood belongings is of utmost comfort for me, and I almost enjoy regressing back into "little Jenny." I have no other option. After desperately needing a painkiller at 4 P.M., I pass out until the early dawn. When I awaken, I look out the window and notice the full-grown tree right outside and the view of the long road ahead. The sky is soft and light. The birds are chirping. There is a surreal quality to the morning, but it is grounding too. There is silence that I'm not used to hearing.

This is breathtaking. Have I ever looked out this window before? I think of all these past years, and although I had noticed this beauty before, I would arise quickly with some kind of dissatisfaction with myself or pressure to get up to work out, and I would not allow myself to linger in bed and enjoy what my parents have so generously given me. Lying there helpless, I see more.

We're sitting in the surgeon's office the following week after returning to the city. My mother, almost in tears, tells him, "In all my life—I'm a mother of three—I've never seen any of my kids or heard of anyone going through such torture as my daughter did this weekend."

He doesn't know what to say exactly, "Well, it looks like you'll have to take laxatives indefinitely."

At that point I think it's okay. *Jenny, at least you're not incontinent.*

The following week I stay with my mom at their Park Avenue apartment. My father is in London. Obviously my mother and I couldn't join him. I'm trying not to take painkillers, only Xanax. I feel so much pulling and gnawing in between my legs, I can't comprehend that this much discomfort can exist in life. I hold my vagina all day. I have to give in to a painkiller. Just one.

Then my mom and I go to see my original internist, Dr. W, and I complain of the unremitting pain and tell him of the country episode. He has been away on his honeymoon and seems confused by this reaction to the surgery and is very concerned. He X-rays my stomach and finds me almost totally impacted again. He sends me to the lab around the corner for a special test that afternoon, where they fill me up with a mineral oil–like substance and take a picture. The radiologist there tells me my new connection, my new anastomosis, is on a weird slant. I ask what that means. He explains that it's hard for the stool to get around the new positioning, where the colon and rectum have been surgically attached. I ask if I will need more surgery. He says I may need a revision. I gulp.

We take the X ray back to Dr. W. He studies it. He also questions the way the surgeon has created a kink or curve in my anastomosis. I ask him, "Will I need more surgery?"

He says, "Over my dead body."

And I'm touched. For the first time, this internist, who I have resented all year, seems on my side. But for now he says he wants me to take eighteen Colace and lots of Milk of Magnesia.

That night I walk the New York streets, barely able to hold myself up, as if I am pushing a five-hundred-pound trunk. *I'm filled with poison.* In the past if I had a stomachache, I could walk for blocks and start to feel relieved. But now I can't walk for long, and nothing is moving inside me. Around ten o'clock, after managing to get myself to 90th and Fifth, I take a seat on a bench at the entrance to the reservoir where I used to stretch before my runs. I sit there alone under the dimly lit lamppost and cry. Then I look up at the dark sky and begin talking to God. *Please God, please help me. What happened? Is there a glitch here? Something not right? Tell me what I need to do.*

I return to my parents' apartment, and when my mother greets me at the door, I look at her solemnly. Then she tucks me in the large cot she has prepared for me in her office den and tells me not to worry, things should start working. With all the laxatives in me, it takes the next few days of straining my traumatized bowels and many more baths to get some relief.

My internist talks to my surgeon. My mother and I go to see the surgeon again. He tells me my anastomosis will stretch in time. He did the surgery like this, he explains, because when it's done any other way, the rectum scars down and narrows and he has to redo it. Whatever that means. Then I ask him if there is any other woman I can talk to who had the procedure. He is very silent for a while and then he says no.

I ask, "What, was mine so severe or something?"

And his words still ring in my ear: "Jenny, when I opened you up, your enterocele was nearly coming out of your vagina. You could have fit a 747 in there."

3. The Family Problem

I couldn't stand Dr. Shark's brown beard, his tweed jacket, or the way he stared at me so intensely. When he spoke, he acted as if he were God Almighty, and as if he thought he was as sexy as all the other girl patients made him out to be. Every time he came onto the unit, he'd signal hello to me, check in at the counter, and then come tell me to follow him out. I'd glance at my reflection in the nurse's glass counter and make sure the flab wasn't hanging out of my ripped jeans, so that Dr. Shark would think I looked okay. Because I'd spent that summer bingeing, I hadn't come into the unit all that thin, and I always wondered if he'd believe that I had, yes, been one of those skinny girls who weighed eighty-five pounds. I think I had a lot of shame for not keeping it up, for losing control. *Did he at least think I looked pretty? Was I still pretty?* He'd take me up in the elevator to his little brown "seventies" office with the putrid orange carpets and fluorescent lighting. I'd sit on his couch in profile so as to avoid eye contact with him, and stare instead at the library of books across the room, noticing all the titles on eating disorders, personality disorders, and Jung. I was curious about what he kept himself busy with, what he thought he was an expert on, and wished I could spend the afternoon reading those heavy texts.

"So, Jenny, how are you doing this week?"

"Okay, I guess. I miss my parents. How long do you really think I'll have to be here?"

"Jenny, missing your parents so much is part of the problem. You need to be here a while so we can get to some of the core issues that landed you here in the first place. Your relationship with your parents is one of them."

The thought of being here much longer seemed excruciating. I would become teary-eyed, and panic. I felt a horrible pang of loneliness, thinking about an indefinite period of time. Like my life was waiting for me somewhere. *But what life?* Then I'd get tired of yearning and longing, and just wish I was back on the unit taking a nap.

Dr. Shark believed that there weren't healthy boundaries in my family, that there was a detrimental kind of enmeshment, and that I was the one who manifested the dysfunction. We discussed the pressures I felt to appear beautiful, thin, and perfect, especially because of my family's place in the fashion world. There was really nothing that complicated about anything we talked about, but Dr. Shark thought there was. He thought I was smothered and not permitted to be my own person.

Family sessions were even worse than my private ones. My parents would travel an hour each way for our meetings. When I saw them at the door of the unit, side by side, their blond and brunette coloring and low-key outfits (a faded pink button-down with jeans, a navy sweater and chinos) working so well together, the familiarity was a big dose of relief at first, but then it turned to heavy sadness. I was immediately transported to the year before, the starving, the bingeing, the ipecac. Then I'd cringe at the reality that I would be saying good-bye shortly. I knew they'd be leaving as soon as they came.

We'd gather in Dr. Shark's office. The smiles and greetings soon turned to silence. Inviting a man in to watch, explore, and dissect our behavior and family roles made all three of us uncomfortable. It was truly invasive. Here I was, trying to get help, asking for help, at a hospital, for God's sake, and yet I didn't want to let the doctor in, or challenge my family's close ties. I was very loyal to my parents.

It seemed like Dr. Shark provoked my parents, and I could see my mom or my dad getting upset by some of the things he said. "Mr. and Mrs. Lauren, don't you think Jenny tries to do things to impress you? Do you put a lot of pressure on her? Do you think she gets enough privacy?"

I was aware that Dr. Shark wanted me to feel like he was on my side, but I didn't want to attack or blame anyone. I didn't want to psychoanalyze everything. I couldn't bear that I was dragging my parents through my nightmare. It wasn't fair. I wanted to hold my mom when she had tears running down her face and said, "I love my daughter more than anything. I've done the best I could do. She's everything to us. My children are everything."

My dad would then pick up for her. "Susan's trying to say that we will do whatever Jenny needs, we want help for her. But we won't take the blame. Jenny has a lot of talent, and she's harder on herself than anyone, even than us. We don't ask her to get As or be perfect at everything, that's her own issue. And she's beautiful. Look at her. Maybe that's a curse she bears. We've given our children everything, all the kids, and there is a tremendous amount of love in this family."

I wanted to tell my mother it would be okay, that I loved her. I didn't want to see them so upset. During one session, I yelled at Dr. Shark, "What's the point of all of this? My parents did the best job they could as parents and better than most. They've only loved me. It's my problem! It's because of me. No one else!"

Then, at another session, he affronted all of us when he asked my parents, "Do you think it is normal to put a ten-year-old girl in the same bed as her twelve-year-old brother?" He was referring to the summer I came back from starving myself at camp. It was the same summer Greg was having difficulty sleeping at night. We all had taken turns lying by his side to help comfort him.

"Now, you wait a second, Dr. Shark, what exactly are you implying?" my father asked.

My mother looked horrified and said, "What is going on here? We did nothing wrong. We all tried to help Greg. Oh my God, Jerry, do you believe this?"

I sat silently watching this transaction. I was absolutely aghast. What was he saying? That something naughty had happened? How could he be reading something into it like that? I simply told him that my brother had some problems around the same time I did. After all, in the olden days, like on *Little House on the Prairie*, and even now, where families live in small tight quarters, beds and spaces are shared by siblings. *Eccch. What was wrong with him? Thinking that way?*

This analytical Freudian bullshit was way too much for us.

I didn't really make much progress in therapy. With all his big words and psycho-lingo I never really trusted Dr. Shark. And it only got worse after his arrogant assumptions. He was the first doctor I really didn't like.

Every week I waited anxiously for my one visit and one phone call with my parents. "Hi, Mom. Yeah, I'm okay. I miss you, though. So much. Are you guys going out tonight? Where? Oh. Um, say hello. Hi, Daddy," I'd start to choke up, "No, no, I'm okay. Really. Just miss you guys. You're coming again on Friday, right?" More sniffles. Then, "Is Greg with B.J. tonight? Where'd they go? Send him a hug. Has Brad called from school? Oh, this new girl, Lucy, came in, really nice. She knows the Ornsteins' sons. Goes to Cornell with them. She's skinny, skinny, and beautiful. I can't wait until I see you guys. No, I don't need anything. Well, maybe another Danielle Steele book. No, I don't need more socks. I don't know when they're going to let me exercise. My body is going to mush. This isn't healthy to be stuck on this unit with no movement or fresh air. Oh, can you bring me one more pack of cigarettes? Marlboro Lights, yep, right. I promise I'll quit when I get out. Thanks, Mom. I love you. Mommm." I'd start to panic, knowing my time was up. "Can't I come home? I can't bear it. Pleassssse. Pleasse, Mom. Mommmmm!"

If we cried while we were on the phone, we were usually forced to hang up. I cried during most of my phone calls and begged to come home. On one occasion a young intern studying to be a social worker came over to me and said, "Are you okay? Come on, get off so we can go chat." I sat with her for about an hour as she made jokes, told me about her boyfriend and the classes she was taking. I ended up looking forward to when she was on duty, when she'd come in popping her chewing gum and wink at me. Those nights I felt a little stronger because she'd get a smile out of me and remind me that I liked to laugh.

I stayed at the hospital four months, and in the majority of my sessions all I talked about was when I could go home and how much I missed my parents and that I couldn't get better without them being near. Dr. Shark disagreed and told me that I suffered from severe separation anxiety.

I keep hearing his words, "Jenny. You do everything for your parents. What about you? When are you going to do something for yourself?"

He argued that I had no means of satisfying myself, and that everything I did—from the way I looked, my dancing, my artwork, even my moods—was for my mother and father. He felt that I was fighting to be perfect to satisfy my parents, and that my sense of self and self-esteem was entirely dictated by my parents' approval. On some level, I knew this was true. My parents were my best friends; they were everything for me. *But so what? What is life for?* I was plagued by nightmares that they would die and that I would kill myself because of it. I daydreamed that even when they died at an old age, I wouldn't be able to handle it. I was obsessed with the fear of losing them, and the fear of not making them happy.

After three months my weight was at a stable 115 pounds; I had gained the privilege of going to the bathroom in a real toilet, of choosing my own food, and of spending a day visiting my parents in New York City. On Thanksgiving my parents and Brad and Greg came to visit. It was so comforting to see them. They told me all about the progress of my Santa Fe–style room. That it was really coming along and it would be finished in a month or so, hopefully when I'd be returning home. They kept emphasizing how beautiful it was, and that it was something to look forward to. After they left, all the girls couldn't stop talking about how gorgeous my brothers were.

In a session at the beginning of my fourth month, Dr. Shark told me that he thought we could begin discussing discharge. He said that I would never fully recover if I went back and lived at home. He handed me a pamphlet for a special boarding school called the Harvey School and said, "I've made arrangements for you to meet the headmaster."

I laughed. "You're kidding, right. You have to be kidding?"

He said, "Jenny, I'm very serious. You cannot live at home. You will never get better at home."

"No way, Dr. Shark. No way. I won't do it. I won't go away for my last year and a half of high school." It wasn't right; it didn't sit right at all. He was so off. I became sad thinking of my parents. I wanted to be home with them. What did this arrogant doctor know? These shrinks send the girls away all the time, to halfway houses or other hospitals, now he wanted to send me away too. It was their answer for everyone.

Dr. Shark's face turned red and he got angry and he raised his voice. "You're so stubborn. You have time to think about it. Be open-minded. Your life wasn't great at home before, was it?" How dare he? Fuck him. He doesn't even really give a shit. He's getting paid for this crap. I left his office weeping and confided in the few friends I still had at the hospital. I missed Lucy, my true confidant on the unit. She had left Cornell after losing too much weight. She was a nice, pretty Jewish girl, and we talked all the time. On her first day, she wouldn't eat, she cried, yelled, and shrieked with terror as they picked her and her flailing arms up and placed her in the quiet room. We nice Jewish girls can really go nuts.

I never landed in the quiet room. I'm sure if I had come in there needing to gain weight and been forced to eat, I would have been in it a lot. After Lucy was let out we became instant friends, and we sat and talked together all the time about life back home. She told me about Cornell and all the pressure there. She knew some people I knew at Dalton. Although she was older, she seemed like a girl that I would be friends with at school—warm, smart, easy to talk to. She used to argue that this place was ridiculous. That the treatment was horrible and that this was no way to get better. She said it was a jail. The times we weren't badmouthing the hospital or crying, she'd blow-dry my hair straight for me or do my makeup. She left before me. Her parents took her out because she promised to gain weight on her own. I wondered if she would really do it. I wanted to leave so badly too. And become thin again.

Dr. Shark told me I couldn't leave if I didn't decide to go to the Harvey School. I was appalled by this. *Is this extortion? Who does he think he is?* My parents were pretty much against the idea too. It seemed a bit ridiculous. So on one visit to New York, I tried to run away. We were in our garage waiting for the car. All of a sudden, I even surprised myself when I started sprinting up that concrete mountain out onto the street and kept going. But then I saw Brad coming after me, and I slowed down and let him catch me. I knew I had to return to the hospital. On the car ride back, my parents promised me that they would sign me out.

At my last session I said to Dr. Shark, "I'm sorry. I'm really sorry. Thank you for all your help. But I'm leaving and there's really nothing more to talk about. I know you think there's only one way, but it doesn't suit me. My family is everything to me. There's nothing wrong with that. I'm lucky to have such a loving family. And truthfully, Dr. Shark, I'm not sure you get me."

He said firmly, "Yes, I do. Yes, I do. It's unfortunate, Jenny, that you don't see that I do."

I left the hospital after four months with AMA status: Against Medical Advice. This would be on my records forever because I didn't want to go to the school he suggested. I had been a good patient. I had eaten my meals, never vomited, never wised-off to authority, and was never put in the quiet room. Most of the girls could be vicious to the help, unruly, and often threw tantrums. I was a good girl and that's the reward I got for it. Always such a good girl and where does it get me? *In a hospital.* I don't think I learned much at Cornell White Plains except to feel more guilty for having a problem. I saw that there was manipulation and betrayal in there. I saw that the girls were treated as "crazy" and that I was considered a threat to myself. I was angered not necessarily by the way the doctors tried to figure us all out (we came in for that), but by how they came up with some wild hypothesis and then tried to fit us into it. They gave us advice that wasn't necessarily going to help, and couldn't admit that maybe they just didn't know what to do with us. I didn't gain self-esteem, I didn't gain inspiration for a healthier life, and I didn't get better. I didn't trust anyone or myself more than I had when I came in. I had gone on the ride, and I saw things, sad, horrible things, a lot of suffering, fear, and sadness. One girl drank the water out of the toilet bowl before she weighed in just so the number would show up higher on the scale. Some girls did jumping jacks together in the bedroom each night between the fifteen-minute check-ins instead of sleeping. One girl chewed her food over and over, then hid it in her napkins. The skin of one beautiful Julia Roberts look-alike had turned orange because she had eaten only carrots for a year.

Truthfully, what was worst of all was how bitchy some of the help and nurses were to the patients. How they often wouldn't listen compassionately when someone cried, how they always looked at us suspiciously, how they sometimes seemed like they just really didn't give a damn. And for goodness' sake, one of the female psychiatrists would come onto the unit every day wearing her Chanel suit and her own bone-thin body. *Now, who was she kidding?*

Within the locked unit of this hospital in White Plains was a world where priorities and goals were talked about in a similar vein. At this place there were other females whose lives were dictated by solemn codes of depriving and feeding one's hunger, where starving and purging was the behavior, where fear and lack of control were the common roots. The females were punished inside this place just as much as they punished themselves before they came in. The world inside wasn't all that different from the world outside that locked door.

4. Blood Ties

I am ten years old and lying in bed next to my twelve-year-old brother, Greg, our bodies and skin only a few inches away from each other. It is near midnight and I am relieved that Greg is sleeping soundly. *Finally. Now I can go to bed.* It is my turn to sleep next to Greg. Sometimes my mother does and sometimes Brad. Tonight I can hear Brad in the bunk bed above snoring deeply. Nothing is keeping him awake, not even Greg's fear. I am holding down the fort tonight so everything will be just fine.

I lie there watching Greg sleep, noticing the contours of his face, his cheekbones, his chiseled nose, his long eyelashes, the soft wavy curls of his dark hair. I notice his light blue Brooks Brothers pajamas and won-der what they feel like. I myself am enjoying the softness of my silk, light pink nightgown with the bow across my chest. And for a moment I imagine that I am a princess, beautiful and feminine, and I am sleeping next to my prince, handsome and strong. Then I think about how Greg makes me laugh during the day, how much fun I have with him, and how relieved I am that the three of us are all back together from camp. But it hurts me that Greg gets so scared at night. I feel badly for him. *What is it that he is afraid of? What does he think will happen? Why can't he sleep alone?* I am happy I can protect him; it feels good to be doing something important and to be needed. And then I experience the coolest most wonderful realization I will ever have. That I am con-nected to this boy like I will never be connected to anyone else. That this boy who looks like me, and even at times acts like me, has been cre-ated by the same two people that made me, and that he is the same blood, the same DNA . . . the ultimate closest possible person there could be. And it is the same with my brother upstairs. Whether it seems narcissistic, or whether someone wants to make it sound ugly or sexual, which it wasn't, it doesn't really matter to me because then, and now, at twenty-five years old, looking back, I think of it as really beautiful. I can honestly say that I think I fell in love with both my brothers that night. *No wonder it's always been hard to find a suitable guy.*

It was always pretty obvious to my friends, therapists, and myself that I idolized them. Not only were they both handsome and charis-matic, but they also gave me, *little Jenny,* their darling and often "trou-bled" sister lots of attention. And vice versa. Through the years, all my therapists have had a field day discussing my relationships with them, specifically Greg, the "middle child," who was for most of my childhood and adolescence my best friend. Greg and I are only two and a half years apart, and it was inevitable that we often went to events together and shared friends. Brad is five years older than I, and although we had our own special relationship, he had his own set of friends and interests that differed from Greg's and mine. He was into acting, computers, technical stuff, less athletic than Greg and me and a bit more quirky. He was smoking pot and going off to college while I was just a mere baby going to pizza parties in middle school.

Greg and I were often mistaken for identical twins. It wasn't just because of how we looked but because we shared many of the same passions and interests. Whether we were drawing huge cards for our mom and dad with colorful design markers, shopping for beads in the fashion district to make cool necklaces, dying T-shirts in luscious colors, bin by bin, on the fields of our country house for our stand at the 76th Street flea market when we were in high school, or hunting for vintage clothing, we were often doing something creative together. We both were also athletic (you could say obsessed with physical activity, he just as much as I, but *I think he ate*) and we would jog the four miles to the General Store and back in Connecticut, swim one hundred laps in our pool, enter a Saturday Night Fever Solid Gold dance contest in public school that we won (he lifted me and flipped me . . . *Jesus, we were good*) or take a Body by Jake and Tina aerobics class together. My brother had no qualms about trying any activity and put equal energy into all of his projects. In high school, he would race back from his Dalton varsity soccer game to get to a Dance Theatre Workshop rehearsal in the auditorium for our two dance pieces. Then he would go home to finish a drawing he was asked to do for the cover of a Dalton brochure. We were both driven. We bonded even in our great desire to hear or see our parents acknowledge us and our endeavors with delight. Brad was less attached to this notion. And for that, I think he was the healthiest of us all. But on a deeper level Greg and I were both extremely sensitive and intuitive, especially to the nuances of emotion and personalities that we encountered, and to the tension and dynamics experienced in our immediate family. And both of us were affected in our own ways, especially that summer of '82.

That was the summer I had starved myself, and he was frightened to be alone at night. Eventually the bunk beds were dismantled so Greg's bed would be on the same level as Brad, and that seemed to do the trick. Even more than the psychiatrist he saw that year, who said we both picked up on our parents' tension, their financial strain, the sadness and boredom we saw in our mother's eyes when my dad went to the track at night, which he had been doing for some months.

The prior year, Greg and I had left our neighborhood public school on First Avenue, where we had been happy and popular, to attend The Dalton School, an elite and competitive private school on the Upper East Side, and where Brad was already in high school. The kids there were like little adults, having conversations about where they'd be vacationing, where they were shopping that afternoon, and whose parties they were attending that weekend. They all seemed very smart. It was unlike my experience at public school; I was no longer one of the few to get As. No longer one of the only Jewish girls, one of the only "special" girls. Even though I made friends pretty easily, I wasn't the ringmaster anymore. At public school I had been much more of a leader, more of a tough girl too. I hung out with my brother and his friends in the schoolyard, popping gum, joking, "acting cool." I also stood up for the underdogs, confronting those kids who teased others. At Dalton I became more reclusive. I concentrated a lot on my homework, dancing, my outfits, and my fat thighs.

It hadn't been an easy year for my parents financially and emotionally. Suddenly my parents were sending their three children to private schools. Where money was concerned, my father was like a fat person who loses weight but still thinks he's obese. He was always in fear that he didn't have enough, even when he was starting to feel comfortable. My mother, picking up on his fears, added to our awareness that we had to be careful. My father worked hard and he provided well for his family, but we still lived in a small apartment, and my parents still struggled. And even though the company was beginning to take off, my father didn't have the means that people assumed.

My father started going to the racetrack at night more and more as an outlet. After dinner, he would grab his Carhartt jacket and say, "Sus, I need to go. I need to blow off steam." My mother would respond, "But Jerry, you went last night. Why don't you just stay and unwind." They'd argue a bit. Then my dad would come over, toothpick in mouth, and say,

"Give me a kiss good-bye, Jenny Penny." He'd suck the toothpick backward into his mouth and pucker up. I'd beg him not to do that and whine, "Dad, stop. You could swallow it." But he'd kiss me anyhow and manage not to choke. The door would slam and it would become silent in the house. My brothers and I knew our mom was upset. We would finish clearing the table, and she'd be staring at the floor. Then she would do the dishes with a sad expression on her face as if she were in a trance.

When she finally finished her chores, she would turn off the kitchen lights, go wash her face, grab her floss, her book, and set herself up cozy on the couch. She might start noshing from the cookie jar or the doughnut box that sat on top of the toaster, taking little pieces at a time throughout the night. The three of us kids often procrastinated about doing our homework. Brad talked on the phone in the bedroom, and Greg and I usually curled up next to my mother like little cats and watched the television while she nodded off. I always felt bad for my mother, that she looked forward to seeing my dad all day, cooked him his meal, and then he didn't spend the evenings with her. I felt like she was abandoned, left to do the dirty work, left with the kids. I was afraid she was bored and lonely. Sometimes I was angry at my dad for coming home to eat and then running off. On the other hand I understood how hard he worked all day, that he needed to have some fun too. And I wasn't actually that upset when he left, because we'd have our mom to ourselves.

I always awoke at midnight as I heard the keys jingle and my father come in. My mother would yell out from their bedroom, "Hang up your jacket, Jerry! It reeks from smoke!" Then my father would come into the kitchen, and since my room was right next door I could see him, so I'd prop myself up and say from my bed, "Did you win, Daddy?" He'd often respond, "I did about even," or, "I got beat up." He never really won. His routine was then to open the fridge, stuff two Ring-Dings in his mouth and wash 'em down with a big swig of club soda. Then the night was finally over. We could all go to sleep. In the morning, my father would awake drenched with sweat, and when I went to say good-bye to him in his bathroom while he was getting ready for work, I could smell the dampness of newspaper print and anxiety all over him.

The track thing was just a phase for my dad. Later on, he stopped going because he admitted that it was a no-win situation and that it depressed him. That year had been the worst of it, and after that I don't recall a time when my parents argued as intensely.

5. Destruction

I do not even know what the date is, nor do I know who or what I am anymore. The reality that I have been opened up—my beautiful, once flat, and often concave stomach, my pelvis, my rectum, all of it restructured—absolutely horrifies me. I feel rearranged, uncomfortable, out of sync with my entire body. Something that I and others in the 1990s had attempted to do with great energy and enthusiasm was to find our bodies—the shape, size, and look that felt right. There I had been, a year before my surgery, finally thin, exercising like a maniac, and incredibly happy with my results. Now, even after surgery, I am unable to run. God, how I miss my runs. I miss feeling my buttocks.

My asshole surgeon sure has a way with words. He says he "tucked in," or "dug around" in my pelvis. He claims that's why I'm in pain or "sensitive" in that area. I feel like he may have had a little bit too much fun in there. I'm sickened that some stranger has decided my fate, that I have given him the liberty to change my wires, to reshape my insides. Will I always feel his hands inside me "digging around"? What if he messed me up? Why is there so much pain? I had so much hope that in time I would be walking and running and living like before. It's almost three months, and I know this surgery crippled me. I basically feel like I have no ass (my surgeon says, "Trust me, you have an ass," since I've put on some pounds). I have nothing to spring off from like the power from a buttock. My butt . . . my butt . . . this is so sad. *Mom . . . Dad*

. . . help! I lost my ass. Will you find it? Or at least could ya buy me an-other one?

My surgeon says he saved me from incontinence. If this is so, does this mean there is a trade-off? Surely life only gets better; the terror must end at some point. But then I realize there are no rules in this game of life. Nothing promises relief, nothing is written in stone: *"You had an enterocele in your buttocks and the doctor fixed it, therefore you will walk like you once did."* Nothing promises me I will be okay. And all these self-help books and doctors say that I need to think positive. Thinking positive won't change what has occurred. I'm just trying to be realistic.

If I cannot feel my muscles, how can I feel alive? How can I get my mind to work? And if I can't get my mind positive, how will my body awaken and come alive and my spirit return?

I feel as if I have awakened in the past few months from a somewhat peaceful delirium. The anesthesia, the painkillers, kept me slightly floating above myself and above what has occurred, in pain at moments but drugged enough to ease some of the emotions. And all these med-ications . . . I already miss those that I resisted, those that I hated hav-ing to take, like the Xanax that I just stopped. Now I crave them. The dulled sensation made everything hurt a little less. They were my shield. Now I still feel that displacement, but everything is getting too bright and chilly today. The cold is going right through me but not even the way it used to. Not like after an invigorating walk or run, my hands and feet becoming frozen, burning sensations caused by the nature of the wind, damp sweat filling my scalp and long ponytail, dripping down my back.

Instead, every day, I feel like I'm going to explode. I am so extended now (or is it distended?) that it is scaring me. I have to start listening to my body. Why don't I accept that I cannot have milk products, coffee, Wasa bread, frozen yogurt; all my old comfort foods are killing my al-ready dying insides. I am very frightened right now that I may truly ex-pand like Violet Beauregarde, who chewed the blueberry gum in Willy Wonka's chocolate factory.

What did I do to deserve my own destruction? And to have to *watch* my own destruction? Is this some message to me or is it punishment because I lived in fear my whole life, which made me inflict harm upon myself constantly? I was in anguish over how much emotion I always felt, but was that so wrong? To hear the music and be able to dance, to run, to walk fast, to feel graceful, to spend a whole day feeling pretty? A few days? So I would inevitably binge and act out one or two days a week and hurt myself. Yes, it was a violent act, and it was selfish, because, tucked away alone in that world, it kept me from being the loving friend and family member that I could have been. But it was a compulsion, the only way I could react, numb myself, and the only way I knew how to live. Am I being punished? *"Here, I'll show you. You had the nerve to disrespect yourself that much, to play war with the blessed life I gave to you. I have given you beauty, intelligence, talent, a family that loves and supports you, and you do nothing with it but fear it and waste it. You never thought about anything or anybody else, you narcissist. I'll show you real pain. And then maybe you'll learn."*

I think, *but, God, it's a disease. I swear it. I've had it since I was ten years old. I've tried to beat it but I never could. I don't know why I have it. I used to think you gave it to me. Maybe I shouldn't have blamed you. Maybe you're angry with that. But I've asked for your help before to free myself from the jail I was in. Every day before this was a challenge for me. Is this supposed to be the greatest challenge of all?*

6. Fair Oaks

I worshipped a girl at Fair Oaks Hospital. Dawn looked like Shannen Doherty, wore Jordache jeans and a gold chain with a cross around her neck, was skinny as hell, and acted like Rizzo from *Grease*. She was tough, she was cool, she was pretty. And she was everything I wished I still was and thought I used to be. But for me it was Oshkosh or Levi's, and beads instead of a cross or Jewish star around my neck. She was a twenty-year-old girl from Yonkers, New York, and had already been in ten hospitals for anorexia. I could tell by the way she hung out and sprawled her legs up over the bend of the couch so casually that she was used to this scene. Hospitals were her thing, and she was very comfortable on her turf. Sometimes she chatted with her choice friend of the day, sometimes she remained quiet, and sometimes she giggled and made wisecracks with her raspy voice, riling everybody up and making us all laugh while we watched the television or flipped through magazines, waiting to go in for our group sessions. When we reenacted family or relationship scenarios, she was very funny. Even the social workers got a kick out of her. I was too damn shy and self-conscious to really get into those exercises . . . to pretend that one of the stand-in girls was my father, and tell him to fuck off. She could do it well. With pizzazz. And an occasional huge outburst of tears. But all in all she seemed rather blasé and unaffected about being there. And that . . . was depressing to me. But still, I was intrigued by her and jealous of her.

I came into this hospital after two months of nonstop bingeing and vomiting. I was seventeen, becoming overweight (and that means even over my goal weight of 123 at the other hospital, *yikes*). I had just started senior year at the Tutoring School and was afraid I was going back to old habits. I asked to go. So my parents and I did research and found this place that was supposedly less harsh and intense than Cornell White Plains.

I was repulsed by my expanding body and my behavior. I just couldn't take it anymore. It was as if some demon possessed me. Like I was under a spell and unable to stop myself from eating. I'd get a craving for food, have one piece of sugar, and forget it; I didn't know where I was anymore or what I was doing. I was gone. Over. *Finis.* IN TROUBLE. My mom continuously asked, "Why don't you call me first?" I never could. Doctors have always said the key to recovery is reaching out. Some bulimics are successful with making that call to a family member, a friend, or a sponsor from a self-help group. Some people can save themselves from taking that first deadly bite, or stop themselves midway. But I never reached that point. I hadn't been strong enough to get down on my knees and beg for the urges to go away. One of my therapists once said that it had to do with my pride.

Even now I just wanted a place to stop acting out, keep myself from stuffing food down my throat, a breather, almost like going to a spa. This wasn't a spa exactly, it was more like a Marriott hotel than a hospital. This was a place to hang out, bide your time *until the eleventh hospital*. There were occasional group meetings, and elective activities were offered, such as art therapy or knitting. At night they even showed us film features on the VCR or we watched sitcoms. There weren't many rules at this hospital except for having to stay out of your room for an hour after meals so you wouldn't be able to puke it up. This is a life for many anorexics—young girls, women . . . some men. They come in and they go out. They gain weight and they lose it. They find a new doctor, a new place, over and over again. It is not as trivial as a game, and yet somehow it becomes exactly that.

I can remember only one other girl's story from that hospital. She was bulimic and addicted to drugs. Ether was her thing. She told her long drug tales to me or the group, exciting herself, getting high each time. It was like hearing a suicide waiting to happen; her future was very clear to me. That she was in a no-win situation. And it was probably the same for Dawn. *Was it the same for me? Nah. This was definitely the last hospital for me.* I barely remember any details from that place. Maybe it was because they fed me lithium for two weeks, or maybe it was because I didn't shit for the entire month I was there and all the toxins had caused brain fog. Just like in the first hospital—prunes, Colace, and all, I still didn't go. Perhaps it had all started then.

I mainly recall feeling very cynical and angry for most of my stint at this so-called hospital. And then one day, in particular, sneaking food back from a privileged trip out, a bag of popcorn and cookies . . . I offered my goodies to all the girls in secrecy. I still had these intense cravings. They just wouldn't go away. I binged. Finished both bags. Didn't vomit, though. Got caught. Wasn't really punished, . . . just was watched more closely. I think I wanted to be bad for once. *As cool as*

Dawn. But even though Dawn got all excited when she caught a glimpse of the popcorn, she still wouldn't have any. Then she became afraid, like a little frightened puppy, and found a corner to hide in and just kept her eyes glued to the television screen.

I stayed there for one and a half months and then decided to get out of there fast. I sure as hell didn't need to stay cooped up at a hospital unit in Hoboken, New Jersey, to binge. Might as well go finish senior year in high school and try as hard as I could not to eat three huge cups of Colombo frozen yogurt every afternoon while walking the twenty blocks home on Third Avenue.

I always wonder what happened to Dawn. What was she so afraid of at home, to keep having to run away? What kept her locked in her cycle, her routine? Is she at a hospital now, at thirty-something years old? Is she even still alive?

7. Dr. Hannibal and the Mayo Clinic Blues

I've been going to see my father's therapist, Dr. H (because he looks a lot like Hannibal Lechter from *Silence of the Lambs*). Dr. Hannibal is the best of the best. Many so-called important people go to him. My dad began seeing him after his health scare and when he found himself getting lots of headaches and heartburn when he was upset. On occasion, when I used to meet my dad there to have family sessions or pick him up before dinner, I'd see a certain football star waiting outside. My dad would say, "Hey, do you know who he is? Look, everybody's got problems."

I like Hannibal. He's strict but he's good and he has dedicated himself to my situation. He really wants to believe my physical pain and suffering is from a normal aftermath of surgery, although he does question the degree of my discomfort, implying that it could be psychosomatic. After a few weeks he put me on some strange drug called Haldol. After the first pill, I had a bad reaction and nearly choked on my tongue. I later discovered that Haldol is prescribed for schizophrenics. What was he thinking? But I see Hannibal is getting wary now too. He and Dr. W can't comprehend my discomfort and my symptoms. *Doctors at a loss? This is getting too familiar.* Together they arrange for me to go to the Mayo Clinic for a full battery of tests. Hannibal says we had better rule out Lou Gehrig's or something akin to that. It's amazing that he feeds me these antipsychotics on the one hand but is sending me off for a thorough physical evaluation. Either I have done such a good job of convincing him of my ailments, or he is just trying to pacify me and my parents. The thing is, I know Hannibal is fond of me too. I know he thinks I'm a smart cookie. I know from the intense way he looks and converses with me. Unless, of course, I'm an original nutcase and he is fascinated. And in the past, before all of this, when I saw him at group sessions with my parents, when I was just my father's somewhat troubled daughter, a Barnard College student with an eating disorder who caused my father agita, I would get an A+ on my report from my dad afterward. He'd tell me proudly that Hannibal told him I was a very sharp, attractive, and intelligent young woman and that he had nothing to worry about with me. *Another doctor. WRONG AGAIN!*

Still, I'm not totally offended by Hannibal. *Even if he is as confused as the others.* Mainly because I have come to him in desperation and asked him for his expertise. But in the psychiatric world, when you ask for help you usually get it in pill form. I do know Hannibal is trying everything possible to provide comfort to me (and my parents). But now, I believe he is perplexed. And there is nothing more scary than the brilliant doctor who doesn't have all the answers.

I'm sitting here this morning in my Radisson hotel room staring out the window at the bleak, gray October weather of freakin' Minnesota. I'm scared for my sanity and deeply devastated by the loss of my independence. Even with all the depression and lack of self-confidence, I was still able to take care of myself. In a way, I think I might have thrived on the anguish, with every sensation so piercing. A smell or a sound could give me a yearning for something slightly abstract, like a desire for love, something sensuous, or perhaps erotic; or for something specific like a physical place, or a place in the past. It's like the way a burning fire reminds me of my experiences at co-ed camp. I associate it with nighttime, with a chill going through my hooded sweatshirt and a fear that the boy whose arm was around my shoulder would have to get up and return to boy's camp, leaving me wanting and waiting for the next time. Anything pleasurable always seemed fleeting. But I lived and nourished myself on the fear of losing everything.

I changed weights and shapes many times in my minuscule twenty-five years. But even when I was thin and had reached a temporary illusion of achievement, I had even more fear. It was scarier than remaining unsatisfied with extra weight. I would call my mother up, yes, even at twenty-three years old, and ask, "Mom, is it okay that I ate an extra piece of chicken? Will I gain weight?" And my mom would say, "Honey, you probably needed it. Your body was craving it. Don't worry, you'll burn it off tomorrow on your run. Stop thinking about it. Go to a movie or something." My mother understood my experience well. When I was in college, our occasional coffee shop lunches between classes were difficult. After we had finished our tuna niçoise or egg white omelet, we would both get very quiet. I'd say, "Mom, I feel so blah. I get so depressed after eating my meals." And she'd admit to experiencing the same. "I know, sweetie, I get a letdown too. But that's why you need to keep busy. Get yourself distracted, go on with the day. How 'bout we go over to Bloomingdale's?"

After most meals I ate with my parents, my dad would notice my frown and say, "Jenny, your mood changed. What, do you think your face is fuller now? Jenny, a person doesn't gain weight overnight." And if my mother complained of being full, or whined, "Jerrrrrrry, why did you let me eat all those french fries from your plate?" my father would say, "Susan, cut it out. You two are crazy." Yes, my dad knew my neurosis, the way I thought, but he couldn't console me. I could feel my thighs expanding and feared the bloated face appearing in the morning.

Through college I lost the weight that I had put on my senior year of high school. I had had enough of feeling lousy and was uncomfortable with an extra twenty or so pounds. I wanted to express myself, my style, and my sexuality. So, as I had done time and time again, summer after summer since I was ten years old, I began my vicious cycle, concentrating on a low-fat diet and a shitload of exercising. All through college I took yoga classes, ran daily, did calisthenics, and I was real lean by my senior year at Barnard. For two years after college, I followed my routine and remained thin. The downside is that there was a lot of bingeing and purging in the mix. *But, hey, no need to pay attention to that . . . 'cause I was looking good.*

At twenty-three, I liked my body. It was the one I finally felt comfortable with. I could actually shower with the lights on. Before, I had spent years flicking off the bathroom switch just so I wouldn't have to look in the mirror or at my bare flesh under the running water. Although, on the days I binged and purged I resorted to my old routine. I didn't want to see the damage, the stretched-out swollen face. I wanted to hide then. But the majority of my days *I had style,* and would strut around New York in a short skirt and high black Varda boots, with a big leather belt lying low on my hips. *Yeah, I'm cool. I can take on this avenue. Uh-huh. Uh-huh.* It was the body I wanted to pursue men with, I wanted to express my sensuality with. It was the body I could face the world with. Everything else that went along with this body, the intensity of the behavior I used to get there or stay there, existed in a parallel universe. Although I lived in some narcissistic shell, it was the only way I could proceed, and cope. I was only in touch with the lines of my muscles, the inner workings of my intestines and organs through yoga practice. Feeling lithe and toned, feeling the strength of my physical core made me feel almost whole. As I extended my leg behind me and stretched toward the ceiling with my arm, I felt cradled, nurtured, and balanced. Tears often came to my eyes when I did such poses. A bittersweet feeling went right through me, a blend of strength, courage, and an intense yearning. The poses were little prayers. The poses represented the physical beauty of the form but, mostly, the realization that beauty could truly exist and be felt within—and that beauty was based on emotions.

I sit here now, amazed at my fate, that I feel and look like a crippled woman and that I am a patient at the infamous Mayo Clinic. I am also amazed at my clarity for the moment, amazed that my hands are not experiencing the uncontrollable spasming of veins or arteries or whatever it is that clenches me throughout my whole body. But what amazes me most is that when I used to look in the mirror and feel fear, I must have known that I was going to lose my body.

Yesterday, after giving me my near fiftieth rectal exam, in front of three other male doctors yet, the surgeon that Mayo has assigned to my case just stands there, and without any ounce of tact or compassion, tells my mother and me that he never would have done the surgery. He says physical situations like mine are too complicated and that surgery never really helps the symptoms. He says they leave it alone in older women, where such a condition is more common.

But what was I to do at twenty-four years old, live with my perineum stretched and my small intestine between my legs for the rest of my life? How can he be so cruel as to make me regret the surgery even more than I already do? My surgeon at home had said that I really had no choice. How can anyone trust these doctors when they all have different opinions? This Mayo surgeon says, "There's great controversy over these matters." Well, I am not *these matters*, I am Jenny, with Jenny's body, Jenny's sinking intestine, Jenny's awful twitch, and Jenny's situation. *What the fuck.*

My mother and I are pissed. We demand to speak to another surgeon to allay some of our fear and hopefully tell us that the surgery was not a mistake. They give us a female surgeon (thank God) who seems much kinder, although she is brutal with my insides. She gives me a painful colonoscopy that I cry through. After sticking that scope all the way up my bleeding and inflamed colon and watching it wriggle and squirm like a snake on the television monitor, she says that I fortunately will not need a revision on my surgeon's work. Small victory.

At this point, I really just wish I had gone to Santa Fe and shot myself.

The Mayo Clinic feels like a Disneyland for the dying. There are tons of people here, some who look pale and weak, some who are pasty and morbidly fat, some who hobble, and many who sit in wheelchairs that are being pushed along by family members. In fact, there are wheelchairs in the lobby of each building, but I don't want to use them. I sure as hell don't look like I need one, but the riotous fact is I probably do. Getting around is tedious because the buildings and offices are often far away from each other; it is the usual mazelike setting of a hospital, with colorful arrows and signs with body parts pointing the way. Gift shops dot the place, with heart-shaped balloons and stuffed animals that say "Get Well" on them and hardcover books on every possible disease. I keep waiting for a Mickey Mouse on crutches to turn the corner followed by a herd of sick children.

I need to focus on moving forward to keep up with my mother as she searches for the next room for the next test. I let her do all the work, get the directions, get frustrated, mutter under her breath, and I just follow her like I have no mind of my own. Like a child. I really can't think straight. My wrists sting (all my joints do, for some reason) so much that I can't hold anything. I've been told it might be from the anesthesia still in my system. My eyes spasm constantly, so I can't even focus on my mom's face or the crossword puzzle we attempt as we sit and wait for hours, and I mean hours, for each test under those awful fluorescent lights. I get jealous when my mother reads her book, because I wish I could escape like that too. There is nothing I can do to get a break from the pain except at mealtime, when I get distracted by deciding what I should eat. And I've been joining my mother for a glass of white wine at dinner. I want to relax, calm down like she does. It doesn't do much for me except help me fall asleep, for which I'm grateful. Then I awake a few hours later in the middle of the night and I cry out to her, "Mommm, help me. Help me, Momm, oh, God." I want her to make it all go away. I want her to make me tea with milk and honey, or bring me three boxes of Pine Brothers honey-lemon cough drops like all the times I was sick in bed as a little girl, watching *I Love Lucy*, and having her dote on me with her usual remedies, goodies, and recipes of love to help me get over strep throat, a common infection of mine when I was younger. I want it to be that simple. Instead now I am asking her to help me get my body back, to help me hold up my insides. I may as well beg her to let me back inside her.

The separation anxiety started way back when. Both of ours. Holding me by the hand, my mother would take me to kindergarten to drop me off, and there were so many mornings when I just couldn't let go. I'd start to stamp my feet and sob, squeezing my mother's arm tightly and begging her not to leave me, to take me with her. I can remember not wanting to part from the smell of her skin, her hair, the touch of her smooth camel overcoat against me, or even the sound of her bracelets clinking. I also remember wondering where she was going that day and if she'd be lonely.

Then, at night I'd cringe when I smelled Lauren perfume, because I knew that meant she was going out with my father. I'd watch her get dressed, put on her makeup, and panic even more when the doorbell rang. It was my father, who was already dressed dapperly enough from a day at work in one of his navy or gray suits, and that meant they'd be ready to leave shortly. Although I had my brothers there to comfort me, it took me a while to stop crying when the baby-sitter came. My mother would almost always call to make sure we were all okay. By the time my parents came home, my brothers would be asleep, but although it was way past my bedtime, I'd be cozied up with the baby-sitter, watching *Charlie's Angels*, waiting up for them.

Then there was camp. The worst experience of separation, of

course, was the summer I was ten. Some of the other times, I would leave home upset, but return weeks later covered with makeup, cussing and popping gum, obviously having dealt with being away just fine. But even as I got older it was tense before I would leave, like the night before I went to stay at the Barnard campus for my freshman year. My mother helped me pack and we started fighting. Stupid stuff. I was being a brat, and she was nervous, acting persnickety. She ended up slapping me. It was easier to go up to college hating her and wanting to get away. *All this, and it was only uptown.*

But for my entire life, mostly every time I parted with my mother, I'd get a knot in my throat and a feeling of panic. I can always picture her bending down, cupping my chin, with tears in her eyes and a shaky voice, saying, "I love you, Little One."

As I lie there praying for comfort, I feel myself slipping away from her. I wish more than anything to be healthy and well, so as not to feel the same separation that always tugs on my heart. Because now I feel a nostalgia that is almost more unbearable, a longing for my mother that is so deep and so profound that the pain in itself is harder to take than the actual physical discomfort. I fear our shared grief will make her sick. Then I remain fixated on that fear, that I will make her die. That somehow, whether I go or she goes, I will lose her.

After many tests, the only tangible results are: I have low B_{12} levels and a bit of anemia, as well as a colon-motility problem, which we already know about. I am probably going to have to live on laxatives. This is not right; a person can't exist like this. They have also diagnosed me with the same thing the physiatrist at Mount Sinai called it: fibromyalgia, which they say is probably causing the joint discomfort. Fibromyalgia is one of those new, hip diseases that doctors are diagnosing left and right for pain syndromes they can't explain. *Hi, I'm bulimic and I've got fibromyalgia.* It does not show on X-rays or in blood. The doctors look for sore points throughout the body from a checklist of fourteen.

They say it's caused by trauma, specifically surgeries, car accidents, lack of REM sleep, and get this, eating disorders, because they are so traumatic to the body and mind. They say there's really nothing they can do for it except use small amounts of sleeping pills and antidepressants. More antidepressants now? *Again?*

By the end of high school I was an expert when it came to antidepressants. I experienced a lot of different reactions from these chemicals. But although there were extreme physical side effects, I really thought the drug was just a mental placebo.

When I first began taking Pamelor, I couldn't comprehend how two tiny tablets would help me eat, help me smile once again. I was afraid the medication would make me lose the control and discipline that had become my best friends. The first day after I ingested the little pills I slept the entire day. I couldn't lift my head off the pillow but kept dreaming that I had gotten up to go running. I kept getting frustrated when I realized I was still dreaming. In the late afternoon I was so dizzy that I still couldn't get up to run. The day had been wasted. At least I slept through the meals my parents would have wanted me to eat. Eventually it became easier to wake up, and the only side effects I had were the dry mouth and the hypertension. I remember feeling like I was floating during my workouts. When I went to St. Martin at my eighty-nine-pound stage, I ran ten miles in the heat, and right afterward I'd get really dizzy and lose my balance. I had moments when I wondered what was happening to me. I actually liked feeling scared that I could die.

After a month of Pamelor, I was hunched over with my arms crawled up in my shirt, my paws hidden like I was a cold, frightened kitty. I used to wear these gigantic cotton long johns from Banana Republic with big thick red suspenders to hold them up. They were so cozy, but I would only let myself wear them if I had run that day, because then I deserved such comfort. My compulsive eating wasn't getting any better. I was becoming more of a stranger to everyone, including myself, and I felt like a freak.

I went off Pamelor and Dr. Bowen gave me a new drug called Nardil. It was an MAO inhibitor, which meant that I was not allowed to eat caffeine, chocolate, cheese, aged meat, or banana peels. Who the hell eats banana peels? And, very important, no drugs or alcohol could be consumed because the combination was lethal. I downed tons of chocolate that Easter and turned a tomato red and my chest pounded, but I survived. After I threw it all up, the feelings went away. They really shouldn't give MAOIs to bulimic girls.

I had some outrageous hallucinations on Nardil. I was on roller coasters and trapped in long narrow hallways. Many times I would fall asleep and could feel myself watching myself lying there in bed and see myself getting up, only to then realize that I hadn't gotten up, kind of like on Pamelor. I didn't have the strength to break out of the trapped place I was in, between consciousness and unconsciousness. It was like dreaming you get up to go to the bathroom but you never really do, and you wake up having wet the bed.

The physical side effects of Nardil were the most extreme of any of the antidepressants I've taken. For the first few minutes after I awoke in the morning I was temporarily blind and deaf. My mom used to have to walk me to the bathroom until the power of my senses had turned on. Then throughout the day if I moved too fast, my lower back would get this weak sensation as if it couldn't hold me up. It was as if the Nardil was affecting my whole spinal cord and nervous system. Dr. Bowen said that my back pain was more likely caused by all my working out.

I began going to my mother's friendly and hip chiropractor, who was located in the building next to my mother's exercise studio. He was used to getting a whole entourage of women from next door complaining about their physical pain and their bodies. I felt comfortable talking to him, and I told him that I really thought my back problems were from the drug. He agreed that it was possible, but he told me that my whole pelvis was arched the wrong way. He said it was also inflamed from all my yoga and exercising and that all this would eventually prevent me from working out at all. He did some healing work on my back, snapping it and twisting it, and I couldn't work out that day. I couldn't breathe without a workout. My life was shit without a workout. The antidepressants were shit. I was shit.

The next antidepressant was called Prozac, the "wonder drug of the 90s," as *Time* magazine had deemed it. The drug didn't have many side effects, except it made me totally wired. I turned from a lethargic and depressed girl into a hyper and silly three-year-old. I loved it. I had more energy to work out and it was really good at mentally deceiving me that I was happy. But the lows were still horrible. When I crashed I was awful and dramatic and threatened to kill myself. By this time I had gained fifteen pounds and was told that I looked good, that I looked "healthy" (probably an anorexic's least favorite word). I was in agony that I wasn't too skinny. I wasn't ahead of the game. I would lose it again. I started to work out intensely but I was not losing weight. I didn't weigh myself, because seeing the number at the 105-pound measure would kill me. I just knew I was there, because my tiny faded jeans that had sagged at the hip were filled out and tight.

I was about sixteen then, and my mom was worried because I hadn't had my first period yet. So I went to a gynecologist for the first time and she gave me progesterone pills to artificially induce it. After twenty days of feeling bloated and gross and moody, I bled for the first time in an exercise class. My stomach had hurt so much during the class that I had to stop. I was really annoyed. I didn't want to have a period. Periods to me meant fat, meant I would become fat, or that I wasn't thin enough. I knew girls didn't get their period if they were too thin. Well, this was artificial, so maybe it didn't count.

Between the antidepressants and the hormones I was gaining weight and becoming angry. I was hungrier too and had less discipline. I was confused. Why was I no longer working out hard enough to be skinny? I was losing the drive. The angrier I got, the more I ate. The more I ate, the harder it became not to. I was definitely not going to take that progesterone shit again. I was not ready to be a woman yet.

Later I tried the drug Norpramin, which didn't do much. I even tried lithium for a few days, but it made me a total zombie and morbid. After that I went back on the Prozac and remained on it for nearly a year. After two months without any antidepressants at all, I felt better than ever. Except, of course, when I got depressed.

I know this fibromyalgia thing is a crock of bullshit, a diagnosis for people in pain that the present technology and science of X rays cannot detect and the doctor cannot figure out. They tell me I better get off the Xanax (dangerous, addictive, bad for someone so young) and give me a small amount of Librium and Kolonopin. What's the freakin' difference?

So, I ask, could there be someone out there, some healer—be it God or a power—to bring some light of interest to this body and phenomenon of mine? To shower reason, understanding? And shall I ask for relief if it is not too late?

They have recommended that I stay out here and admit myself to the Pain Rehabilitation and Management program. My mother is planning to leave. She has to resume her life in New York, take care of my father, return to her docent job for the Costume Institute at the Metropolitan Museum. It will probably be easier if she is gone. The guilt hurts too much anyhow. But I can't believe they can't do anything here for the pain, and I don't see how this program can help if I can barely walk, sit, stand, or see straight.

8. Pain Rehab

Everyone in Pain Rehab is diagnosed with fibromyalgia, arthritis, or nerve damage. One middle-aged woman had incorrect brain surgery a few years ago and has painful headaches all the time. Another woman was cut incorrectly during heart surgery almost ten years ago and has difficulty taking deep breaths. One young woman fell ice-skating and limps from awful nerve pain in one leg that they say can't ever be helped. There is one guy about my age in a wheelchair whose legs were crushed by a boulder at a construction site, but he is doing really well and starting to walk. He's actually cute; I find myself fantasizing about him. When they ask me what I have, I say that I think the surgeon pulled me together too tight during colon/rectal surgery . . . that is, he sewed up my rectum too close to my vagina and maybe even my groin. They all look stunned. I explain to them that nobody really knows what is wrong, which is why I'm so scared. Then I tell them about the fibromyalgia. *Now they can relate.*

The first morning I am called into the boardroom, where all the doctors meet to assess my situation and progress. I stagger in, eyes spasming and joints pulling everywhere, and I try to sit down with eight doctors all staring at me like I'm crazy. It feels more like we're about to make some business deal; they're all dressed in regular clothes, the men in tweeds, the women in fall skirts, and they're seated at a long table. I feel like I'm Melanie Griffith in *Working Girl*, when she comes in on her day off in sweats, and is about to make a pitch to the board of directors that will knock them out of their seats.

There is silence, and then the head of the program, who is handsome in that spectacles-and-finely-combed-hair way, with a lanky runner's body, states matter-of-factly in his affected bullshit Harvard drawl, "Jennifer, we have come to the consensus that you are suffering from depression."

I just stare at him and start to scowl, but then I laugh. I keep laughing until I finally say, "Hey, you're really smart, huh? You figured it out. That's it; I'm depressed. Hey, no shit. Considering I was once pretty and talented and basically had it all . . . and now I've been cut open, rearranged, have to hold my vagina all day in pain and can hardly walk, move, or take a shit. Yeah, I'm depressed. You got it right on the mark. By the way, how was your run today?"

It feels so foreign to be this mean . . . to be this desperate. When I was at the hospitals for eating disorders, I was a model patient. I couldn't even imagine behaving that badly. Even though I disagreed with Dr. Shark I was polite about it. I have always been such a nice girl, afraid to be rude or disrespectful of authority. But it feels great to be a bitch. This time I am fed up with these arrogant doctors and I have nothing to lose. They always think they have all the answers. They think everything is caused by depression these days. They blame everything on the mind, especially when you're a female. I remember in Santa Fe when I went to the clinic with a 102-degree fever, covered with huge lumps on my neck and my groin, the doc said, "It doesn't look like you have mono. Do you have a lot of stress in your life? Have you tried Prozac?" I called him back after another doctor found pneumonia in my lungs and asked him how he got his MD. I really wanted to tell him to take his Prozac and shove it.

I stay at the Mayo Clinic a whole fucking month for nothing whatsoever. Every night, all I do is try to vomit after drinking the whole bottle of wine I've ordered from room service, let the phone ring and ring, and cry myself to sleep. I stop going to the pain program completely because it is too tiring to walk downstairs to catch the shuttle. Besides, I don't know how they can expect me to fill in worksheets with huge pie charts on them, with circles to divide how I plan to manage my days, when I can barely manage a minute. But I do go to one session on sex and intimacy. *This should be really interesting.* I figure, what do I have to lose.

I can count on one hand how many times I've had sexual intercourse. Although I can't count how many guys I've messed around with . . . especially in Santa Fe. I think to myself, "I've been celibate for basically six years." How sad, how utterly pathetic. Just when I was dying to have it, I had to go and get sick. My endocrinologist once said that the reason I wasn't going out and pursuing sex like all my other girlfriends might have something to do with my amenorrhea, lack of periods. She suggested that it could be hormonal discomfort that held me back. But I knew why.

I didn't want to lose my virginity in high school when all my friends were doing it. I looked at my mother as a role model. My father was her first and only lover. I thought that was beautiful. My parents seem more liberal now, but they used to be pretty traditional. My father used to say, "Don't just give it away," or "Don't get used," so I thought that meant *don't do it*. "Be unapproachable," my father also said.

When I took my sophomore year in college off and lived in Santa Fe, I met the special man. It was a mystical experience. I was standing in front of the market locking up my bike when all of a sudden I just turned my head. A dark-haired guy with green-blue eyes was sticking his head out of a pickup truck that was driving by, and he smiled at me. I swear it was like I knew him, and I was compelled to wave. I saw him a week later at a coffee shop and he asked me to join him. He was writing in his journal and wanted to read a poem to me. Then he showed me all his drawings. I noticed his Carlos Castaneda book too. *Hmmm, a philosopher type. An artist. A thinker. And so handsome. That's it, this is love.* We left and he walked me and my bike three miles home. We spent the entire next two days together. I knew I would lose my virginity to him. There was a softness and kindness about him. I felt safe. We made love the second night, and the following morning he combed my wet hair after a shower, and we sat watching the sunrise. He was a wanderer, a spiritual nomad who left the very next day with his one-way ticket to Hawaii, although he promised to be back sometime. He still sends me fabulous letters.

But after that, I started seeing a funky bohemian musician and I felt pressured to do it. My roommate was sleeping with the drummer from the same band, and one night we all got carried away drinking beer. And I figured, *well, now that I'm experienced like her* . . . But after one time, I didn't want to do it again with him. He didn't love me.

Then I met this gorgeous troublemaker whose fiery charm and flirtation was enough to drive me to desperation and people-pleasing measures. The very first night he came over, it was like he cast a spell. I remember him backing me up against a table, and we made love standing up. I was completely smitten by his blue eyes and his sexual energy (that preppy boarding school kind of cool), and within a few weeks, even though he treated me rather unkindly—even having slept with my roommate while I was sleeping downstairs—I lusted for his attention. But it wasn't as if we were dating. There was a big group of us that started hanging out together. He made himself completely at home, bringing his pothead friends to our parties, getting hammered at our house. Those days were, in a sense, the high school craziness I had missed because of my problems. I enjoyed it until he became cruel. We'd fight all the time and he'd say mean things, tell me I was fat, which really hurt (it was right after that I started dieting and exercising frantically again), and yet I still was infatuated with him. One day he stared at me with those devilish eyes and I let him seduce me again. As I let him enter me—I remember thinking this feels so good, and I was like putty—it didn't matter that he forgot the condom or that I was fat. It was literally the fourth time I made love. I got pregnant. What a mind trip. I felt punished. I went back to New York, because it was definitely time, had an abortion, and waited six months to have an AIDS test. The anxiety and fear while waiting for two weeks for the results was excruciating. I vowed that I would never put myself in that position again, feeling guilt, fear, punished, or *fat*. And so I have remained reserved. I wanted respect from someone for what I was all about, and I thought that sex should be sacred. Sometimes, if I think too much, I wonder if the D and C I had at nineteen could have caused my enterocele.

Whatever fears I had about the actual act of intercourse didn't take away my yearning. I made love through my dancing, through my yoga, to my canvas while I painted. What if I can never express this passion through my movement again?

Now I'm sitting here in *Sex and Intimacy 101*. I'm in this tiny room with about six other women and one man who's in a wheelchair. It is absolutely horrific. I can't hold myself up, my whole body is spasming, my vagina's killing me, and to top it off, we're about to talk about *doing it*. And at this point I'm convinced I'll never make love ever again. I imagine my story splashed across the front page of the *Enquirer* that reads, BOTCHED SURGERY, 25-YEAR-OLD WOMAN'S GROIN PULLED TOGETHER TOO TIGHT . . . NEVER TO HAVE SEX AGAIN!

All the women who have this pain or that pain for various reasons are busy complaining. *But none of 'em have had their pelvis smushed together.* And one woman who has fibromyalgia specifically annoys the shit out of me because she's all whiny and she says, "I keep telling my husband to stop pushing me. I mean, he always wants to have sex, and I just can't take it anymore. I mean, Goddddd."

Then the leader of the discussion group, Peggy, asks her, "Well, do you tell your husband to be more gentle and maybe discuss trying other ways?"

The woman answers, "Well, I've told him I'll give him a blow job or to just touch my breasts," and I can't comprehend that this woman is actually describing to us in detail her sexual requests. What is she, retarded or something? I mean, the question didn't call for that response, maybe a "Yes, I've tried to talk to him." I start to cover my ears as she graphically goes on, and I surprise myself as I start to almost convulse and begin to cry silently.

And then Peggy turns to me, astonished to see some emotion coming out of me, and asks, "Jenny, what's going on in there? Tell us. It's okay."

I start to yell, "You all sit here and complain about sex and how your husbands demand it and you can't stand it, and that you have a headache or a pain here and there. Well, guess what? I don't think I can ever have sex again, I've been sewn up so tight. And you guys take it for granted. What I would do to express my emotions through my body, my movement? It's the most beautiful thing. The most beautiful way to communicate to someone your feelings and that you love them. Why don't you stop complaining and just go for it . . . just try."

Everyone in the room is just silent. And then the woman speaks, "I'm so sorry, Jenny. You're absolutely right. I never thought of it that way. I'm gonna try."

And then everyone else in the room agrees and thanks me that I've given them a great perspective, even the cute man in the wheelchair who can still have sex with his wife, and I can't believe I'm actually envious of him.

After the group has finished, Peggy walks me down the corridors to biofeedback. She says, "Ya did real good in there, today. I'm proud of you."

And for the first time I don't give a shit that someone tells me they're proud of me. I'm still stunned and suicidal and not excited to be on my way to have some nurse stick some measuring device up my ass so I can learn to relax and squeeze the muscle.

Before I get on the plane to go home, I take whatever Librium is left that the doctors have given me for my muscle spasms and anxiety. I drink alcohol the whole ride, don't even try to conceal my hands, which remain on my crotch praying for mercy, and for the first time I don't give a shit if the plane goes down.

9. Home

"I can't believe you're not happy they didn't find anything at Mayo," Dr. Hannibal says, looking confused.

I say bitterly, "No, I'm not happy. I wanted a disease, something to explain all this, at least then there would probably be something they could prescribe, or if I was dying, this pain would be short-lived. I can't do this. I can't live like this."

I keep trying to imagine myself taking the whole bottle of Xanax that I still keep next to my bed. I tell Hannibal that sometimes I think of doing it, swallowing the whole goddamn jar. He says that it wouldn't kill me and it would be pretty stupid, that I'd just lose feeling in a limb, or have a small stroke, and be worse off. He gets a bit nervous when I say, "Well, not if I put a paper bag over my head simultaneously," an idea I've read in some book on death and suicide.

Hannibal urges me to be strong. He says, "Do not bow down to your body. You are smarter than this. I have written books on chronic pain and its effect on the psyche. Believe me, this will pass. One day I will meet you in the park to go Rollerblading. One day it will be over." Then he tells me about some great composer who went to hang himself and the noose broke, so he changed his mind, and then he lived on to become incredibly renowned. I try to explain to Hannibal that I have no desire to die, to go, to leave. I sob just thinking about leaving this world, leaving my parents, my brothers. I sob and sob because I can't believe what I am truly saying and thinking, that I am actually considering suicide, that I think it could actually bring me relief. I also get really scared when I think, *What if it's the same on the other side? Or the next life.* I hear myself, and I know I sound crazy. And what's crazier is that I talk a good game, but I could never do it, never end my life.

In all the years, even with the feelings of shame and self-hatred, even the worst kind of fear and anguish over a binge, extra pounds, or the belief that I was doomed by my illness, I never, ever truly considered suicide. They were passing thoughts on bad days. At the hospitals I'd hear about girls cutting their wrists, threatening to kill themselves. I was never one of those girls. The thought of not getting a chance to overcome the eating disorder seemed like a worse fate. But this is different. I can't get a second of physical relief, and I don't have much hope that it will pass. The option of killing myself to find respite from the pain remains with me minute to minute for a sense of solace, but I keep saying to myself, *just get through this minute.* I figure I can always decide later.

I lie alone in my parents' bed, unable to walk, while my parents are away in Europe. It is my dad's annual fall trip to Milan and London to see fabrics, and this time my mom has accompanied him. Half of me can't believe that they both actually left while I'm in this state, but the other guilty part is relieved that they get a bit of a break from me. Especially my mother. Anyhow, I know that there is absolutely nothing they can do to make this hellish experience any better. But that harrowing thought, along with the constant realization that nothing will give me relief, makes me angry at them for leaving. And then I panic.

I call Nikki and tell her I can't take it. In all our fourteen years of knowing one another, since she had come as the eccentric new kid in the fifth grade, this is the first time I have just straight-out begged her to help me.

She says, "You get your butt down here, now. I'll make you comfortable with warm socks, pillows, blankets."

"But Nik," I cry, "it doesn't matter where I sit . . . socks, no socks, comforter, no comforter . . . I want to rip off my body, not my clothes."

"I know, honey. Please, please, come down to me." She often pleads and I don't give in but this time with all my might I lug myself downstairs to a taxi. I'm really afraid. I get to her 20th Street and Third Avenue walk-up, a tiny, special Nikki-smelling cozy home with flowers, candles, and pictures of her friends all over, and she is running around the house cleaning up, trying to get everything ready. She looks gorgeous, with her long chestnut hair piled high in a twisted knot, her light almond–colored eyes shining with life, her body lithe and toned in black leggings and a faded blue tank. How can I let her see me this way?

She says, "What's going on, Fur?" she asks, using the short affectionate nickname she has always called me.

"Look, no muscles . . . look at me. I can't stand or sit. Am I dying, Nik? Should I kill myself?"

"Not today, but Jesus, Fur, you're like a rag doll." She looks horrified.

"I know, would you believe it?" as I gasp for air. She distracts me as she proceeds to talk of everything going on in her life. I envy her energy, her compassion for me, her beauty.

She says, "You promise if you're going to do something rash, you'll call me first okay? Say good-bye, at least." She's good with the joking thing. "You know you shouldn't be alone like this," she adds.

"Nik, it doesn't matter where I am, who I'm with, I don't want to burden anyone."

"Fur, honey, we'll get to the bottom of this, I promise." She states this with the same seriousness she had when she was the only one who backed me last year in my persistence to find a diagnosis. She begged me not to tie up my legs to run. "I don't think you ought to be doing this," she said. "Something is definitely wrong, and you could be hurting yourself." She was so right, but did I listen?

We end up at a nearby Indian restaurant, and I hurry to order a huge Frangelica, the sweet hazelnut liquor, the only thing getting me through these days . . . Amaretto and Xanax all day, no food, then a huge one of these.

I get lost, sentimental. "I'm gonna be all right, Nik, right?"

She is realistic. "We'll see, but I think so." She looks worried. "No more drinking tonight, okay? Are you gonna sleep over?"

I think, *no, I can't. I better go home so I can return to my trance.* I take a taxi back to my parents' and hobble into their high mahogany bed. I stare at photographs of my family that surround the room, at their bedside, on their dresser: me, eleven, roller-skating gleefully in the park; my brothers and me, the three of us grinning cheerfully, sitting in a group as tiny children on our grandparents' porch in New Jersey; me, five, playing in the sand in a little white blouse and pinafore looking dramatically pouty; me, three, swinging on a tire looking goofy in a plaid shirt, suspenders, and ripped, patched dungarees. Then Greg and me, very young, barefoot in the Hampton dunes as twins in white T-shirts and faded blue overalls; me, fifteen, all chiseled and tan in a shimmering, tight orange dress; then Brad and me in recent years, in black tie and dancing at our cousin's wedding (my arms skinnier and more toned than ever); and then me at twenty-two, hugging my father and smiling brightly at my college graduation.

I stay alone for ten days in this Park Avenue house filled with painful photos, folk art that I have encouraged my father to buy, trying to think of those good times when we went antiquing all over New England, and then I panic for air, and I think I'm going, fading, dying, slipping away.

I call my parents in London every two hours. When my mother goes to Spain to visit one of her oldest and dearest friends in Madrid, I call her there. She says, "Linda can't wait for you to come here to Barcelona. She wants you to meet her son. He's so handsome. You'll love it here, honey."

"But, Mommy," I cry. "I'll never get the chance. I can't breathe. I can't walk. I can't even watch a goddamn TV show. Mommy!!!" I howl, "Please help me. I love you so much. I miss you. Don't hang up. I love you. No, don't go yet. Okay. Okay. All right . . . okay."

I hang up and lie there in some concocted curled-up position, everything pulling me apart, as if a child is having fun with taffy. Nikki keeps calling me to tell me that she loves me, which is enough to remind me that I still exist. How I want to be skipping down the New York City streets with her as we sing, "Lollipop, lollipop, oh lolli lolli pop" or "Kumbaya, my lord, Kumbayaaaaaaaaa," and trip over each other's laughing bodies. Then I start to fixate on the memories of the past, dressing as pink ladies for a school dance (wearing hot pink Ralph Lauren jackets, polo player and all), and sending anonymous roses to the boys we ached and longed for together, and then consoling each other when they didn't acknowledge our gifts.

Then I replay the many times we walked to and from Dalton together. I have a memory associated with Nikki for almost every uptown city block. Each day after junior high, we'd hang out on our school corner at 89th and Lex waiting to catch glimpses of the high school boys' varsity teams loading onto the school bus. After we flashed our wide grins, full of braces, and batted our eyes at some adorable guys in their baseball uniforms, Nikki and I would giggle, give each other a high five, and then continue on our journey down the avenue.

Back then it felt like there was nothing I couldn't do, that there was no possibility of embarrassing myself. When I remember how much we loved each other, and how fearless we were, it gives me a feeling of strength. It also makes me realize that even during the hard place of my budding adolescence, I had normal times too. And then, one morning I'm calling her at 6:15 A.M., panicking and barely able to sob, "I can't breathe, Nikki. I'm losing it. I don't know what to do anymore. The seconds, minutes, are endless."

She makes a call to the physical therapist she's been begging me to see all year, and by 7:30 A.M. I'm there with glazed eyes, trying with all my energy to explain my situation. Everything and everyone is spinning around me; I grip the armchair to support myself. Can the physical therapist tell that I am sinking? Can he figure out what is wrong? Can he help me, please? I think of how he has strengthened Nikki's weakened ankles, and how she delights over being able to run again after many years. She has said, "Tommy is amazing. Tommy is the best. You really ought to see Tommy."

Tommy is a charming and athletic man who has worked with people like Gene Kelly (there is an autographed picture) and Yankee ballplayers. He applies heat packs to my groin. Nice warm heat. It doesn't do much. He watches me try to stretch. I know I have horrible breath. I don't think any of this is helping. With his subtle and low-key way, he listens and he tries to find the exercises he can think of for me, having never had experience with such a strange surgery. No one has had experience with this surgery. He does not deny that nerves were cut, and that for certain there could be damage. I make a plan with him to come three times a week.

Then Princess Diana dies. I learn from the television news that she's been in a car accident, as I lie in pain, in my parents' bed, feeling sorry for myself. This is just way too much for me to handle. I start crying and can't stop. This is the most morbid thing I've ever heard. I try to call my parents, but no one answers at their hotel. Every television channel keeps showing beautiful, elegant Diana in different flashes from when she was young and innocent and married to Prince Charles, to when she is older, sophisticated, and holding the hands of a child in Africa. I think of how far she'd come. What a real person she was. How brave she was for being honest about her battles and for changing her life. When I first heard of her sneaking food from the kitchens of the castle, bingeing and purging, I thought of the terror she must have felt after stuffing that food into her mouth, knowing that she'd then have to go wear some evening gown for an event, or be photographed. She must have been really lonely. Like a lot of women with eating disorders, I felt like I knew her closely. I remember feeling so proud of her (and repulsed at the same time because of my own shame) when she shared her struggle with anorexia with the world. I would become irate at the media for attacking and mocking her constantly, with cheap newspapers like the *Enquirer* featuring photos of her in a bathing suit with blurbs that read, PRINCESS DI BATTLES CELLULITE.

I watch the television, praying that if I watch the news over and over they will say she is going to be okay. I keep imagining her fragile body dressed in a silk, cream Ralph Lauren gown, but crumpled in agony, mangled. When I awake sometime in the very early morning and hear that she is no longer alive, defeat racks my bones. I call my parents again, finally getting through to them. They haven't heard, because they went to sleep before it happened and are just waking up. My mother exclaims, "No way! Are you serious? No way. Jerry, Jerry, Princess Di. Oh my God."

It feels like the whole world is dying.

10. My Only Option

My mom, dad, and I sit in Hannibal's office. I cry, moan, and drool. I threaten to kill myself. I sit there letting the poison of defeat eat away at my body. I am ready to lash out and jump and spew venomous attacks at all who I blame and hate and love at this moment. My parents try to interject about me in third person, but I don't let them. Hannibal says that there is nothing else anyone can do. He has made a call to the Mount Sinai emergency psychiatric ward, and there is a bed there for me to fill, and he suggests I take it. I experience a sickening and familiar feeling. I had already admitted myself twice to eating disorder units during high school, both of my own accord, but this seems much different and more extreme.

I sit there sobbing violently on Hannibal's Berber couch, which is scratching my thighs, and rehash my life in my mind and ask myself how exactly I have gotten to this point. Thoughts, memories, images of my early hospital days flow into my mind . . . the commodes, the daily weighing, the skeletal cheerleaders . . . meatloaf covered in gravy, Sustacal chocolate pudding. I remember Brad chasing me after I have tried to run away from our car on a visit back home after three months away . . . and then him catching me and crying, "Jenny, you need to go back. I'm so sorry." I can feel the terror in that car ride back to the hospital. I cried hysterically with a lump in my throat. My mom cried too, in the front seat.

I think about the good times since then, the life I have led since those scary days. No more hospitals in college. *What a relief. The worst must be over.* My great year off, exploring Santa Fe, dating, having fun, painting. I think about how much I painted back then, how I had found that great love and returned to college and worked hard. I see an image of myself feeling pretty, ethereal, and light and dressed in a white, wispy Morgan le Fay dress at my "Image of the Wheel" painting exhibition my senior year at college. *A great finale it was.* I remember that following summer in Santa Fe, dancing with B (my crush of the century) in my living room, feeling desired, beautiful, and in lust. I remember road trips with friends to White Sands and Carlsbad Caverns, oohing and aahing at the terrain and my independence. *There is a land outside myself.* I remember life after that in New York City, standing in front of a huge wall with friends watching as I paint a huge mural of wheels for a film festival in Soho, thinking, *Hey, this could be a cool life.* I remember photographing the nooks and crannies of some great apartment in Chelsea for a possible spread for the home magazine I was scouting for. I remember thinking, *How great! Maybe I can go scout homes in Italy and in Spain . . . travel the world.* I remember helping Brad and Greg hand out flyers for their first film at Slam Dance, a film festival in Park City, Utah. I was so happy that they wanted me to be a part of it. I remember taking off with some guy I met there and going back to LA just for the hell of it and because I felt free.

I remember mostly that I had a life.

But then, soon after, the twitch started.

I had made many vows since my early hospital days that no matter how bad my behavior was I'd never end up in a hospital again.

The first night when I arrive—after they give me some kind of sleeping pill and laxative—this large hippo of a woman dressed in a hot pink sweat outfit keeps opening up the door of my room, ranting and raving some kind of biblical blasphemy. I'm not even afraid of her. I don't care if she murders me. I just let myself fall into a disoriented sleep. Hippo Lady usually sits very silently, though, during the day, with a childlike pout. I think she is schizophrenic; they say she's been here for months. She's actually kind of endearing. She's my favorite patient, because her behavior truly fascinates me, although usually I'm too distracted by the gripping in between my legs to notice the others. I wish I could feel comfortable enough to sit and read or chat with one of them, but I can't. I'm in so much pain that it's hard; I feel like all I can do is focus on trying to hold myself up.

The second day, the doctor who runs this unit spends over an hour with me, listening to my symptoms. He says that the most important thing is that we tend to the pain and make sure I move my bowels. I can't keep taking these laxatives; they don't even work. It's so horrible. But HE BELIEVES ME. . . . He believes I'm in real pain and something is fishy here. Unless, could *he be patronizing me?* For some reason, I feel like I can trust him. It's about all I can do anyhow. He does have a nice smile.

I spend most of my time in here waiting. The only thing I look forward to is visiting time. Edward, one of my best friends, who I first met in Santa Fe, comes to see me and brings me Ben and Jerry's. I eat it all, of course, which mixed with all these laxatives makes me feel like I'm gonna explode. Edward, in his South Carolinian accent, chats and chats voraciously about his hairdresser boyfriend, his Buddhist chanting, and the gold lacquer paint he has chosen for his room in the designer showcase. I feel my facial muscles attempting to curve upward into a smile as I listen.

Joan (my college advisor and close friend) visits early Thanksgiving morning, which really cheers me up, although she has a few slipped disks and is also in pain. I keep saying to her, "It's just not our year." It's just like Joan to show up at the hospital to see me when she herself can barely stand, still looking superhip in her black pantsuit and funky black spectacles as artist-professor meets MOMA curator. She looks at me, shaking her head. "All right, okay. This time you did it. You exhausted yourself silly. You're really a wreck, aren't you? Okay. We're gonna deal with this. I hope they're giving you some Valium."

Nikki comes a lot. One night she even stays for a group meeting about meds. It is really a pathetic discussion, and as we sit in a circle, the vision of all these mentally ailing people—including me, who everyone thinks is a famous actress for some reason (love that!)—is really too much to take. There are people drooling, some muttering under their breath, and some touching themselves in their private spots or picking their nose. Nikki just starts to laugh uncontrollably. I look at her like, *No, Nik, don't do it. Don't go there. Oh, no* . . . but I can't help but laugh too, and then everyone just stares at her and she is very apologetic, saying that she obviously belongs here too.

But the visitors I look forward to mainly are my parents. I stand by the door until I see their faces. I cry from relief when I see them, and I cry for fear when they leave. I call them on the hour just to ask them to help me. I call my dad at work, and his personal assistant puts him on every time, and he says, "Hi, my daughterkey." And I break out in a sob the second I hear his voice. I am acting like a baby, and I am one. I feel helpless and long for my parents' hugs. And when they come I can smell the night chill of Madison Avenue on their pristine outfits, and I feel even more lonely for a world that is far away from me now.

Dr. P (for Dr. Positive) is the first doctor I've talked to, even in all my years of therapy, who doesn't look at me and treat me like I'm crazy. The first week he comes into my sterile white room, which smells of fresh detergent and buzzes with fluorescent lights, and he wakes me out of my delirium. I had been lying there on my narrow cot trying to find a comfortable position for at least a minute, rehashing my situation over and over again. *No one can help me . . . no one. Why the fuck am I in a mental institution? Why has it ended up like this? I was already in two hospitals for the bulimia, but I was getting better. Those hospital days are far gone. But now I'm back here and they think I've gone mad. I am not mad, I swear . . . or am I?*

Dr. P pulls a chair close to me as I try to sit upright on my cot and asks me to recount the past year and tell him about my background. He says, "It sounds like you've been through the wringer, Ms. Lauren. So we're going to sit here as long as it takes, and I want to hear everything, where this all began, and what exactly is going on now. Okay. So please make yourself comfortable. Are you all right there or would you like to sit in a chair?" At first I am unenthusiastic. *This is bullshit. Why tell another fuckin' doctor?* But, from the beginning, he actually seems nice, and interested. *What the hell.* I give him the rundown, to my surprise, in a calm and articulate manner. Dr. P interrupts me at one point and says, "Please don't mind that I'm taking notes. I just have to take a few. I understand that it can be annoying." *Wow. Who is this guy?* He also nods his head, and interjects every so often with a question. *I am talking to a living, breathing person who is actually listening.* He takes out a drawing of the anatomy of a woman's body and makes a request: "Ms. Lauren, I'd like you to take a look at this and point to all the areas that you feel pulling or throbbing. I'd like to map it out." He seems fascinated by my situation . . . as if he is addressing a puzzle he is going to systematically solve. He has an air of confidence, expertise, and professionalism that makes me feel like I can trust him. He ends up sitting with me for almost two hours. Funny how they send me to a psychiatrist to shut me up, and he's the first one to listen and tell me it ain't in my head. He actually says to me, "Okay, Ms. Lauren, this is the truth. You have had major surgery. You've had nerves cut in the most sensitive area. It's very serious. We're going to have to assess exactly what nerves have been cut and possibly damaged. And you've gotta be in a hell of a lot of pain. So I want to address that immediately, before anything else. I also think you're dehydrated, so I'd like to give you some electrolytes. And if you're willing, an antidepressant, because believe it or not, it's been proven that it helps with the neurotransmitters that cause pain." I'm willing. I like this doctor.

He provides Demerol and Valium at the nurses' counter for me to request when needed. He agrees that it's absolutely ludicrous that I'm not having bowel movements, and he stresses that a stool softener and laxatives are necessary for now. He is emphatic that the dehydration could be causing a lot of problems. He educates me that it causes constipation, enhances physical pain and depression. And he plans to feed me intravenously the next day to balance my electrolytes and see if I feel a little better. Then, after finding some odd things on my blood tests, he is having my gallbladder checked for stones because he thinks this might be causing the irritation . . . but I know deep down this isn't the case. I do give this doctor a lot of credit for trying to help me, although I'm not pinning all my hopes on him. Still, every time he comes into my room to check on me I feel a bit of relief. *Please stay with me, Doctor. Please don't leave me alone in my head and this body, this awful room, this nightmare. Come back, Doctor . . . come back, please.*

The bottom line is that I feel stuck with this situation, a gruesome one. I wonder if I will ever stop hearing the wheels of my stretcher being rolled down to the recovery room.

Accepting my fate seems so hard now. If in time I lose the pain and feel my physicality again, I think it will be possible to overcome this. There are lessons I am learning. The pursuit of perfection and of control (this story is common) drove me down to the ground. Trying to maintain that state of comfort with my body, I needed to see and feel with the concave stomach, the solid buttocks, the chiseled face, the music of hunger in my ears, that zombie techno music. But it was all so addictive that it dehumanized me and made me crumble. Sometimes I feel relieved to have to let it go. That narcissism kept me so alone. And when I came out and said, *Here I am,* that was just a picture . . . *charismatic, outgoing, shining Jenny,* I presented a lie. Only those who really knew me knew that my closest relationship was with my obsession, my intangible quest for control . . . *my hunger, my fullness, my anxiety, my longing for the tantalizing unknown.* But nothing ever relieved my anxiety.

What would have happened if B had loved me, and what would happen now? I would be afraid to look into his eyes and not feel that powerful penetration when a soul discovers another soul. In fact, I fear most not looking into my own eyes and being in touch with my own soul. I am also afraid I will never walk on the desert in cowboy boots that are sturdy beneath me, with legs that stand strong, and I am afraid I will never experience the vastness of the terrain and horizon and the tremendous inspiration I smelled and breathed there. All my senses seem different. I am alienated from myself, unable to feel familiar things, invaded by the unknown hands of a stranger who played Twister in my pelvis, a man covered with a green mask who said, prior to the event, "Now get ready for a new body," and meant it.

I think the worst part of all this has been this slow, tortuous break. It is as if I have been drugged and I am trying to reconnect all the pieces of my life in order to move on. I try to imagine the two years before the surgery. I want so badly to remember it and feel it, just so I can feel less dead. I want the smell of the paint, the noise of the heat gurgling in the basement studio, the clobbered feeling as if I were drunk, the wondering why I couldn't think straight or move with ease, the *Am I crazy? Why am I going limp, weaker, weaker, and weaker?* Chewing piece of gum after piece of gum . . . chew, chew, chew . . . as I tried to stop worrying that something was wrong and threw paint onto the canvases and the floor.

I want to move on from these past two years, become Jenny again. Will the summer sun and heat feel wonderful against my body? Will the cold snow feel refreshing on my cheeks and in my nose? Will the crunch of an apple taste delicious and pure? Will normal breathing resume? Will creativity spew out of me again? Will I kiss again? Will I paint my wheel images or something new?

Do I control my fate now?

I do feel a little better. Is this Serzone antidepressant working, or the Valium? Or is it the fact that I'm being heard by this new doctor? Is his understanding a placebo? Who cares. He gives me what I most need, what I had lost: hope.

11. Dreaming of a Man

It started in junior year of college when B, my forty-seven-year-old art professor, came up to me at the 125th Street studios and asked, "Hey, am I in the right place? Is this Crit?" When I stared up at this tall, gangly man with wild blue eyes, distinguished graying hair, and a loud, dominating voice, I immediately became tipsy. I felt heat lingering throughout my body.

"Uh, yeah, you're in the right place."

With a bit of a haphazard look he replied, "Thanks. Hey, nice necklace." It was a single leather strand with a large cobalt blue gem hanging at my neck. I wore it with a black turtleneck.

The first time he gave me a critique on my paintings I hated him. He seemed haughty and obnoxious. He wasn't that impressed with my big bold colored paintings of women. He said they were too flat. He thought I should move in a different direction with my paintings and challenge myself. I missed the next class because of my grandmother's funeral, a sudden heart attack, but rumor had it that he had pissed me off. The next class, when he came to my studio, he flung my overused paintbrushes out the window onto the streets of Harlem and said, "Now what the hell are these?" My face got red and I couldn't stop giggling. Nerves. But it was funny. And then, it was all over for me. He continued to describe the colors I might want to experiment with. "Jenny, not so bold all the time. Why don't you try some soft, pastel tones, experiment." My stuff was draped over the radiator and he pointed to it and said, "Look, look at that. Look how subtle that pink oxford shirt is laying over that faded army-green bag." It was that moment when he sounded like my father, when he would describe a tie or shirt he had designed. He sounded like he had the Lauren sensibility. And I was crushed.

I went to the art department's office to see his work in his catalog. It was explosive, bright, and frenzied, and about nature. He was inspired by the self-taught. So was I. And he went to Santa Fe in the summers. So did I. *Hmmm.* B would get all nervous too, when he saw me. Then I would feel giddy. I wanted to believe he felt something like I did. *He must, why would he act like that?* But I started to become embarrassed and self-conscious around him, and it was uncomfortable for me. The oxygen just wasn't getting to my brain.

Annie Lennox had set the backdrop for our romance and our week fling (if you could call it that). I played her *Medusa* CD all through senior year when I fantasized about him. And although I didn't have classes with him during that year, I saw him around the studios and at the weekly Visiting Artists lectures. When I tried to come up with excuses to talk to him, it was obvious I was smitten. That summer after I graduated, B didn't waste any time, and called me as soon as he got to Santa Fe in late June. He left a message at the Native American art gallery where I was working that he'd like to take me out. We met at a coffee shop, then went to a hip cowboy bar. As he knocked down the whiskey shots and leered at my bare legs in my miniskirt, he made me laugh with his animated gestures, his stories, and his flair for self-deprecation. He played it well, cosmopolitan, chic art professor meets wild, eccentric cowboy-artist. He was lusty and energetic and I was falling fast. "After I have another whiskey, want to go grab dinner?"

"Why not?" I said, laughing flirtatiously. *Holy shit! It's happening.*

Of course he brought me back to his place after dinner. Within ten minutes, he roared loudly and grabbed me from his ottoman, where I had been lounging, cozily wrapped in his huge camel wool cardigan and staring into his hungry eyes. "Jenny, Jennnny. I've wanted you all year, roarrrrrr."

It was surreal.

I began to surrender most of my pent-up passion. But I held back. Couldn't give myself completely. I knew I could never really have him.

And I had hang-ups. *I want you so much, but it's not right. I was your student and you're twenty years older, for God's sake. What do I have, an Electra complex? And I hear you're just a womanizer, you'll just be using me. Is this really happening? After two years of being infatuated with you. Holy shit . . . I was right. Told ya, Mom, told ya, Dad, that there was something here with this man. I can't sleep with you, though. Not tonight. Not yet. I can't be too easy. I can't give myself to you fully. Then it'll just be a fling. Want more. Because I think I love you, but I can't love you if I barely know you . . . and you don't know me. I can't sleep with you because I want you to think I'm special, respect me. Is this okay I'm doing this?*

I went home. He picked me up the next morning to work out at the gym, where he complained of his bad knees and how old he looked. I just did my run on the treadmill, looking at him every so often while he peered back at me, pretending to read his *New York Times* through his tortoiseshell spectacles while riding the stationary bike. Afterward he said, "I'm getting out of shape. Better work out more." Again he added, "I'm old, Jenny. Old." I said, "I don't want to know how old you are. Now shut up with that."

"Hey, uh, Jen, you want to have dinner Wednesday? I have to go to Abiqui with my class, but I thought maybe, uh . . . ?"

"Sounds good. What time will you pick me up?" *He asked me on a date! Yee ha!*

I had to be perfect for that date. I had to be the fucking perfect picture. I worked out like a fiend for two days, sat in the sun getting tan during my breaks from the gallery, had my upper lip and armpits waxed, and I waited. Waited for what I had been anticipating for the entire past two years. I wore a white dress showing every lean curve, with my short black tuxedo jacket. I was running around barefoot when he arrived, and I remember how he stared at my feet. After I put on my red heels we were off to my favorite restaurant. An elegant, very white place in the midst of brown adobe that served Southwest-influenced Asian cuisine. As we walked in, it felt like everyone was staring. He was very tall, regal, and striking in his olive green blazer and cowboy boots. I felt glamorous and pretty next to him. I was half proud, but also half confused at the turning of heads, like maybe people were wondering if I was his daughter or something. Through the course of the meal, I tried to let go. I sipped on my white wine slowly, because I had noticed earlier in the year that after a few sips I couldn't think as straight (maybe something with my blood sugar) and I'd feel like gagging (the beginning of acid-reflux problems). Anyhow, I didn't want the alcohol to blur our conversation, because I wanted to talk and get to know each other. I wanted to tell him who I was. And I wanted to know about his past divorce and his painting and what he was all about. The attraction was so chemical, so physical. Still, I had this notion of what I thought it should and could be. He was more reserved on this date, fitting the mood of the restaurant. He seemed a bit self-conscious. Maybe just low-key.

"So, Jenny, tell me how the Lauren empire began."

I was shy at first, but I was articulate enough when I talked about my father, his work, my uncle, how the business all began.

"Well, put it this way, it started with some ties. My uncle designed some ties and then sold 'em to a few big places. Everyone thought he was crazy, he'd never make it with his fantasies, but it happened. He was a dreamer but he worked hard. My father joined a few years later and has been heading the menswear ever since." I didn't want to play up the family stuff. His asking this question made me self-conscious about who he thought I was. *I'm just Jenny—creative, emotional, passionate, frightened, and vulnerable Jenny, who just wants you to take me and make me feel even more alive than you already do.*

"But tell me about you. Tell me about your painting," I said. I didn't want to intimidate him with this conversation about the powerful men in my family.

"It's going fine. Not like it used to. I'm excited to go up to northern New Mexico next week after this seminar I'm doing to have lots of time to paint. Starting a whole new series. But it's been so hectic. Jenny, the past few years have been so crazy."

We also talked about my painting. I asked him to tell me the truth, if I had any talent. His answer was sweet, and *tactful.* "Well, Jenny, you have a lot more in your paintings than I did when I was your age."

During the meal, I ate my roasted chicken slowly and delicately. I felt fine eating with him. Something made me confide in him that I had a problem with eating. After all, I had shed probably twenty pounds since arriving at Barnard. And then there was that time when the head professor said in front of B, "Hey, Jenny, you're getting a little too thin." I never forgot the mortification. But now I felt I could confide and told him I had battled anorexia. B startled me with, "You know, my sister died of that." *Whoa.* We didn't say anything more about it.

We went back to my house, and I felt like a princess in a king's arms when B and I danced, bodies meshed together, in the living room to "No More I Love You's." In bed, he opened up to me. Told me some of his fears, how he couldn't sleep well at night, how he was depressed over his divorce. Afraid his career was flagging. We didn't actually make love (I still wanted to wait), but he slept well in my arms. It was a beautiful night, and the image of us dancing stays in my mind always. Maybe even a bit more than the feeling.

That weekend he ended what had only just begun. He took me out for sushi. I noticed he was pensive, quiet. For a moment I thought that maybe I didn't even find him that attractive. He said, "Jenny, I can't do this. You're just too young. And the art world is tough. You were just my student. I have a reputation here at stake." As Annie Lennox would put it, I turned a whiter shade of pale. "I don't know what this attraction is about," I told him. "I just thought we should explore it. I don't understand." I started crying, thinking, *Don't let him see this, it's pathetic.*

I lay in bed that night feeling as if my heart was dropping, and the ache inside was bitter. He called and said, "Are you okay?" I said, "I'll be fine, just fine." Loss, rejection, inflated hope. I wondered if it would kill me.

A week later I saw him getting out of a car and opening the door for a tall, leggy blonde. It turned out she was his girlfriend. I smiled and waved, with cold cynical eyes.

Then, at a benefit two weeks later, I was with a good-looking male friend, and B was drunk and eyeing me from across the catered tables. He called me the next day and said, "I guess you're doing fine now. That was quick. Handsome guy."

I said, "Yeah, right. Just fine." He'd never know.

One morning, a month later, I awoke to hear Annie Lennox's lullabies playing loudly outside my home. I ran outside in my pajamas praying that he had come back to love me. But that kind of shit happens only in the movies. It was just my neighbors.

Eight months later I saw him at an art opening in New York.

"You still living in Santa Fe, Jenny?"

"No. Didn't you get my Christmas card? I think I told you I was back."

In front of his little posse of art farts he said glibly, "Oh. Uh, yeah. I have it on file somewhere."

The sick, twisted worshipping of a man twenty-three years my elder. Friends said, "It's typical to fantasize about a professor, especially you, Jenny, being so intense. But you're letting it rule your life. It's become an obsession. You've got to move on."

Four years later I still wake up longing for B after dreaming of him.

12. And Life Goes On . . .

Within an hour of leaving the Mount Sinai psychiatric ward, I can be found bending over the toilet bowl in my bathroom thrusting my fingers down my throat. It is a little late to rid myself of the morning's hospital food but I just want something so bad to feel familiar. As I catch myself performing my old ritual, I panic and then stop. *Jenny, what do you think you are doing? DON'T DO IT.* I know that my body, and my mind, and my soul, cannot withstand this behavior anymore.

I am grateful that Dr. P has agreed to see me as an outpatient three times a week; otherwise being back at home and dealing with myself might be completely unbearable. In fact, Dr. P's sessions are the redeeming highlight of my week. Most important, they get me out of the house. I like going to his office, which is right outside the Mount Sinai psychiatric ward, so I can peer in through the glass window onto the unit to see if Hippo Lady or any of the others are still there. Part of me is glad to be released from prison, but part of me wants to go back in there to feel safe again. Then Dr. P greets me warmly like I am an old friend, and I chuckle, happy to see him. Dr. P thinks the Serzone is helping me. I don't know about that. I feel kind of zoned out. I recount my days to him and tell him little odds and ends from my past, but I spend most of the sessions complaining about the pain.

I've been laughing a bit more—well, wanting to laugh . . . there's a difference—and I call Nikki and Edward and can talk on the phone for a little while. Physical therapy, my only outdoor activity other than seeing Dr. P, is just plain depressing. I look forward to going, but then I'm usually in too much agony to do the exercises. Instead I lie there with heat packs on my groin and stimulators on my knee joints for the constant throbbing. When I leave either PT or Dr. P's office, I go grab a bottle of wine from the nearest liquor store and rush home in a cab with it. Drinking white wine has become the prize waiting at the end of such torment. I don't care that it's fattening. Just pouring the liquid into my glass calms me down.

In July of this past summer, right after the surgery, I had a much more positive outlook. I did way more than I am doing now. Although the pain was excruciating, I had more fight in me. Even in Connecticut at the house right before that weekend I got impacted, I had attempted to join my mother for her morning walk to the general store and back, but we had to call Dad to pick me up. Then in the city, I grabbed myself a frappuccino from Starbucks and went to the Metropolitan Museum to look at art by myself, but I got violently upset when I couldn't remember whether a painting was a Cézanne or a Manet. I was an art history major, for God's sake.

These days I am lucky just to get to both therapies. Most of the time

I lie around waiting for the discomfort to go away. My mood is starting to lift, but it's usually after I throw some Bailey's in my coffee for breakfast and have my wine at night.

Sometimes after my sessions with Dr. P, I go to a Japanese restaurant near my apartment to relax. I usually drink plum wine and eventually come to wonder how the hell I ended up sitting here downing sushi all alone. Am I being destructive or am I being kind to myself? Each day I think, *Clean yourself out, let go of all the toxins, feel light,* and yet since starting the Serzone, there is a part of me that doesn't give a shit. Although I hate looking in the mirror now (not chunky yet), I can't seem to have a day where I can go without eating, let alone eating only a little. I am ravenous. Sushi's been my thing lately. I wonder why—maybe I'm craving salt? And the energy I receive from the food still depresses me because I can't act on it. I can't stand it. Oh, the rush I get, the athletic feeling. How I want to run far, feel my muscles, burn this protein, take a great shit . . . go to Japan.

I always feel at home in a Japanese restaurant. I want to go to Japan badly, to see the serene and slick beauty. But I wonder if I can go there with comfort of mind if I don't feel lean, singular, linear, as if I will not fit into the clean angles I imagine there. It's the same way I am afraid to go back to Santa Fe without the desert-terrain muscles I once had, the feel I had in my jeans and cowboy boots. Why can't I look out of eyes that sense and see the surroundings but separate it from the knowledge that I am there in that space? Why can't I leave my body?

Why can't I feel like I deserve to love and be loved, even if I feel fat or covered with cellulite or big-breasted? Why do I want to strip myself bare?

13. Periods

My mother always attributed my erratic mood swings, my food behavior, and my extreme sensitivity to the fact that I barely ever got my period. Before my surgery, in my whole career as a female, I had six periods, with three of them induced by taking a progesterone pill for fourteen days prior. The normal age for a female to begin menstruating is from thirteen to sixteen (sometimes even earlier), so by twenty-five years old I should basically have had, well, twenty-five minus, say, fifteen years equals ten years, times twelve months equals 120 periods. (Give or take a few for various reasons, most commonly STRESS.) Six periods instead of 120 periods. That's just a bit bizarre, but given my eating disorder since age ten, the gynecologist always said that it made sense. Surprisingly, and ironically enough, I've been getting my period since my surgery. I've had a period about six times within eight months. My theory is that the anesthesia, the painkillers, the Valium, and the fact that I can't run or exercise the hell out of my body are the reasons I'm finally getting them. My mother thinks that my internal problem, which they supposedly fixed, could have been interfering with normal processes. Who knows?

I had my first period induced when I was almost sixteen. Most of my friends starting getting it three years earlier. I started to feel a little bit left out. But it was really my mother who felt that it was very important that I begin my reproductive cycle. I fearfully agreed to ingest the artificial hormone and see what all the hype was about. For eight days nothing happened.

One night in my sleep I dreamed of nothing but the color red, vivid, like fire, and then it turned a magnificent purple. The following morning I had to stop in the middle of my exercise class and hurry to the bathroom because of my cramps, and then I saw the same deep red on the toilet paper. *Is this it? Is this it? I got my period! I got my period! It just drips out of you just like this? Blood just pours freely out of you? It feels like a wound. It's so messy. Ecch.* I couldn't quite fathom the whole thing. It felt so new, so strange, so abstract. So unnecessary. *Every month? I don't think I can get used to this.*

I rushed to call my mother at the country house. "Guess what, Mom?" Then I sang, "I got my question mark . . . I got my question mark!" hoping to make her proud.

She gasped, "Well, mazel tov!"

But somehow I managed to hex my periods away after that. I was afraid they would make me fat. *Or make me normal yet.* And, yeah, obviously maybe I didn't want to grow up. Simple answers. I wanted to control what I couldn't control. But I did. After that I got my period a few times on my own through the course of seven years. I went to endocrinologists and none of them understood why even at a normal body weight, or even heavy, I just wouldn't get my period. They said I suffered from perennial PMS. After that first induced period, my breasts often hurt, my cravings for food were endless, and my bouts with anger, upset, and feelings of defeat became more frequent. When I look back, I really think my hormones did play a major part in my depression and bulimia. Or were at least an underlying cause.

Although I had starved at ten and fifteen, I had never binged the way I did after getting that first artificial period. Today I have been told that low estrogen levels are linked to many health problems, not only osteoporosis, but also to the nourishment of a woman's pelvic region. When I went in for surgery, my estrogen levels had been severely low. Perhaps not getting periods for years added to the weakness of my pelvic muscles. My colon. The prolapse of my organs. This happens in older women, they say. I never grasped how important balanced hormones were. I should have listened to my mother early on when she stressed how crucial it was that I get periods, and pleaded with me to take the artificial progesterone more often. Perhaps I really did do this to myself by never respecting my body. *At all.*

14. New Year's Weekend

In the early hours of New Year's Eve, I lie in bed recovering from the flu, still in chronic pain, talking on the phone with Nikki while she procrastinates about getting ready for the night. We begin to reminisce. We read to each other from our journal entries, fragments of writing from long ago, a dramatic poem, letters we had received from each other one summer, a sweet love note in our yearbook from a boy. All these thoughts jotted down and saved represent so many feelings, memories, associations about men, our troublesome families, our dreams, and so much fear and loneliness. But oh, how we laugh about where we are now and how many goddamn people we grew up with who are married and having babies. At least Nikki is pursuing an acting career, running a private tutoring business, and designing jewelry. But she still feels like something is lacking. We ask each other, *Should we care? Where have our lives gone? Why does it seem so much harder now to find someone to love and love us back? Is it our high expectations, our fears, our narcissism, or just bad luck?*

When Nikki goes to her party, I stop laughing. I am slightly envious because I am not going out too, although every year the ritual ends in the same empty feelings. Usually everyone is too wasted to say or do anything all that interesting. I don't think I ever had a boyfriend on New Year's Eve, maybe just a fling or a crush on someone who was kissing another girl. A swig of champagne at twelve o'clock. What was I celebrating anyhow? Still, I miss the battles to find cabs all night, as all our friends hold hands shivering, with feet aching from heels (yeah, right). No, but I truly miss all the four o'clock, morning coffee-shop-dulled yakking. "Did you see her dress? Did he even look at me once? Could you believe how rude so and so was?"

In truth, am I more relieved not to have been part of it? When I imagine what the night might be like, it reminds me of all the bullshit, the power plays, the turning away at the door of the bars, the clubs, especially the infamous Dorians (the preppie-murderer bar) in high school. My friends getting made up all glamorous with sweet-smelling lipstick, and kissing ass to the bouncers. I didn't want to work that hard. *What, so I think you're a scumbucket and don't want to kiss you, so you won't let me in? No, asshole, I don't have a fake ID. Yeah, I'm Greg's sister. Oh, now you'll let me in, oh great, now I'm cool. Fuck you.* Everyone rushing for the drink, the lighting up of butts. *Whooh, we're in. Oh my God, we are so cool! We have a life.*

But with my unyielding physical pain and shame over my changing body, I don't feel I even have a choice whether I can participate or not. I'm afraid now that I do not want to want. Even the thought of a night out on the town and the possibility of having fun or meeting someone special seems more painful. I'm losing any hope and desire for a man in my future. I lie awake trying to put myself to sleep so I won't feel these emotions of loss and deprivation.

And then I start to fall into a deeper melancholy, as I begin to think of my parents and the exaggerated fear that I have always had of their deaths. At camp I used to imagine that the director would gather my two brothers and me after morning reveille and tell us our parents had been in a plane crash on their way to Europe or Nantucket. During my most awful times, that idea of them leaving me has always seemed unbearable. Now as I lie here and feel helpless and without purpose or dreams of experiencing great sensual pleasure, I dread more than ever that they will leave me too soon. I am so afraid I will not get better and stronger, and if my parents were to die now, I could never endure it. And too, that if they get sick, I would not be there to care for them. Sometimes I feel like I want to die before them so I do not experience the grief of losing them.

I remember once, in a family session with Dr. Hannibal during senior year, surprising myself when I admitted to him in front of my parents, "Sometimes I'm so scared of my parents dying, that sometimes I think if they died, I'd start living."

There was no reaction of shock on his or my parents' part. I think my dad even said, "Dr. Hannibal, I know what Jenny feels. I was very close with my parents. I had those fears. Jenny is very sensitive to us."

My mother looked as if she understood too. The stifling power that parents and love can have on their daughter. That they had on me. I think I was the only one astounded by what had come out of my mouth.

In the morning, when the phone rings, it is hard to pull myself out of my usual stiff and embryo-shaped position. But Nikki convinces me to meet her for brunch at Sarabeth's Kitchen. As she shares her stories of the night before, I struggle to hold myself up, leaning on the table, gripping my thighs, and still overcast by the dismal feelings I had gone to sleep with. Although I smile at Nik and am happy to be with her for the continuation, recount, and finale of this horrific year, I can't help but feel distant and afraid. What will this year bring? Will I get stronger? Will I get better? Will I really be okay? But hey, it is New Year's Day.

15. RX #?

I think it may be entirely true what they say about men having a lower threshold of pain than women. This is the fourth time in a row that I have had the pleasure of watching the same man gasping and sobbing as a physical therapist manipulates his toes. Today when he comes in I'm, like, *Oh, shit, it's the whiner. Oh, we're in for a treat.* He lies down on the table, rustling his Wall Street suit, and doesn't even undo his stiff Brooks Brothers suspenders. He must have to hurry back to work afterward. Maybe that's why he's so upset. I continue to do my stretches, and I wait for the histrionics. A few minutes go by and all of a sudden the cries begin. I can't help but turn my head to stare at his chubby pouting face as he tries to breathe. I'm truly amazed. I feel really bad for him. I kind of want to throw up because it's making me more aware of my pain, which I am trying to forget. The physical therapist is barely touching his toes. Meanwhile, my feet are beginning to hurt all of a sudden.

When the guy gets up all flushed and discombobulated, he asks me, "Hey, what happened to you?"

I just can't hold back.

"Oh me? I had colon, abdominal, and *rectal* surgery. No big deal."

That shuts him up pretty fast.

I watch how people move. I watch how they walk. How they hold their bags. How they use their utensils when they eat and how they pick up their coffee cups. How they type at a computer. How they open a door. How they cross their legs sitting and how they fall asleep waiting in the doctor's office. All these simple actions. I have always taken them for granted.

Now they feel different. I have to think about it when I try to do any of these things. Do I look strange? I catch myself going to flush the toilet in an upward motion; it feels unfamiliar, but I can't remember which way to do it. I find myself having to pick up one of my legs manually to cross it over the other while sitting and gripping the arms of the chair to hold myself up. When I go to walk, I don't know whether my legs should turn out or stay straight. Got myself all confused, my body messages seem like they're crossing lines. I try to explain how hard it is to pick up a fork or hold the blow-dryer but my parents or doctors say it doesn't look that way.

Like a junkie, I turn on the light so I can find the right meds, a 20- and a 10-milligram Prozac so I don't kill myself, a 5- or 10-milligram Valium for the spasms, and Synthroid for my low thyroid levels. I have gotten very used to this tray by my bed. I am twenty-five years old, and the tray looks like my eighty-year-old grandmother's. Prescription bottle after prescription bottle. Percocet, Lortab, Darvil for the extreme pain,

Naprosyn for period on top of pain. Prilosec for GERD, as well as every other thing for antacid: that gross mint green bottle of Mylanta (which my mother swears by), rolls of Tums, Digel, and Levsin for abdominal cramping. Leftover Serzone antidepressant from my one-month trial. Klonopin and Librium from the Mayo Clinic, and oh so many *laxatives*. Three bottles of milk of magnesia (eeech), Colace, Sennakot Extra, and stool softeners, Fleet enemas and phosphate soda, mineral oil, magnesium citrate, and weird-ass health food store ones like Swiss Kriss, Aloe Lax, fig fruit cubes, and can't forget the gallons of Go-Lightly that sit in my refrigerator, oh yeah, and the prune juice, and the Smooth Move and herbal teas that sit in my cabinets. My tray. Is it filled with medicine or poison?

These medications . . . what do they do to you, for the future of your body and mind? My insides are never getting to know the real me again. I try not to worry (pop a Valium) about taking all this stuff but how can one not? In fact, I'll chuck the ones I don't use right now; I already threw out the Ativan, the Zyprexa, the Haldol, the Xanax. I was totally addicted to Xanax. Last summer I would find myself just standing and staring off into space on some street corner trying to hold myself up for minutes at a time, unsure where I was. *Madison, Fifth, Palookaville?* At Mayo, when they told me I was too young to be on that stuff, I thought, *Oh, is that why I can't remember anybody's fuckin' name or phone number?* I must thank God immensely for Percocet, especially in the early days of my pain. I do prefer the injections, but I'll settle for the pill. But, God, I have a request: PLEASE INVENT A PAINKILLER THAT IS NOT CONSTIPATING SO THAT I DON'T HAVE TO TAKE A PAINKILLER FOR THE CONSTIPATION. Ahhhh, then we have my ultimate concoctions; like a scientist I mix up all the laxatives . . . *How 'bout five doses of Milk of Magnesia, a handful of Colace, five Sennas, and a few Ex-Lax for the bang . . . ah, yes . . . will act like dynamite . . .* None of 'em work.

Last week I had to go back to Dr. D (the gastroenterologist from before the surgery who measured the size of my butt twitches). He sends me for another defecogram to see exactly what's going on eight months after surgery and why I still can't take a shit. The test shows that my small bowel still falls or, as the radiologist describes it, "makes a loop" into the space. I don't get it. Why is it still moving in? I thought the surgeon closed the space between my rectum and vagina. In fact, what the fuck did he do? I still have no clue, even though he has tried to explain it many times.

Now Dr. D says, "At least it's a lot better than before the surgery."

Yeah, sure it is. Every day of my new life I feel like Mike Tyson came and beat the living daylights out of my stomach, or as if I was in some car wreck and came out with a mangled pelvis and stiff and achy limbs; and to top it all off, like with whipped cream and a cherry, I cannot shit!! *AAAAGH!!!!* All right, so before the surgery, I suffered for months from the twenty-four-hour nonstop rectal spasms and walked the streets endlessly, not wanting to stop because if I did I could feel the bugs crawling up my ass, and my mushy tushy getting mushier, and had to stand to move my bowels, and thought I was dying and wanted to jump out of my window . . . but now you say *it's a hell of a lot better.* What does that mean? That I accept not shitting, most of the time? Was it too much to expect that after this surgery I would be able to sit on the toilet and go to the bathroom with ease like a normal person? Had too much damage been done? Was it too late? Whining, I cry, "Why isn't it all better?" I think I paid my dues.

Dr. D gives me a checkup, and as he touches and presses on my stomach, I yelp in pain. My *entire torso hurts! Don't touch me, you asshole!*

He tells me and my mother that the pain must be from the chronic laxative *abuse.* I want to scream. *You have gotta be kidding. You guys all told me to take this crap! You all said, "You've got to clean yourself out somehow. Let's just deal with today."*

Every time I gulp down those laxatives or stick 'em up my ass, I think *my poor colon. I know you hate these foul things and, oh, you miss your darlin' resected part of your sigmoid . . . I know, honey.* I really want my colon back. The original. LAXATIVE ABUSE! *Thanks a lot, fuckers.* To my surgeon personally, thank you for saving me from suffering the worse fate of incontinence (which I still hear buzzing in my ears) and I truly mean that, but thank you for also sticking a cork up my ass.

Dr D tells me to stop taking laxatives for a week and that we will do another marker test to check my colon motility. I will swallow a capsule filled with markers and next week they'll take X-rays that will show where the markers have moved to in my colon, or whether they moved at all. What if they find out that my colon is barely moving, or it's like a turtle, or they don't find a damn thing? And what if the markers are hiding? Dr. D had to convince me that no matter what, the markers will light up because they are inside me somewhere. If the results suck, Dr. D says I might need to try taking injections of this stuff called Sandostatin. Of course I have obsessively looked for all the information over the Internet, and it scares me because it is some kind of hormone that stops excess growth, and it is often given to people with tumors, cancer, and AIDS. And why exactly is it that I have to take such serious stuff?

But the worst part about all this is that I have no trust. I don't trust the doctors, the tests, and I don't trust that my body will reveal the mystery behind the pain.

The only medication that doesn't sit on my tray that my grandmother takes is heart medication, and it is really my heart, more than anything, that is breaking.

16. Visiting Grandma

I don't know how I manage, but somehow I get on a plane with my mother to visit my ailing grandmother in Boca Raton, Florida, for two days. My grandma Mary has dementia and I know my mother needs the support, and it's about time I do something for her. Even though I spend the first afternoon there lying on my stomach on the tacky blue-and-white diamond carpet in our hotel room, staring out the huge window at the ocean yonder and getting sentimental because I cannot run on the gritty sand with the waves cascading over my feet and ankles, I'm not that upset, because *I have the mini-bar.* I'm on my third Kahlua.

But finally it's time to make our way to the Stratford Living Residence for the Elderly to join my grandmother for dinner. I'm glad I made it here. Except I hope I can get up in my buzzed state. Plus I'm sort of afraid to see my grandmother because I hear she looks very old and fragile and she doesn't speak, so the silence will be excruciating.

I miss Grandma Mary. I hate watching people change, lose their spirit. Now she's a little old woman in pain who doesn't seem to want to be here. But why would she? She lost her husband years ago, we live far away, she doesn't have much money left, and they don't play poker, her favorite card game, at the nursing home.

The soft smile that comes over my grandmother's face as my mother and I walk in her tiny apartment is enough to tell me I did the right thing. I start to cry a bit, but then I get it together. *Shit, she is tiny . . . whoa. Skin and bones. Better get her some of her favorite foods, like a bowl of Heavenly Hash ice cream.* We'll have to go to the supermarket and stock up her fridge. It is really hard to believe that her kitchen is relatively empty, considering her cabinets used to be a bulimic's dream, or rather, nightmare, because she was always a major nosher. My grandmother would snack on Poppycock, Cheez Doodles, and Chips Ahoy without gaining any weight, although she wasn't necessarily thin either. But she kept her shelves overstuffed with the best crap, things you'd never even heard of, all the junk food you could buy *with a coupon.*

We wait for the nurse to help Grandma get dressed, and suddenly she appears in a fresh white cotton cable Ralph Lauren sweater and slacks, with her short dyed blond hair combed and her lips *and teeth* covered with red lipstick, and her cheeks dotted with rouge. It always amazes me how older people take care and put themselves together better than I do. *Especially now.*

My mother says, "Mom, you look beautiful," and I say, "Yeah,

Grandma, so pretty, come on, let's go eat some macaroni, and then we'll play rummy cue afterwards." As we walk and both hold her arms (*although they don't realize they're holding me up*), she waddles, and she squeaks a bit when she says, "Aaaw, that'd be nice."

At dinner, I drink glass after glass of wine so I can get drunk again, because those small bottles wore off mighty fast and I need something to deal with the pain. My grandmother knows I had surgery but has no clue as to the extent of it, and I don't find it necessary to explain my whole deal to her. She's got her own troubles. But I do ask about *her* gallbladder surgery from years ago, although she doesn't remember much of it. She's had a lot of surgery—stomach, heart—and I don't recall her ever complaining. *Wow. Maybe I should take some lessons from her.*

I have to say, Grandma Mary was my favorite "elder," and I always looked forward to our weekend visits. My parents used to drop us kids off at my grandparents' house at the Jersey Shore or at their Florida winter rental, and we always had a great time even though my grandfather was a bit of a character, a man who acted tough but had a tender heart. He would order us around and yell, "Hey, Horse's Ass, did you hear what I said? Get me an ashtray." But then when we rushed from the kitchen and rested his ashtray or his Pepsi beside the jar with his floating teeth on the table next to him, he would smile and there would be a glint in his eyes that told us he was just kidding around. And he made up for his bullying with all the other goofy nicknames he gave us. Brad was Benny the Gonif, Greg was Jake the Plumber, and I was Sarah Bernhardt (*I'm not sure that one was so great*). Although Grandpa Sonny sometimes got to us, he never was successful at riling up my grandmother, although he would try constantly. He would sit in the TV room watching baseball and chain-smoking, with his huge belly puffing out of his undershirt, and all the while keep hollering at my grandmother to fetch this and fetch that, but she would just ignore him and keep on doing what she was doing. Considering they met when they were in grade school in Bayonne, New Jersey, ran a moving company together, and were married for over fifty years, they obviously had their routine down pat.

And Grandpa was indeed fat! He could stuff down a whole seeded roll with lox and cream cheese in one mouthful and then have four more. He would get up early and go out to get bags of bagels and appetizers and come back all proud and say, "EERF, EERF. So eat up. Mary, start the bacon and cut those tomatoes." *They obviously weren't Orthodox Jews.* EERF meant "free" spelled backward, and my grandparents were very into bargains and even a little gambling here and there. Their favorite kind of weekend was to book a hotel room at Atlantic City and play the slot machines.

When we were very little, Grandma Mary would take us to the boardwalk to play video games and eat candied apples, and to see R-rated movies. And as cuss word after cuss word rolled off the screen from *Saturday Night Fever* or *48 Hours,* she'd say, "Oh boy, oh boy, Susan is going to kill me." We would giggle and then afterward Grandma Mary would whisper, "Okay. It's our secret. Don't tell your mother."

At the house we would watch all the game shows with her and she would get the correct answers before all the television contestants. I always begged her to go on *The Price Is Right.* Grandma Mary was valedictorian in high school (so she told us many times), and she was very smart. She read a lot, all the bestsellers and all the *Enquirer*s that lay in bundles in her living room. And she never could miss her late-night soap operas, and would let us stay up with her watching *Dynasty* and the others into the wee hours of the night.

Then she had her card game nights with Lil and Gertrude and Rose and the *junk food.* It was all lined up in crystal bowls on the pull-out table: honey-roasted peanuts, potato chips, Nibs caramels, licorice, marshmallows. Greg and I both kept going back for more, and to watch Grandma and the girls cackling with laughter and spewing gossip while they played. But Grandma could also get very serious during a game and then we would return to the guest room and let her concentrate. In the early days I usually felt sick after staying over and munching all weekend. As I got older I tried to resist the sweet temptations, but it was hard. *It must have been all the sugar, artificial food colorings, and white flour, calling my name.* But weekends there were always like a slumber party and the food was supposed to be part of the fun. I have to admit, though, I ended up having some big binges at my grandparents' house, and then I didn't look forward to visiting as much.

I once asked my mom if she enjoyed her childhood and felt close to her parents, and it actually makes me sad to hear that my mother spent most of the time alone because my grandparents worked all day, the nanny left early, and her brother, Charlie, was ten years older and went off to the army. She spent a lot of hours waiting for them to come home and even used to cook their dinner. But she says, "I was fine, I had my good friends Madeline and Isabella, my cousin Suzanne. I was just fine. But no, I wasn't close with my parents, not the way we are." It hurts to think that my mother might have been lonely as a child, but that may be why she's so readily available for her own kids.

After dinner my mother and I take Grandma to Super Shop and Go. As my mother loads up the cart with ginger ale and canned peaches, my grandmother and I sit by the bubble gum machines. I get a ring from one of the machines for her, but it won't fit over her swollen knuckles, so I put it on. And then out of the blue she asks, "Jenny, are you getting your *whosey-what's-it* these days?" I am amazed that she remembers some of my ailments.

I say, "Grandma, would you believe it, I get my period now, ever since the surgery. Isn't that wild?"

She exclaims, "Well, holy moley, whaddaya know!" Then she says, "Any fellows in your life?" I laugh, because for a withering woman, she's still pretty with it.

"Nah, Grandma. Nobody yet. Been too busy lately."

She says, "Eh, you'll find someone. When the moment is right."

I stare at my grandmother and think how lucky I am to be with her . . . for maybe one of the last times.

17. Inspiration

A few weeks after surgery I hobbled into the Corner Bookstore in the Nineties on Madison Avenue. I felt drugged and could barely balance, but I was captivated by all the covers and their elite selection so I stopped to get lost in them. I heard a customer asking the knowledgeable man who's been behind that counter for years for his advice on which Dubus book to buy. He suggested the newest one because he claimed it was his richest work. Dubus wrote it after he stopped to help a disabled motorist, only to end up getting himself hit; his left leg was amputated above the knee and his right leg was shattered. I was inspired then. Although he had already been a writer, he kept on writing. We only get one life, one body, one mind (maybe . . . don't know for sure). That thought helped me and also frightened me for months. I did not believe that I had the will to endure my own tragedy like some people had.

Since then, I have become obsessed by those who have dealt with a tragedy and not only healed but have used the creative powers to do so. Nikki bought me tons of Frida Kahlo books, likening me to her. *Yeah, sure, if only I could paint like that.* But I never knew she had that bus accident and that a pole went right through her pelvis, and how she lived in a brace and with horrible pain. She was extremely prolific, and her work was extremely profound.

Matisse did those wonderful paper cutouts with his toes when he was in a wheelchair later in life. Nothing stopped him from creating color.

Christopher Reeve is writing and acting, although paralyzed. There are people all over dealing with horrific blows, people who live in pain. They still have families, they still have lives, and they still can exercise their passions. And I will too, because somewhere within, I pray that I am stronger than I've known.

This morning when I drink my coffee after popping all my pills, I lie in bed for fifteen minutes of grieving time, feeling achy, twisted, and stabbed at the knees. I find myself saying out loud in a goofy manner, "Ooh, so achy. Ooh, boy," like I seem to be doing every morning, attempting to have a sense of humor about it all. I try to squeeze my shoulders together tight and then relax them and bring my knees to my chest. *Ooh, no good, doesn't work.*

I tell myself, "*Don't think about it. Don't let it get you down. Get up. It's a beautiful day. Besides, you have ten million things you want to do, all these ideas that you've jotted down and have sprawled all over your apartment. There are papers underneath the bed, in your coat, tucked into your drawers, thoughts in your head.*"

I turn on the radio, and I remember that line I enjoyed and cried bitter tears at, from the movie *Good Will Hunting*, when Matt Damon says to Robin Williams in a therapy session, "It's like I hear the music and I just wanna get up and bang, bang, boom." It's right on my target. I start to dance, thinking I am in Jenny's old body, the body that at any physical weight felt light and attuned to the rhythm of music. And every time I danced in that body I felt like my life had meaning, that I was born again, and that if I didn't have that ability to experience that, I might just want to die. At twenty-two I asked myself why I gave up my dream of performing, whether I had denied myself and pushed away my true love. But, I thought then, I can dance now for myself. I can dance in my house; I can dance in the Sheep Meadow of Central Park; and I can dance alone in the rugged hills of the desert terrain. I can dance for me.

But this morning, in this new form, I want so badly to dance, and I try. The music, the beat, the sensual sounds, make me yearn to move in my special way, but everything aches and I can't get my hips and pelvis and arms to move with the fluidity of the old Jenny. I keep trying like I have many mornings since surgery. I make a daily attempt to resist my ailing body. My physical drive is still deeply alive within me, and it fights to come out.

18. Dissecting My Life

There was a time in high school when I thought I wasn't going to go to college. I didn't even know if I would make it through the SATs or senior year. I imagined that I'd just fall apart, stay a mess, and anyhow, *some of the most successful people never went to college, right?* Thank God for Linda, my headmaster at the Tutoring School, for not counting half the school days I missed, and for inspiring me to go for it. I was bewildered when I got into the only three colleges I decided to apply to. I got accepted to Sarah Lawrence, and I thought that was where I would attend because it was small and perfect for outcasts *such as myself.* Only, when I saw a guy wearing a skirt on the day of my interview and noticed that a lot of the girls in their dorm rooms were knitting or doing jigsaw puzzles, I just didn't feel like it was the place for me. I also got into Skidmore and debated about going there because they had a terrific art program and it was near the cultural town of Saratoga. I remember being wowed by the window seats in some of the dorm rooms, but I felt displaced. It seemed too far away. I was homesick for my parents already.

But when I opened the fat acceptance letter to Barnard College, I was flabbergasted. I never expected to get in, thought it was a total stretch. *Gosh, I'm not such a fuckup. They like me . . . They like me.* I was thrilled. When I visited the campus I was amazed that I had never known there was this little college environment in Manhattan. I fell in love with Riverside Park; it was so lovely and so different from the East Side. I chose Barnard.

I've always wanted to believe I was smart and capable. *But of course it was more important to be thin and beautiful.* With my moods and my hang-ups, I often couldn't trust that I would get things done on time, or at all. Somehow, though. I always did.

I talk about this with Dr. P, and he urges me to write. He takes my work home. I e-mail it to him sometimes. We discuss it in our sessions. This is really different from past therapy, where the conversations drone on, the same cycle of stuff, sadness, anger, bullshit. I have found a way now to make this whole thing work. For the first time I feel excited about dissecting my life. I have created a new kind of dialogue, with a doctor who seems to believe in me and my intellect. More important, I may finally be believing in myself and my life enough to ask for help.

At my next appointment with Dr. P, when I go to sit down on his couch, I realize that I am feeling a bit blue, a bit down, unlike the past week when I felt this hyper-elevation and surprised myself with my witty, joking manner. I enjoyed babbling to my family, hearing them laugh with gusto, a hint that they feel some relief that maybe *Jenny is feeling happier*. Even with all the yucky pain in the knee and wrist joints, and catching glimpses of the side view of my silhouette in the glass windows of stores, which I usually avoided, I truly was happy. Almost jovial, almost free. But yesterday I began to feel the fatigue and frustration coming, and then the dwindling of these fabulous feelings.

With past therapists, I found myself talking as if no one was there. With Dr. P I can feel the presence of his emotions, and mainly, his empathy. I can feel his desire to listen to me, because his eyes get wide, and he is ready to interject at any second. And Dr. P really hears me, unlike the many anal New York shrinks I've tried. The ones who need two shrinks themselves and many cigarettes and keep an apple on their desk for the "perfect snack," who tell me on the phone before I even meet them to bring a check, because the consultation fee is two hundred dollars. "See ya!" I feel blessed to find this doctor after all these years. He's from the West Coast, and I keep thinking this is why he's so laid-back and doesn't look at his watch one single time during the session. There's still a formality here, though; he is the first doctor to call me Ms. Lauren, which I like because I feel his respect, and as if I am being treated as an adult; but I still can't help but chuckle when he comes out in his suit and tie and calls me into the waiting room. He's definitely not like my therapist from Santa Fe, who wore Hawaiian shirts and brought his three cats to the office.

But God bless psychiatry. It's kind of like medication. Some doctors just don't work, or you're allergic to them, or the side effects can be more harmful, or you've just got to try another. Even though I had some good doctors, I still wasn't ready to be "fixed." I had my eating disorder, my separation anxiety from my parents, and that was that. Group therapy, two private sessions a week, and even my hospital stays didn't stop me from my compulsions.

I tell Dr. P that maybe I'm thinking way too much. I feel like a psychologist myself, as if I'm reading a case study, dissecting each piece, noting the common themes running throughout various time periods. It all seems like obsessive repetition. Babble and calorie counting, and prayers to God for freedom. It went on for years in my journals. Like I was hypnotized. Especially the two years prior to surgery. I prayed to God constantly for help, for color, for light, for my prince, to rid myself of the demons, for freedom to pursue my creative endeavors and for freedom from my disorder. These requests maybe were more blatant because I was becoming physically sicker, but what is apparent to me now is that I, who didn't and still don't know if I believe in God or whatever, who joked that God resembled Obi-Wan Kenobi from *Star Wars* and thought that God was just about as real as Santa Claus, was desperately asking for help for change and, in a sense, some kind of salvation.

I begin to get in a better mood as I tell Dr. P about how I am dealing with my days. Whether it's Prozac or just having to haul myself out of this situation, I feel more in touch with humanity than ever. Even with my physical discomfort, I find myself smiling at people, naturally saying to those sharing the elevator, "Hello, how are you today?" and goggling at babies, baby-talking, "Why, hello theeeerrrreee. Aren't you a sweetie." I always used to be afraid that people in my own building and my neighborhood would know me. I wanted to be private, protect my secrets; now I go into the deli at the corner where I never looked the cashier in the eye (in case the next time I came in I wasn't buying carrots but loads of ice cream or something), and I know the three guys behind the counter, so I give them each a big smile. One remembers me and says, "I know, honey. Two cups of coffee with a wee tiny bit of skim milk and three Sweet'N Lows, right?"

And I say every time, "Now, make sure it's real hot, all right?"

He grins widely, "How hot?"

"Really, really hot!" I blush and we both crack up.

I continue telling Dr. P all about this change in me. I describe how I was sitting in a cab waiting at a red light and noticed an ordinary guy crossing the street, a little chubby, a little disheveled, with straggly long black hair and a mustache, drinking a Coke. He looked so lonely. I caught his eyes and grinned at him. He looked back at me, startled. I realized I might never have noticed him before. Why had I never had the impetus to connect with people before? The other day I saw a handicapped woman ahead of me driving a motor cart. Instead of cringing and looking away, with the thought that I should feel guilty that the world did this to her and, *Oh, I can't bear to look,* and *I can't stand this horrible world,* I stared right at her with a cheerful expression. Then I held the door open for a guy about my age who was holding a cane and looked so sad, even though the weight of this door was hard to manage for me. In fact I'm smiling most of the time now at all kinds of people, *even beautiful, tall, thin women.*

Before, when I walked the streets or, shall I say, strutted on the streets, I was very lonely myself. But I kept my eyes focused ahead with peripheral vision antennae trying to not be seen and at the same time hoping to be noticed. *Look at me/Don't look at me.* I'd walk by a bunch of construction workers and cringe in defense and repulsion if they whistled at me; but if they didn't, *did that mean I wasn't "hot"?*

I tell Dr. P about my nightly ritual meeting my parents. How I would hold my breath as I waited for my father's initial greeting and comments. Through the course of the meal, my father might make his infamous comments, "You look gorgeous," or "Your hair looks so beautiful and natural today." "You look so chiseled," or "Your hands are so elegant." "I love the way that blazer fits you perfectly." I would feel a nagging pang. *Stop looking at me. Leave me alone. Why do my looks always matter? But gotta keep it up. I will walk thirty blocks after dinner.* But if my father didn't say anything, then that might mean he didn't think I looked good and he wasn't proud of me. I became obsessed with being beautiful for my father—and I rebelled and was often obsessed with looking ugly for my father. It was the same on the New York City blocks, as I constantly searched for the external, the reactions of complete strangers, to validate my existence.

But now things are feeling different. I tell Dr. P that I'm enjoying looking at people, noticing the different types, walking without fear and that fuck-you scowl or blank expression, the "I'm so cool, don't even think about approaching me" look that I often gave off out of insecurity.

I think some of my defensiveness came partly from living in New York City and being exposed to the chaos, the stares, the crude remarks. I always felt very vulnerable as a woman in this city. Even as a little girl, just going out of the apartment seemed like going out into the jungle. I hated the whistles and leering. I have experienced so many tactless comments from men walking the streets of the city that I always felt like I needed to have my guard up.

But I was at war with my feelings of insecurity. *Is there something wrong with me for resenting the stares, the comments, the attention of men? Should I get so angry? Am I too sensitive? Am I gay?* I knew that my strong reactions came from somewhere, and over the years I could tell therapists were trying to pry something out of me, waiting for that so-called trauma that I had perhaps blocked to come to the surface. But this angered me also. *No, I was not raped or molested. No incest. Nothing. Wouldn't that just be the easy answer, Doc?* Perhaps it's a cultural thing. Perhaps it's the typical stuff, the confusion women feel with being an object of desire, and our twisted relationship with it. I can't blame anyone, not even men, because I was too guilty of playing right into all the bullshit anyhow.

I constantly got mixed messages from my father and brothers. Here they were, sensitive, kind, funny, and yet everywhere we went, they were constantly staring, gaping, and discussing various women in front of my mother and me. I couldn't ignore how they tore them apart or how they put them on pedestals. If she didn't have good legs then, "She's a mess," and if she looked like some skinny Audrey Hepburn model it was, "Oh my God, she is the most beautiful little thing. Look, look!" I would turn to see if my mother was upset, because I felt like they weren't being loyal to us. Only sometimes she would say, "Guys, stop staring." Maybe she wasn't angry because she didn't doubt that my father loved her and was faithful. But I couldn't take it. It made me angry that they were not only rude, but so weak, that a woman could make them gawk like that. That basically they appeared like desperate fools. And it always affected how I interpreted my own looks. I didn't know what I looked like in comparison, if I ever was as pretty as this one or that one. I found a jealousy within that I was not comfortable with. And in many ways I became convinced that all men were the same, that any look I received from them was some kind of judgment.

Then there was the confusing message about skinniness. When I was eighty-nine pounds and wore my rubber dresses, all the guys came on to me. In the tenth grade I was voted "the most sexy," still weighing in the low nineties. Even my father, who tried to force orange juice down my throat, still made remarks at the time like, "You are the most beautiful girl I've ever seen." I thought that perhaps I truly was only beautiful when I weighed less than ninety pounds. Especially because when I gained weight and was on the chunky side, guys seemed to lose interest, and my dad seemed displeased.

Women sometimes leered at me too, with really mean expressions, and that was even worse. I always felt really close to women, forming special bonds with them, many of whom were older, like counselors at camp or older wise women I met in Santa Fe. I was the type who could be a best friend as long as my disorder didn't get in the way. Which it often did, preventing me many times from joining in or calling back my girlfriends.

It wasn't just New York, or my dad and brothers. It was also me. I was my worst enemy. I walked the city streets feeling harassed by my thoughts. I had a big chip on my shoulder, always preoccupied with "my pain, my torment." *Ahh, it's so hard being me.* In my four years at

Barnard, even though I walked around that huge Columbia campus daily and sat on those infamous Columbia steps, where everyone hung out to mingle, and eyed an occasional man, I really only met a few guys, and nothing ever evolved because I was always too distracted and afraid. Thinking, worrying, moving, rushing. Went from class to class with obsessive thoughts circulating in my tight head. *What's my calorie intake? Did I run enough today? I feel fat. Do I have the right amount of eyeliner on? Are these shoes stupid? Oh, I'm so hungry I could faint. What should I have for dinner? Gotta get to yoga class.* Then in the last two years of college, *Did B notice me today? I can't wait a week to see him. Fuck, I can't bear it. I love him. Oh yeah, shit, gotta do that paper, which means I can't paint tonight. Maybe I should go to that party. Feel too fat. Forget it. I'll stay safe and snuggle up at home, watch an old movie . . . but maybe I'll meet someone cool if I go. But what would I wear? Will I actually make it through senior year?*

I tell this all to Dr. P—and this change I'm beginning to notice through my old writing and as I "try" to move around the city. That I want to start living for me, for what I want, to see and notice the things and people around me, instead of worrying about how everyone is perceiving me and my appearance. I want to walk around less harassed. A tumult of tears begins, and I say to Dr. P, "God, I feel like crying. I'm having some glorious revelation . . . that this whole goddamn lifetime, I wasted it all, worrying whether I was five pounds up or down, and the truth is that nobody else really cared." It was only me who truly noticed, and I made my own hell for myself. I mean, sure, it's great to have a "perfect" body. I know this, but not if it means sacrificing everything else.

I continue to Dr. P, "Nobody is walking around these days whispering, 'Gosh, Jenny got fat.' "

To this he responds, "But, Jenny, you're not fat."

19. The Big Event

*B*ig News! I call my parents to report the breakthrough: I have finally gone to the bathroom on my own. Yes, I report the news to them the way another daughter might call with news of a promotion. This new medication, Colchicine, which is actually for gout, seems to be working. Yesterday I run to the bathroom to pee and without laxatives and without even thinking I just go. Then I realize what has just occurred.

My mother is ecstatic, and then my father grabs the phone from her and says, "I can't tell you how happy I am. I really, really felt bad for you. I mean that is deprivation of something wonderful in life. I'm so excited for you. Did you scream it out of your window? I'm sure all of Third Avenue knows by now." *I can't actually believe we're talking about shitting.*

We ramble on in our good moods over the occasion, and talk about lots of things. I love when my dad is chipper on Sunday mornings. It means he might want to have a meaty chat, which could entail a wide range of conversation from the most trivial of matters like our opinions on the latest movies, to the deepest of subjects, like his life at the office. Today I dare to ask inquisitive questions. I find myself inquiring about what's going to happen to the company when they're all gone. We go into a whole long discussion on the matter. Then he tells me about the will. Only my dad would bring this up matter-of-factly, who he's giving to and all. *Thanks, Dad, cheerful thought.* He talks about his work, how hard it is sometimes. He is really opening up to me in the way he usually does with Greg, who is the listener, the consoler; and Brad too. *The boys.* I would listen but feel as if I wasn't really supposed to get involved, but today is different.

Then we get onto some more weird subjects and my dad jokes that his three favorite things in life are, "food, sex, and suntanning." He tells me how he asked a close associate the same question and his answers all had to do with fashion, like wearing a gray flannel pinstriped suit, a cashmere turtleneck, or linen pants. My three favorite things? Right now? Smiling, listening to music, *and shitting*.

My dad always asks these kind of generalized questions. We've spent whole dinners on questions like "What would your last supper be?" and Dad would tease Greg that it would be those lemon Hostess Cupcakes he always liked for no good reason, that Brad would need a six-course gourmet French meal, and Mom, a steak and her bag of peanut M&Ms. I never know my answer. I probably wouldn't want to eat anything. I wouldn't want to feel uncomfortably full. I'd want to feel empty and light when I died. Of course, after my dad brings up this kind of question, I have to ask the more morbid one, "How would you rather die, in a plane crash, by drowning, or in a fire?" And then I always think of the Holocaust and how family members would have to choose one over another for the Nazis to kill first, and how I would never have been able to do that.

When I get off the phone, I try to read the Sunday *New York Times* but fling it aside because I am too hyper. I call up Nikki and chat while adorning a letter I am sending to a friend with all these stickers of cowboy paraphernalia, cars, motorcycles, planes, and colorful doodles. I am definitely regressing back to childhood. I used to trade stickers and stationery at camp, was obsessed with collecting stickers in a huge book, and now I'm doing it again. Like a kid who sends a letter from camp to their M & D, I'm decorating an envelope with stickers, to a guy yet, what the fuck?

Nikki says, "Gosh, you're in a really good mood. Do you think, uh, em, maybe you're a bit manic?"

"Nikki, Jesus, no. I'm not manic, but this Prozac is fucking amazing, and I'm just happy."

She says, "Maybe I ought to start taking it."

I think, *But Nik, I was going to kill myself*. I was figuring out which way to do it. I'm not taking this because I wanted to. I needed to, and now I want to because I never knew I could ever feel happy again. I'm just happier than I've been in a long time and I believe that I deserve it.

Before she comes over to hang out, my dad calls me again. "I'm really so excited for you. I just had to congratulate you again on your great accomplishment and your cheerfulness," and then in baby talk he says, "I wanna buy you something."

Oh, no. I think Dad's in his "I'm so proud of you. Let's celebrate and spend some money" mode.

And then he astonishes me when he says, "Whadda ya think, a car?"

A car? *HOLY SHIT.* My dad is actually offering to buy me a car. I've wanted a real car for so long. I bought a $2,000 beat-up faded red 1975 Mercedes in Santa Fe that broke down on me every other day. Had it shipped back to New York and my dad gave it away when the mechanic in Connecticut said it was too late for the old rusted heap of junk.

I exclaim, "Dad, are you nuts? I'm not even strong enough to drive yet these days. I can't even fully sit up straight. I don't want anything; you know that. I just want to be okay."

Meanwhile, in the back of my mind I'm thinking that if I say yes to a car, he'll say, "Well, um, uh, I didn't exactly mean a car." I think to take the opposite approach, do reverse psychology.

I say, "Not today, right?" and he says that most of the stores are closed on Sunday. So I say, "Well, Dad, I'll think about it. Thanks, though."

My dad cracks me up. Whenever he's in a good mood he wants to buy a toy . . . a $1,000 toy. I used to resent this LET ME BUY YOU A LITTLE SOMETHING, because if I bought anything on my own, like from a flea market, he'd say, "What ya pay? They ripped ya off. Don't go spending my money on shit." But if he bought it, it was okay. One thing he always told me I could buy freely without boundaries (and without checking with him or my mother first) was books. He believed in learning, in culture, and in educating oneself. Art books, novels, he would buy them all for me.

Money is not a simple subject with my parents and me. It is one of those blessing-and-curse kind of issues. Even though I worked since high school—at clothing stores, exercise studios, and galleries—I still have always been totally reliant on my parents financially. On tax day, I have often joked, "Oh, it's that day. Well, I wouldn't know, because I don't really exist. But at least I have a Social Security number." I am always aware of how fortunate I am. But my parents also often reminded me of this. Especially if I pushed the limit, which they'd see when reviewing the credit card bill. My mom would call me at the apartment, "Now explain to me why it's so high this month? How could you spend all this money? What if you had to support yourself?" *Giving it freely but then throwing it in my face.* If I got annoyed my mom would then state matter-of-factly, "I'm allowed to say it, Jenny." I could definitely ring up a bill, but it wasn't like I was going out to clubs every night or big-to-do events. But somehow between food binges, books, CDs, and art supplies, I managed. And then I'd ask my mom if I could order a Ralph Lauren Collection dress, or some of the simple cashmere sweaters, and she'd exclaim, "Jenny, you're too young to be wearing such an expensive item." They were very moral. Sort of.

It was also a reason friends might resent me, and so I got into a habit of picking up the tabs for a group at dinner, a lunch date, and even for some of the guys I dated. I had a tremendous amount of guilt. But I also enjoyed making other people happy. Then my mom would continue reviewing the credit card bill and call me up and say, "Jenny, what's this place? A restaurant? Did you pay for everyone again?" And in the background my dad would raise his voice, "Is she taking all her friends out? What is this? It's my money, damn it." He was right, but if I'd rather pay for everyone than buy that watch or that bracelet, wasn't it my prerogative?

There was part of me that liked that they could take care of me, *come on, who wouldn't,* but also, more important, I knew that they liked it. My last year of college, my parents said to me, "Jenny, we don't want you to ever worry. We will always take care of you. You just keep painting." But it didn't comfort me. I actually got a wicked knot in my throat, and the feeling that I was nothing and could never amount to anything. They never told the boys this. Just like they never forced me to get in a car and said, "Now drive." They said, "Don't worry, the boys can drive you." I finally learned when I went to Santa Fe.

In my senior year of college, when I considered the possibility of working for the company (I would have wanted to be involved in home furnishings or the new paint line), I mentioned it briefly to my parents. My father would say, "Jenny, believe me, you don't want to. It's tough. There's a lot of pressure there. You don't want to put yourself in that position.

Now, it wasn't that my dad didn't think I was talented, but he always was trying to protect me. Unfortunately, both my parents ended up indulging me and it backfired. I sometimes thought that if they had put me in there, maybe it would have given more meaning to my life, maybe it would have made me stronger. I knew I could do it, if I tried. But it was never really an option. My father and uncle wanted us kids to find our own identity, so they never asked if we wished to work there.

I know I was my parents' little girl. The baby they had waited for. My father always said, "Your mother and I weren't going to stop until we had a little girl. Until we had you." It was bittersweet. A catch-22. Because even though I knew how lucky I was to be cared for, to be spoiled, it affected my self-esteem profoundly. They truly did want me to explore painting and my artistic endeavors, to have the freedom they never had. Sometimes I think it was too much freedom. And yet, *there was no freedom at all.* But I want to cry just thinking about this, how everything they did was with wholehearted good intention. To love and protect me. *But it smothered me.* And it kept me completely tied to the umbilical cord. I always vowed in therapy to discuss a plan as to how I could become self-sufficient and gain some freedom, but then I got ill, and now that I have all these doctor bills, I can only thank God for having my parents' support.

At first I was kind of angry at this car offer, even though I knew my dad was half kidding. And after taking some time to think about it, I'm no longer upset. My sickness, my surgery, it's put both my parents through the wringer. I know my father sees the change in me, the warmth coming out, the grooming starting; he's beginning to like me again and it feels wonderful. This is really his way of saying, "Thank you, God, my daughter's going to be okay."

PART THREE

1. Coming Back to Life

The other night before I went to sleep I combed my hair, looked in the tiny mirror that hangs on my bedroom wall (I have no full-length mirrors), and I thought to myself, *Jenny, you are not dying. Now pick yourself up.* I saw strands coming off in clumps. White dandruff all over it . . . *ecch, never had that in my life.* I looked at my teeth–stained yellow from acid, coffee, medication—I have been afraid of toothpaste, afraid there is something in it that I'm allergic to. I usually gag and my colon starts to spasm. *Funny, I used to be afraid there were calories in it.* But I went into the bathroom, washed my face, and brushed my teeth. Then I studied my skin, noticed the broken capillaries, dry patches, untweezed heavy eyebrows that joined at the middle, and the light mustache growing back. I have been incapable of looking at myself, sometimes because I feared the image I might see, and sometimes because the pain was so bad I couldn't even bear to stand up and stagger over to the mirror.

But now it's getting easier. I feel a bit stronger and I'm bathing every day. Washing and blow-drying my hair is the most difficult part, but it helps that I got it cut into a bob. My mom forced me to go to the hairdresser. Mary, who has been my friend and my hair doctor for the past ten years, the woman who would shape and style it so I'd look pretty for my big events, my art opening, my graduation, an important date, was so horrified at the condition of my ends that she just chopped them off. Once she had told me my hair was a wreck from all my dieting; this time she said it must be a disaster from all the medication and anesthesia. I don't mind that it's short; it's easier to care for.

I was traumatized for months by the harsh reality, the physical pain, and the fear that the surgeon did something wrong. I regretted the surgery. I thought that I was ruined forever. And then I stopped caring and I hardly got out of bed. But I awaken now, eight months later, with the realization that I may just have to come to terms with this changed body. I may have to accept that my legs roll all the way outward when I lie in bed, as if they could roll inside out and back again. And the throbbing pain—it too may be here to stay. And what to make of all those doctors telling me those are just feelings. "Ignore them, stretch, exercise, go on with your day."

Only, then I met Dr. P, who exclaimed just how serious my surgery was and that it would probably take two years to adjust to my new shape and feelings. And today at the marker test, which shows the same thing they found at Mayo, that I have impaired colon motility, the doctor also says, "You have a long recovery time ahead of you. The surgery really changed your body."

These past few weeks I spent days torturing myself looking through old photographs. I even compiled a whole group to show Dr. P—the dramatic evolution, the changes my body has gone through my whole life, from healthy little girl, to anorexic girl, to overweight girl, and then back to muscular, body-obsessed woman. He finds it amazing and helpful. I find it utterly depressing. Especially because in some of those pictures I remember thinking I looked so fat, but now I could see that I wasn't. If anything, I was sexy. I stopped looking at those photos after I ripped a whole pile of them in half.

I realize I must accept the truth. That, yes, my pelvis, my stomach, my legs are changed. I can't go back. As I eat and go two times a week to physical therapy and do my ten minutes on the Stairmaster, I have to stop thinking about what I was before, the dancer, the athlete.

·   ·   ·

About two months after the surgery, my Buddhist friend Edward drives me upstate, while I moan and cry in pain, to see a Tibetan healer who used to be a heart surgeon in Tibet. As we enter her tiny home, the smell of boiling herbs and burning incense remind me of my old yoga classes downtown and the boutiques all over the West Village of Manhattan. Then a beautiful woman with a long gray-black braid, wearing an oversized beige cotton outfit that resembles cozy pajamas, comes out from behind a divider, smiles at me, winks at Edward, and then motions for me to follow her.

She takes me into a dark candlelit room, where the hypnotic sound of rhythmic chanting plays in the background, and has me lie down on a massage table. I notice all the shelves are lined with huge bottles of plant leaves and tea bags. There is also an altar, copper and brass figurines, offering bowls, and a paper scroll resting on a low mahogany wooden chest in the corner. *I'm really hoping she'll give me some opium.*

Then she says softly, "Can I take your hand?"

I nod yes. She closes her eyes and takes my pulse. *Please, God, give her some answers. Please reveal something to her.*

I watch how graceful she is as she accentuates every simple movement. She gathers up needles, bends over me, focusing intently, and pokes them one by one into my skin with ease. I get frustrated because I don't even notice the electrical shocks through my system like I had experienced the year before my surgery during my appointments with my West Side acupuncturist. I want to feel something. Anything. Some kind of life force. But there's nothing. I lie there silently, deeply saddened, and wishing she could just say some special prayer, ring those Tibetan bells, and make me well. As she sits by my side, she tells me that it will take time for me to get better. Then I ask her if I shouldn't have had the surgery, if she would have done it.

She says to me, "What's done is done. Tibetans believe what is past is past. We are in the now. You must be in the now."

But I'm not Tibetan. I'm a Jewish American Princess.

I   want   the   past   back.

2. The Healing Seminar

Dr. P and I discuss whether I should go to an upcoming healing semi-nar that will be held here in New York at a Marriott hotel. There will be lots of lectures offered on the benefits of holistic and spiritual ap-proaches to health and healing, and I'm interested in hearing the vari-ous authors and practitioners speak about alternative medicine.

Dr. P laughs when I show him the thick brochure filled with photos of all the great "healers" and guest speakers that will be participating. He describes them as "packaged from the seventies." He says it will be great entertainment and I might as well go. I tell him I will play it up and wear my beads and some bohemian outfit. He chuckles and says, "Now, don't forget your Birkenstocks." It is fun laughing with him. But then I feel the color draining from my face when he says, "Now, a few months ago, you could have never handled something like this, when you were too vulnerable and susceptible and everyone was whispering that you were nuts." He keeps laughing and continues talking. I'm not laughing anymore.

"Nuts"? So they really did think I was nuts, huh?

I ask him if he thinks I am nuts.

"Dr. P, when I first sat there squirming in pain, describing all my symptoms, were you thinking to yourself, This girl is looney? When I leave our appointments, even now, do you think, Wow, she's a nutcase!"

He smiles, grabs a folder off his desk, and inches his chair close to me. I am nervous with him so near, afraid I might blush. As he opens the folder and points to the picture he had drawn of a woman's body on that distinct piece of yellow legal paper months ago, he asks, "Do you remember this day, Ms. Lauren?" I nod my head yes.

He continues, "From day one I knew you had been through hell and back and that there was something really big going on. I addressed the symptoms and the pain first. Remember, I gave you Demerol and

Valium. And I wanted you to get hydrated and to rest? But I knew then, you were not insane, nor will you ever be or go insane."

I ask, "So you'd tell me if I was schizophrenic?"

He says, "Ms. Lauren, you are not schizophrenic."

"Bipolar?"

"No. Absolutely not."

I ask, "But what about Frances?"

He says, "You mean Frances Farmer?"

"Yeah. Like in the movie. I just saw it. She went insane from that Hollywood world. People go insane. Maybe I've gone insane."

He laughs, "She was also an alcoholic and a drug addict, Jenny. We don't know what pills she was on or anything about what she was putting into her body."

Oh.

He says, "Now, yes, you could suffer brain damage if some horrible accident happened, and therefore lose normal functioning. But no, you are not nuts, nor will you ever be. When you came to me, you were at the end of your rope and that's basically what the doctors told me. So I'm glad you brought this up and that I could clarify this for you. It is very mature of you. Therapy like this is all about the dynamics of relationships, on all levels."

I'm not nuts. *I'm mature.*

Dr. P is brilliant and witty, but not in that I-am-God-and-will-use-lots-of-rhetoric-and-big-vocabulary-to-make-you-feel-small kind of way. Although he seems to focus on more of the scientific, mathematical, and logical side of the brain, he tolerates my New Age side. And just because I am mystical and open-minded does not mean that I am not also down-to-earth and practical. I take everything with a grain of salt. We blend well. As I continue telling him about the healing seminar, I see the laughter in his eyes. He is not doing a good job of covering it up. I call him on it flirtatiously, "Excuse me, Dr. P, do you find something funny?"

He begins to smirk, and answers, "No . . . well, uh, yeah."

"I'm getting to know you well, huh?"

He tries to stop joking and says, "A lot of people work from the top down, I work from the bottom up. I have two degrees in biology but also two degrees in psychology. I understand a lot of everything but sometimes . . . uh . . . well . . . I'm sorry for laughing."

I'm not sure what he means exactly, but I guess he's trying to say that *he thinks some of these people are full of shit.*

I explain to him that when my internist, Dr. Worthless, sent me around looking for a diagnosis, each doctor ended up referring me to another one. I had to go to all different types—a nose, ear, and throat specialist for the choking, a neurologist for the spasms, a gastroenterologist for the bathroom stuff, an endocrinologist for the amenorrhea. I see both sides of the spectrum, but at this point I'm open to insight from anybody who understands that the body is a whole, not a bunch of parts. Alternative medicine understands that everything in a person's constitution is connected, and that one internal function depends on another. If a specific area of the anatomy is causing pain, it may actually originate in another part. For instance, scar tissue can affect the entire fascia (the layer beneath the skin and muscles). So, in my case, if my abdomen is filled with really tight scar tissue from my surgery, it can cause everything to feel uncomfortable, my neck muscles to spasm, and make it difficult to take a deep breath from my diaphragm. If I can't take a deep breath and get oxygen circulating, then the lymphatic system doesn't drain and the liver, the spleen, and the kidneys don't do their jobs as well. Then weakness and other immune problems result. One thing plays off another. I've always been aware of this. Our bodies give us clues all the time.

I started doing yoga when I was fourteen, and by the time I was looking for my diagnosis, I was getting all kinds of hints about what was going on with my body from my practice. I would tell my internist Dr. W that my legs would go limp during inversions and that after doing a shoulder stand, which supposedly massages the thyroid, I would get all tingly and weak. I explained that when I did breath of fire, where you breathe in and out through your nose to strengthen and purify your colon and stomach muscles, my belly would distend, my muscles go lax, and mainly, that I couldn't do half the poses I'd been doing for ten years. Dr. W would say, "I do yoga." But then he'd still look at me blankly, as if my reporting these sensations had no relevance.

But then after getting the diagnosis of the enterocele, Dr. W began to speak in my language. He told me to sit in child's pose; he actually didn't even know the name, but he showed me the position, and told me that it helps pick up the intestine. *It's a little late, Doc.* Then to top it off, he tried to address my ass twitch in a spiritual vein. He asked, "Do you ever tell these spasms to fuck off? Why don't you just try clapping your hands and say STOP."

Dr. P tells me that I should be open to help and getting information, but that, yes, I should keep that "grain of salt" attitude. Just be a spectator, he advises. Then I report the gruesome details from a visit yesterday to my gynecologist, where I was informed that lots of woman suffer from lower back problems because the stool just sits there and pushes on the uterus so they get that bearing-down feeling that I still have. She thinks this is exactly what is happening with me. She says I should get myself some gloves and stick my hands in my vagina to push from that direction on the stool to get it out. *Well, let me just hurry and get a pair. Maybe a few in different colors.* The fact that I can talk about the most intimate things with Dr. P is truly a blessing.

A month later I attend the three-day intensive seminar at the Marriott Marquis in the theater district. It is a huge festival of love with yes, a lot of crystals, Birkenstocks, and juicers for sale. The place is inundated with searching souls, people who float from lecture to lecture looking for the meaning of life, illness, and death. And I am definitely one of them, dressed all in white, wearing sandals, and covered with translucent necklaces. The celebrity authors spark an illuminating electricity throughout the hotel. There are lectures on the benefits of acupuncture and chiropractic treatments, as well as more general ones on global consciousness and the healing of America. There are discussions about life and death, and a consistent implication is made that illness is a metaphor for unhappiness. Or the soul's wish to move on to another level. Some of the concepts frighten me. I have asked myself constantly whether I made this happen. And I do, on some very basic level, believe I have caused my illness. Whether it's true or not, it's a lot to take on. When I get home, the aftermath from my overanalytical philosophical three-day circus is great confusion. I am also rather nauseous, like after I've had too much flaxseed oil on my salad or drunk too many vegetable tonics.

The following week in therapy, I tell Dr. P about one of the lectures I attended on the nature of illness, led by a cancer specialist. A bald woman in the audience had addressed the doctor. "I have breast cancer and I find myself feeling pretty lousy and depressed most of the time. I'm not having such positive thoughts. Will this keep me from healing?"

The doctor said, "Yes. Most likely." And then went on to answer the next person's raised hand.

Dr. P gets angry and says emphatically, "That's exactly my problem with many of these so-called experts on healing. They end up making people feel like it's their fault they're going to die, or their fault they got sick. Which really in the end does not make anybody get healthier. They have to be careful of the impact they have on people. It can be very negative too."

I'm torn. Did my phobias, my fears, and my narcissistic obsessions cause me to have this crisis occur? *Does that mean my plane's gonna crash 'cause I fear flying?* On the flip side, *how inspiring!* If I address these issues, overcome the bulimia, the fears, the aching of desire, I can heal and have a better life.

The woman's question is the core issue that the medical doctors, alternative health specialists, psychologists, and patients grapple with all the time.

Most of the speakers said to worry less and to think positive. But I got the greatest kick out of one lecture when a fuzzy-bearded guy said to get rid of the clock radio by the bed, the blow dryer, the cellular, the heating pads, the plastic containers, and the bacteria-harboring pets. Next, he instructed, buy yourself flowers (but watch the mold), love and accept your body (but, yes, eating sprouts really would be ideal, and watch that ice cream, don't have caffeine, and sugar is poison!), *oh, and do not forget to protect that childlike spirit of yours.*

I joke with Dr. P that Fuzzy Beard ought to drink a little white wine, smoke a few cigarettes, and chill out. We squeal with laughter at Fuzzy Beard's expense. The only thing I don't tell Dr. P is that I've also decided to get rid of my clock radio. Just in case.

3. Falling in Love with My Doctor

Dr. P keeps a picture of Cupid and Psyche as his screen saver. He listens to Tangerine Dream music, one of my favorites. He is a Stanley Kubrick fan. He has my Christmas card up, with only a few other photos, on his wall. He was incredibly enthusiastic when I showed him slides of my artwork. I like the way he looks when he's not wearing a suit, in his cobalt blue button-down, or his black V-necked sweater. *I'm sorry, but Dr. P is cool.* And I am so afraid that I'm falling in love with him. I mean he's the only male presence around me these days, besides my father and brothers, of course. But I become annoyed when Nikki laughs flirtatiously and asks, "How's Dr. P? I just have a feeling about you two."

And then my mother occasionally jokes, "How's your boyfriend?" referring to Dr. P, and I get really angry.

I tell them both not to do this. Don't turn something and someone very important to me into a "love thing," into something ugly, well, I mean, something inappropriate. And I don't want to go up to the hospital and start blushing (which I do). Don't put ideas into my head. Because deep down I am very vulnerable to what people suggest—and to the fact that this man is saving me.

Is it normal to fall in love with your shrink? I mean it's not really love, but I do look forward to our session as if it's a date. In fact, I can't wait to see him, the man who has no ring on his finger. But I purposely don't fix myself up or put makeup on or anything because, God forbid, he might think I have a crush on him. *Well, Doc, I have something to tell you. I have the hots for you and I want to have your baby.*

I consider his possible responses. His clinical response, "Well that's okay, it's very natural," or my nightmare response, "Well, this is a problem, Jenny. I can't see you anymore," or the fairy-tales-can-come-true one, "Well, gosh, how about a movie tomorrow night?"

Then again, he really might be married. I can't ask him. It's not my place to ask him anything. At least I gathered up the courage to find out his astrological sign. *Because that's very important.* When I inquired, he turned red and chuckled. I realized my question was probably inappropriate. I downplayed it, "Uh . . . thought you might be Pisces, they all seem to understand me. Instant compatibility, but who the hell knows about all that astrology crap." We talked more, about some deeper stuff, and at the end of the session, Dr. P says, "By the way, I'm an Aquarius."

Does Dr. P know I'm starting to have fantasies about him? He must know. This must happen all the time. I wonder if he just sees me as a needy little puppy craving love and affection. But I don't think I'm as pathetic as I was.

I tell Dr. P that more than anything I hate feeling needy, that I hated panting at the door of his unit, waiting for my parents to visit me in the hospital. This year has been humiliating. Then I related those same feelings with the ones I always had about romantic relationships, that it's all based on a narcissistic desire to be loved, to be approved, like, "Hey, you're okay, and you think I'm okay, so now we're worth something." I hate being that vulnerable. I think that's why I used my other behavior, my obsession with food and exercise, because then I didn't have to *need* anyone. Needing means wanting, and wanting means usually not getting. At least not getting enough.

Relationships have always been a scary concept to me. I watched both my brothers and my best friends invest years at a time in a significant other, only to hurt and bleed and move on one day. For years you mold your life around someone else; you share, you learn, you become attached, addicted—until it's over. Then your heart is broken, you make changes, you kind of heal, and then you just move on to the next. I've watched everyone fall in love, as I remain uninvolved (perhaps infatuated with someone, or some idea of someone), and they all ask me my advice. Somehow I give pretty good feedback for someone who doesn't have the experience, hasn't been in a relationship longer than a few months.

Is it Dr. P's presence that is soothing me—the fact that he tells me I am smart, that I have a lot going for me, and the flush I see on his face sometimes when I enter his office and we smile as we greet one another? Where does it go from here? For how long will he see me, when will he abandon me? Why do I fear abandonment? My parents never abandoned me as a child. I try to think *what happened? Come on, Jenny, what happened as a child, what perverse thing are you not recalling?* Have I blocked out some hideous crime or injustice done to me? No, no, no, I was never hurt, or neglected, except maybe not heard at the dinner table. And still I was able to squirm my voice into the conversation and sometimes even dominate the conversation. Why am I so vulnerable, so sensitive to the effects of others, to the effect of a man?

This is very uncool of me to not respect boundaries. I did it with B too. I tend to do it with older men. I think it's because I find them strong, wise, and passionate about what they do. They're lustful for life. I mean, look what I grew up with. My dad, my uncle . . . But I think it's also because many older men have already dealt with their own demons. I think boundaries are a load of crap anyhow.

And Dr. P is fucking brilliant. Being tall, dark, and handsome only adds to his mystique. He also has a sensuality in the way he moves and the way he speaks. He gets beeped and I listen to him return the call in this almost "diplomatic" way, like "Hi, it's Dr. P?" in this warm, open way, as if he's asking, "What can I do for you?" or "What is it you need?" all with one greeting. So I ask myself how am I not to fall in love with this man? I don't think he feels any attraction for me. But he seems to be intrigued by my stories, my insights. I tell myself, *Jenny, don't do this.*

Don't get these sick ideas in your head. You can love him, but love him for saving you, for listening to you, for believing in you, and for being your doctor.

But I already worry about him, like when he gets on a plane, I pray he'll have a safe trip. Or I worry that he works too hard and doesn't have any free time, and does nothing for himself. Maybe he's having the time of his life. But that's what's so strange about therapy. You feel close to this person and you can't really ask, "How are you? What'd you do this weekend? Oh, here's a check for listening."

I want to ask him, "Are you a happy person? What do you like to do besides this? Do you have brothers and sisters? Where are you from? What do you believe in? When were you first in love?"

Sometimes I wish I could "shoot the shit" and just come to see him as if I were normal, a friend. And there is part of me that doesn't want to know. Doesn't want to know if he goes home to a wife, has a girlfriend, a boyfriend. I like the unknown, and to find out about his soul just by the way he responds to my words and thoughts, and the way he treats me. Maybe one day we really will be friends, or he will just be the great doctor who helped me through a very dark time in my life.

4. The Audition

When I was nine years old and in the fourth grade, my mother picked me up from Dalton one afternoon to bring me and my friend Eliza to Lincoln Center for our auditions at the School of American Ballet, the most prestigious ballet institute in the country. I don't think I can remember ever wanting anything more in my life than to make it into that school. For years I dreamed of dancing, performing, and becoming the likes of Merrill Ashley, or Maria Tallchief. But my mother had warned me for months not to be upset if I didn't get accepted, because she had heard that it was very tough, and that they looked for certain body types.

She explained that sometimes even the most talented young dancers weren't accepted because they didn't have enough of a turnout, or because their height wasn't right, or because their body structure wasn't one of a future ballerina. She said that it was like breeding horses there. In fact, she said, it would be worse if I got in and then they told me to leave at thirteen, because a lot of girls were kicked out when they start going through puberty and their bodies begin changing. My mother had done her research, and she was already afraid for me.

Still, I prayed and prayed that I would get in. Maybe I would. After all, my ballet teacher, Nina from the Harkness School, told my mother that I was a fine dancer. I loved her classes, and sometimes I even became sad thinking of leaving her for SAB. But if I got in I knew I wouldn't be that upset.

When my mother, Eliza, and I entered the backstage of the center, there were dancers scattered all over the fluorescent-lit hallways. There were children, teenagers, women, and men clad in leotards and tights, hanging all about. People's bodies were contorted in all different positions; legs were leaning high up onto the walls, backs were bent over, and arms were stretched toward the ground. There were women sitting in splits and straddles, smoking or eating yogurt and conversing with one another. Children came leaping and pirouetting by, and classical music could be heard emanating from the rooms where dance classes and auditions were taking place. I was overwhelmed. But any excitement I had felt turned into fear.

Eliza and I were led to a dressing room where other young girls were changing. I had a knot in my throat as I took out my new black Capezio leotard and pink cotton tights that my mother and I bought the prior weekend. I was going to wear my old ballet slippers, though. They were my magical shoes, broken in to my feet and to the way I liked to move. I couldn't take a chance using a different pair. I hurried to put on my outfit so I could rush to warm up. Eliza and I met my mother outside and she pointed us toward the room where we would be auditioning. She said she'd be nearby and headed to the corner where other mothers were standing about.

Eliza and I didn't say a thing to each other while we stretched. There were at least forty girls hanging out by the entrance. They varied in age and size, some were tiny, some chunky. A woman with a Russian accent, dressed in a long black skirt and tall boots, and holding a pointing stick, walked by and entered the studio. Within minutes, we were divided into groups by a tall male and told we would begin shortly, that our gum should be spit out, and that any extra layers, such as sweatshirts or plastic shorts (these are worn by many dancers to force perspiration to lose water weight) should be taken off so our bodies could be seen entirely. Although I was already concerned about my figure at that point, I was more worried that my dancing ability wouldn't be quite up to par than I was about my physique. *Imagine that.*

When Eliza and my group were called in, we entered the huge mirrored space and were led to a barre that surrounded the walls of the large room. The Russian woman stood at the front, and a small group of adults sat in one corner. The woman did not say a thing to us and then nodded to the pianist to begin playing. Then she spoke, "First position, and plié . . . one . . . two . . . three and relevé one . . . two . . . three and grand plié . . . one . . . two . . . three . . ."

We followed her lead as if we were taking class. I recall holding my breath for most of the tryout and not being able to understand her thick accent and messing up some of the exercises. I didn't feel comfortable at all. Whatever confidence I had was slipping away. By the time we were doing our adagios in the center I was very frustrated. I had no way of telling if I was doing a good job. The woman didn't smile at any of us the way Nina did. I didn't feel any joy when I heard the music. I wanted it just to be done with. I was sure I wouldn't get in.

But somehow Eliza and I were both called back. We were to wait until all the groups performed and return afterward with the others who were also chosen.

After sweating through the whole rigmarole again, we remained hovering outside the studio anxiously.

The minutes were endless, and the kids around me were all yapping nervously.

I couldn't speak.

The tall male came out of the room, and everyone gathered around. He pointed to her and her, and she and she, and Sarah, and Tanya, and Felicia and . . . suddenly the visions of myself twirling around under spotlights and being lifted into the sky by a handsome chiseled male among falling artificial snowflakes, and getting presented with large bouquets of red roses, and hearing whistles and deep-pitched "Bravos" and bowing over and over to the sounds of the enthusiastic clapping of the huge audience in Lincoln Center turned to a pale ominous screen and to a blank silence. There were no more shouts of "Lauren, yeah . . . Lauren!" No whispers, "She dances like a nightingale." There were no proud parents smiling from afar or bragging to the couple standing next to them, "Ever since she was young, she wanted to be a ballerina. Her dream came true."

What a surprise! I didn't get in. Oh, yeah, and Eliza did.

Oddly enough, after dropping Eliza off, I didn't cry to my mother on the way home. But I remained silent the entire evening through dinner until I went to sleep. I lay in bed rehashing the audition in my mind. *What did I do wrong? Was it when we went across the floor, did I not jump high enough? Was I not graceful enough, even though my parents always say I am? Was it the size of my thighs?* When I exhausted myself silly, I finally found the one positive aspect about not being accepted to SAB. I could still attend Nina's classes and wouldn't feel badly about saying good-bye. She liked me and she thought I was a good dancer. She even winked at me and said, "Beautiful, Jenny," almost every day. But still, maybe I'd audition again the next year. Try again. There was nothing to lose with making another attempt. My dreams weren't completely squashed, were they?

I have to say that I think I handled the letdown and the rejection like a mature little woman. But the effects caught up relatively quickly. Within only a few months' time, I would start my nearly lifelong career of starving myself. *Wrong body type, huh? I'll show them.*

5. Finding Some Answers

Somehow I manage at nine months and two weeks since the surgery to put on a pair of my new golden Sierra Asic running shoes and walk the five long avenues to the 72nd Street entrance of the park. It is difficult, and I have moments of frustration, but when I get to the lower loop I feel more hopeful. I just want to stay in the park and listen to my Walkman playing the Deep Forest tape. Instead of pounding the pavement, I let myself stand there to watch and think. The park is cold and sparse on this Saturday morning, and there aren't many runners, so I take the time to reflect. I so badly wish I could just start running, but I find myself looking into the sky and thanking God for at least getting me this far.

In the past I would walk or run, focused ahead on the task I had to do. I didn't notice most people or the landscape because I was working hard, every ounce of my energy had to be put into my workout; fear was alive and kicking and I had to flee from it. And I didn't talk to God the way I did today. At the end of my yoga classes I would *Om* three times with everyone else, but I would be thinking, *Let's go already.* I didn't look into the eyes of other people sitting in lotus position bowing *Namaste* to one another. It made me embarrassed, and it seemed trendy. I was never once happy when I *om'd*; in fact it left me hurting, yearning, sad. I wonder why I never thought to thank God in those *oms* for what I had.

My dad always believed in God, and I always wondered how such a logical man could believe in Obi-Wan Kenobi. I didn't get it. *I want tangible proof, Dad!* I also thought it had to be a Jewish God, or a Catholic God, or a Buddha, and that made it seem so confusing. *If there's a God, why do we all believe in separate ones, why is religion divided, and why does it cause wars and prejudice and hatred, Daddy? Why can't we eat bacon, my friend Lisa does?* Judaism is my heritage and my culture, not the foundation for what I necessarily believe in.

I know a lot of us find God when we become ill. I realize that this is common, but that is because in our deepest pain we have to let go. We let go of needing to deny, of needing to be practical. We have no other choice but to begin believing and there is nothing wrong with that. I think I was afraid to believe in God, because maybe then it meant I thought I was special, or that I was needy. And if I was educated, how could I believe in something so intangible, so hyped, and so damn inconcrete? The thing I realize is that, who cares why or what or how we believe? Belief is the strongest power we have; in a sense, it is finding some confidence within and allowing our hope to live. It hasn't been easy for me, but I'd rather believe than not, because not believing is saying that you basically have it all figured out, and I don't.

6. Going Away

A few months ago, when I first started downing whole bottles of white wine at night, I told Nikki that I was afraid I was turning into an alcoholic. She said, "Fur, you're too neurotic to be an alcoholic. You'll also get bored."

Well, she's right. I've had enough.

In Connecticut this weekend, as I sit on the rocker under the portal, looking out into the distance at the greenery and the beautiful budding flowers of June and sipping wine while I wait for my mom to serve my dad and me lunch, I realize this has to end. It's already a year since my surgery, and I've been bullshitting and wasting time. I'm not getting well.

Over a meal of tuna salad, lettuce, fresh tomatoes from our garden, and *potato chips* (yes, I now eat it all, even the mayo, the olive oil, and I save room for an ice cream sandwich for dessert), I tell my parents that something is still really wrong. I should be able to walk and sit comfortably, and I need help. I would like to go somewhere to get better, a physical rehabilitation center, a place to address the physical pain and get stronger. I am floundering in New York and Connecticut. And drinking too much, I tell them as I pour more liquid into the glass and my dad says, "Jenny, that's enough."

My mom suggests the Canyon Ranch Health Spa in Arizona. She tells me that she's been thinking about it, that maybe they have some kind of program. I've been there before, and each time I joined the other type A personalities and participated in every single class that was offered, from the walk at 6 A.M. up to Restorative Yoga at 5 P.M. But going now would be completely different. Whoa. Can I handle that?

The lure of getting in shape, even with this physical pain, is enough for me. After dessert, I return to my rocker with my freshly filled wineglass (it may be one of my last) and the cordless phone. As I become increasingly more tipsy and excited I slur my questions to the reservationist, who is eager to make some kind of scenario work for me. Yes, they have a physical therapist on call that I can see daily (but I will have to pay extra), and they have a newly built Health and Healing center that offers twenty-four-hour medical coverage, acupuncture treatments, and nutrition consultations. *I smell the dry desert air already.* I hang up so I can report in to my parents and do some major begging. *But am I sure I want to give up the wine?* Alcohol is not allowed on the premises. *Oh, well, I knew it would have to end.* When I fill my parents in on the details, my father is hesitant at first because it is ridiculously expensive, but it doesn't take much persistence on my part. God knows they'd do anything to stop me from self-destructing. My dad says, "If it can help you, then okay. Just don't expect a quick fix." *Wow, I must really look bad.* I call back an hour later and book my trip. During the rest of the weekend, I am more hyper than I've been in a long time, as I dream of becoming toned and strong, of being able to feel my body again, of miracles.

Within a few days, I say a sentimental good-bye to Dr. P (promising to e-mail him religiously), to my family, to Nikki, and to alcohol, and I am on a plane to Tucson, Arizona, for a one-month visit at Canyon Ranch.

7. Tucson

Ah, the sun-drenched desert, the exotic green plant life, the ever-changing sky, the subtle contours of the surrounding Catalina Mountains. Ah, the adobe homes made from the earth, the miraculous monsoons, and the little jackrabbits and lizards. Just being back in the Southwest is making me high. *Who needs alcohol?*

I used to feel anguish over the beauty of a place, because it made me want. What, I don't know. *But, oh, such a deep ache I felt.* Now, instead of those times in Santa Fe when I would feel overwhelmed by the open sky, it's as if the desert is welcoming me with wide arms. I think it kind of helps that I'm at a resort, a very pretty one, no doubt, and that all the people at Canyon Ranch are so friendly. There is a constant buzz of activity and energy. The whole team that works here is spunky, from program coordinators who help plan your days to exercise instructors and massage therapists. And most of the hotel guests are enthusiastic too. It's like being at summer camp.

But the first week isn't that easy for me. I am relieved to be away from New York City and the noise from the year, but I am angry that I can't just go hop right on into a Funk Aerobics class or even *walk* comfortably to the studio. I hear a Madonna song coming from one of the exercise rooms and I feel the grief welling up. I also have to do a lot of storytelling to all the medical staff at the Health and Healing Center, as well as to the instructors and healing therapists, but I know it's necessary so they can set up an appropriate program for me. After a while I actually *want* to explain my situation. Especially because I'm embarrassed to be staying here for so long. First of all, it's very expensive and second, I'm not using it as a fat camp. "I'm not here to lose weight," I say, "but to get well." (Although, yes, about ten pounds would be beneficial . . . I've become *just a bit bloated*.) I give long, detailed accounts to the receptionists, the servers in the dining room, and even the maids. They all say, "Poor thing. Poor thing."

I work with Naomi, an incredible yoga teacher with a tiny, solid body and a long, white-gray mane of hair. She wears a lot of batik tops, teaches Pilates, and is a flamenco and salsa dancer. She is the perfect instructor to work with because she has suffered many injuries from all her years of wear and tear. She has a toolbox of knowledge and insight to help me. The first time we meet she takes me up to the Yoga Dome, which is where most of the Spiritual classes are offered. I am so happy to look out the triangular window at the mountain view instead of at mirrors, like they have in all the other studio rooms. I lie down on a mat on the wooden floor, and she guides me through subtle body movements and breathing techniques. She has me start with just curling and uncurling my fingers. She plans to use a movement therapy called Somatics, which helps to unlock negative cell memory trapped in the body. Naomi says that what I've gone through is a horrible trauma and that I must not overdo it with exercise or force myself to heal. She says she wants to treat me gently. It's as if I am a baby just learning to use my body, and I need to retrain my muscles very slowly and ease them into recovery. I laugh as I think of sprinting a third time around the Central Park Reservoir, squeezing my ass as hard as I can. *Gentle. Uh-huh. Okay.* Naomi becomes a good friend and my second week there she takes me off "campus" to go see the movie *There's Something About Mary,* and we giggle together the whole way through.

I also see a physical therapist twice a week. When I meet Bob at the Health and Healing Center, I grin immediately. He reminds me of a golf instructor. He wears a polo knit and L. L. Bean shorts, eyeglasses, and is balding. As Bob helps me stretch, and suggests I "brace" my tummy (which means tighten or whatever I can do to feel it), he smiles brightly and tells me about his three daughters. Sometimes he has to change our session times because he has to drive his oldest one up to Tempe for her high school soccer games. We laugh a lot during our sessions. With all these private ones, it's impossible not to bond with these people. And unlike other guests, who usually leave after a week, they all know I am staying longer. They also can tell I'm basically up shit creek.

Even though I'm not strong enough to do hard-core laps, I love getting in the pool. The water is soothing. Every morning I attend the gentle swim class that is recommended for those who suffer from painful joints and arthritis. I am the only twenty-six-year-old among the sixty-plus group.

I go to tai chi or chi gong in the afternoons, although I can barely balance to get any chi moving. I still find the process of trying distracting enough to help me with some of the pain—along with Tad, a tall, dark instructor who resembles Keanu Reeves. At the end of the first class, when I start bawling because I am mortified that I can't even stand upright and feel like a fat, mushy whale in front of him, he comes over to me and says, "Hey, you look like you need a hug."

I let him wrap his arms around me (although I wonder how many girls he offers his hugs to but . . . *so what*). I become a regular in all of his classes. I am shocked to discover in his yoga session that I have remained as flexible as a rubber band even though I feel as if I have nothing supporting me from my center. I'm still like a rag doll, and suffer the excruciating joint pain, but in order to get to watch Tad and receive a soft massage from him when class winds down, I manage to bear it.

Then there's Suzanne, an acupuncturist who I see two times a week. She is pretty and bohemian-looking with many braids down her back. Now *she* is really fascinated by my situation. To many of the healing therapists I am a great project. I am the epitome of a person whose chi and energy flow is very fucked up. She enthusiastically sticks needles along all the meridian spots in my body to help me heal. I try to read a book on Chinese medicine that explains all this. Like how my pulse can give a reading of what's going on with my internal organs. How there is too much heat or dampness in my spleen, liver, or kidney . . . but I just can't grasp it. I figure, I can leave it up to her. And I appreciate it when she fastens a small plastic cuff on my earlobe that I wear for days to help me with my sugar cravings. But I still have a double portion of the chocolate frozen yogurt at lunch and dinner.

Speaking of which, the food is great here. I eat very balanced meals, cereal with fruit in the morning, protein, veggies, a small bit of grain and salad for the other meals with a yummy low-fat dessert. The servers are all friendly, and one of the guys is so gorgeous that I pray every day he will be my waiter, but he's always assigned to another table. Tara is usually my server and is very cool to chat with. I attribute having ingested my last Sweet'N Low ever in this dining room because of her. She's studying to become a nutritionist, and she brings me a book about the dangers of artificial sweeteners. After years of putting it on everything, even my fruit, since I was nine years old, I can't help but wonder if it has harmed me. I read that it's actually linked to irritable bowel syndrome (digestive and *bathroom problems* of a wide range). Yikes!

I consult with a doctor at the Health and Healing Center who tells me that my bowels are suffering from a yeast syndrome (meaning I lack the good intestinal flora and have too much of the other). He suggests I take digestive enzymes and acidophilus to help add some healthy bacteria. I follow his advice because the truth is, even with the Zantac antacid that I swallow every morning, I still feel my whole esophagus close up and have difficulty breathing as my meal goes down.

I try other healing treatments that the ranch offers, but I respond the most positively to Bella's craniosacral work. Two late afternoons a week I go to see her so she can simply place her hands on my head or on my spine for an hour. It seems like she's doing absolutely nothing, but during the sessions I get lightheaded and feel as if bones and muscles are shifting all over my body. It's almost like voodoo. Afterward I am much more relaxed and head to dinner excited to be a bit more pain-free and to chat with the servers. One teenager who delivers my broiled trout and steamed vegetables is a born-again Christian. Finding faith is what got him off drugs. He tells me all about it and invites me to his religion class. I go with him one night. *Why the hell not? It can't hurt to learn something new.*

A few weeks later, without having had any alcohol, I look in the mirror and I finally recognize my face. And I'm back stretching in a yoga class looking out to the mountains and I feel a returning surge of energy when I am doing a pose, and the sensuality and natural flow of motion comes with a little more ease. But I still wake up most mornings depressed after having disturbing dreams throughout the night.

I think it's a good sign, though, that I'm feeling attracted to men again. The physical movement, breathing and relaxation techniques, and the sun and beauty here must be helping to unlock my sensuality.

Sometimes at night, when I play soft music in my room, I think about Dr. P and miss our conversations. I tell him this in one of my weekly e-mail updates that I address to "Sweet Doctor." I even joke about my longing for him and ask him to marry me. When he writes me back diligently, he responds with his usual balance of professionalism and warmth. He doesn't answer yes or no, but tells me he is happy I sound like I'm doing so well.

I am getting a bit stronger physically, although I have a major setback after I try a Funk Aerobic class one morning. I have to spend the rest of the day in bed. My acupuncturist warned me that I was doing too much, and she was right. So I just stick to the series of short weightlifting routines an exercise physiologist prescribed. I meet him every other day and push myself through it. *After fifteen minutes I can't even lift my water bottle.*

In the afternoon during my breaks, I go visit Kate, a program coordinator who I really hit it off with. She used to date a guy from Santa Fe, is easy to talk to, and we chat about life and the books she's reading on self-improvement. She brings in Iyanla Vanzant's *In the Meantime: Finding Yourself and the Love You Want* for me. *She's obviously still working on getting over that guy.* I confess to her my crush on Tad, the tai chi/yoga teacher.

My third week there, Tad invites me to a party. I'm psyched. I drink a bit of white wine there, and before you know it I am back at his place lying with him on his bearskin rug. It is a beautiful hour. Nothing gets too serious, we just do some yoga. *Uh-huh.*

Shortly after that, I find out Tad also likes to bring home one of the program coordinators, as well as other guests. What should I have expected? He also has a thing for hallucinogenic plants. I know this type. Met him in Santa Fe. It's okay. I get over it after I grieve and bitch to Kate, Suzanne, Bella, Bob, and Naomi. And to some of my massage therapists and the receptionists. But his name usually stays unrevealed, of course.

Then, while I'm still trying to get Tad out of my system, I end up meeting the gorgeous waiter. In the pool. He is on a break from working in the dining room. I am doing some slow laps. We have noticed each other before but never really spoken. I make the effort while I have the chance. Embarrassed to get out and expose my bathing-suit-clad body and mushy thighs, I smile from the ledge, bat my eyes, and get his attention.

"Hey, do you think you can grab me some flippers?"

He smiles and politely says, "Sure, of course."

Then he jumps in, dunks his head, and swims over to me. He says he's seen me for a while. He asks why I've stayed so long. I explain to him that I'm doing physical rehabilitation. We talk for an hour. He asks me what music I like. I tell him Sarah McLachlan, Fleetwood Mac, Sting. "Basically all of it," I say, "but not heavy metal. It's too angry." He laughs and says, "I agree." He was a music major in college. He graduated but still needs to finish his thesis on classical music. I'm impressed. His name is Kyle and he is gorgeous, a Polo model–athletic–Princeton type, with sandy brown hair and a swimmer's build. He is nice, very nice. The polite, brought-up-well-by-the-parents nice.

He starts showing up at the pool every day an hour after lunchtime when I am there. It surprises me that he seems to be hoping to see me, that we find so much to talk about. One day he asks, "So do you have a scar?"

"Yep. A big one," I say.

"Can I see it?" I am confused by his curiosity. But then he says, "I'll show you my scar if you show me yours." And then he lifts out his left hand and I notice for the first time that he is missing a pinky. He explains that he got it caught in a washing machine when he was three.

He was pretty lucky not to have lost his whole hand. When we get out of the water, I desperately try to wrap a towel around my bottom before he has a chance to check me out. And then I clandestinely undo the snaps from my Victoria's Secret body suit (which I wear instead of a normal suit because it's more pliable and less tight around the pelvis) and I whip it up quickly and show him the vertical scar up my belly.

I say, "Here. See? Pretty bad, huh?"

He says, "Yeah. Awww, I'm sorry you had to go through that." There is a sweetness that exists between us, and a softness about him that takes my breath away. We make plans to go to the movies.

I end up going with Kate to hear him play his guitar at a coffee shop instead. I am blown away by his talent. When he does a great version of Sarah McLachlan's "Ice Cream," I melt.

I stay at the ranch for one and a half months. I can't get enough of the place. It's like one big gigantic hug. Deep down I know something is very wrong. Even though I go through the motions of doing all the activities, I still suffer from great physical discomfort. After only ten minutes on the stationary bike I feel as if my ribs are pulling my whole body apart. Forget that I can't even feel my ass. In truth, none of my muscles feel connected. But I cherish the people, the friendliness, and feeling like part of a community. My spirit is fighting to get well. This environment is truly helping and, miracle of miracles, I'm even going to the bathroom about twice a week.

I decide I want to stay in Tucson for a while so I can continue working with some of my therapists. I also have a budding romance with Kyle, but the real reason is I just don't want to go home, back to the scene of the crime.

I come up with a proposal to teach an art class at the ranch. Even though they already offer watercolor and pottery, I propose something freer, more like art therapy. I will get lots of different supplies: paints, crayons, beads, paper, origami, Magic Markers. It will be like a kindergarten for adults. It will be a hands-on exploration for all the people who forgot to keep their creative juices flowing. For everyone who stopped drawing a long time ago because their art teacher once told them their tree didn't look like a tree. It will be especially for those who say, "I can't draw. Only stick figures." Yeah. I'm going to do this. After all, the whole place is like one big playground. I name my class Art Feast. People can binge on art materials, not food or exercise. It will be perfect for Canyon Ranch, especially because their motto these days is that the road to good health is to create a balance of body, mind, and spirit.

I meet with the owner of the ranch, thank him for everything, and tell him I'd really like to be part of his team. I hand my proposal to him all typed up. He reads it and we have a great talk. Then he sends me to Human Resources, where I meet Dorothy, the woman in charge of Special Events and Activities. She likes what I have to say and tells me to give her some time so she can see if this class could fit into the schedule.

Originally I was supposed to leave Sunday, but after I tell my parents on the phone how great I'm feeling, they agree to let me stay two more weeks. I haven't mentioned anything about my class, but I figure we can talk about it the coming weekend when we'll all be attending a family friend's wedding in Colorado Springs.

When I arrive at the Broodmoor Hotel I greet my whole family in my parents' room and they are suddenly very happy to let me stay longer at the ranch.

My dad exclaims, "You look incredible. Wow."

Greg is in from LA too, and says, "Jenny, you got into shape fast. You're looking like you used to."

My mom smiles and says, "Did you find a dress to wear tonight? If not, you can borrow one from me. But it may be too large."

Brad and Amy just give me big hugs. Neither one ever mentions a thing about my appearance. And I'm always appreciative of their sensitivity about not focusing on my looks anymore, because they know it has only screwed me up in the past.

I have found a dress to wear. I went to a mall in Phoenix with Kate and found two cheap dresses and tight cardigans from Dillard's that will do the job. I was surprised that I fit into a size 6. I know I have lost some weight but I haven't paid that much attention to it. I'm usually in too much pain during my short workouts to care. Anyhow, I still am not toned. I don't know what Greg is talking about. I don't look like I used to. And I sure as hell don't feel like I did.

The day of the wedding I slip on a black sleeveless dress with slits up the side, throw on a petite black cardigan that ties midchest with a satin bow, and put on a pair of simple black heels. I blow-dry my hair straight, do my makeup with only a bit of eyeliner and blush. But by the time I am done I am in so much discomfort from the effort that I have to lie down on my hotel room bed and rest for half an hour. I want to cry. But I choose to take a Valium instead. This is going to be a long night.

Finally I get up, redo my eyeliner, and go downstairs where everyone is waiting. I smile largely. *Yes, I'm here. I made it.* My dad shakes his head and sighs when I come toward them, saying, "Gorgeous. Just gorgeous, my daughter, Jesus." Then he jokes, "I'm glad I told you to go to that place," taking credit for the idea. I think to myself, *Let him enjoy this me, because it probably won't last for long.*

After the ceremony I stand proud for the family pictures. I keep sipping champagne. I get very drunk. I laugh a lot at the dinner. When all the great songs come on I dance with my brothers and parents as if I can feel my ass. I pretend.

My father says, "You're amazing. Look at you move. You're obviously getting better. You still dance the same." *I'm about to topple over, Dad, but thanks.*

I flirt with some of the groom's friends. When they pass around the cake I say, "Oh, no. No thank you!" One of the guys laughs and asks, "What do you have to worry about?" and he leers at me hungrily.

No one has a clue. I am actually amused. I realize I am a good actress. I take another Valium.

By the end of the night I am nauseous from the pills, and drinking and eating way more than I would have if I had been at the ranch. It's safe back there. You really can't fuck up while you're a guest unless you walk to the Allsups gas station down the road and get some Twinkies. I could never walk that far.

In the morning I cannot get up. I literally can't move at all. My whole Raggedy Ann–like body is actually stiff, my joints ache, and my temples pull. But heck, it was worth it. I did have fun. But I can't wait to go back to CR so I can fix myself and get some bodywork fast. I also am looking forward to seeing Kyle again.

I stumble to breakfast, where I tell my parents about Art Feast. They like the idea of the class, but not of me living in Tucson. They just don't get it. "Why there?" they ask. I decide to just see what happens, if indeed the ranch even accepts my proposal. And then late that afternoon, for the first time in my life I don't feel sentimental at all when I leave my family and get on a plane to go back to Arizona. Because now I have a mission that excites me. I can't let them shoot down my idea, or deter me from having a goal because they'd prefer me to be back in New York City, only four blocks away from them.

8. Growing Pains

But now I'm 4,162 miles away from my parents because it is the summer before my senior year at college, I'm twenty-two, and I'm in a doctor's office in Florence, Italy.

"Dr. Capriatta, I'm feeling pretty weak. My lower back hurts. I seem to get dizzy a lot," I say slowly in English so he'll understand. When he takes my vitals, he seems alarmed. "Your pulse is damn low," he says.

I call the United States to run the forty-something number by my internist. But Dr. W says, "Nothing to be worried about, you're an athlete. You always have low blood pressure. Besides, did you eat breakfast yet?" "A bite of bread," I lie. "But my coccyx hurts. Lately, I feel really sore there. Sometimes it hurts and I feel weak running."

Dr. W assures me it's not a problem and that I'll be okay. "Probably just banged it; you're bony there anyway," he says. That's true, it always stuck out when I did sit-ups. Even when I wasn't thin. I leave the doctor's office, and that afternoon I try to run along the Arno in Florence. God, it smells like shit. Here I am doing something healthy but I have to inhale the fumes of the speeding Vespas and the sour fermentation of the river. It doesn't make sense to put a dirt track right there, does it?

Running hurts so much. I do it every afternoon, though. Even when I am so exhausted after my three-hour intensive morning Italian class in the basement with twelve Columbia University students. But I push. *Sick of this mushy ass . . . got to get thin again . . . been exercising like crazy for the past two years . . . but no great results . . . run those five miles, even if it hurts, Jenny . . .* beginning to get scared of dinner meal *. . . I'll just load up on organic fruit* even though I can't straighten up after all this fiber bingeing. I begin listening to the funky Italian techno music, speedier and tackier than the American variety. I love it. I wear my Walkman around my waist on a tight belt to help suck my stomach in and spend all the time changing the radio dial until I find the perfect song, the beat that takes me somewhere else. I begin to race-walk hard, lifting and squeezing my arms, and I find that even with the great music, I can only run a little. *Something is wrong with my lower back. What is going on? I'm probably just out of shape.* I like the walking better anyhow. Strengthening, elongating, and strutting to the sound of the rhythm, feeling like I am dancing, gliding, and in touch with my muscles. And then everywhere I go, museums, cafés, discos, I am gripping, unrelaxed. Begin to walk on hunger. Notice some progress. But don't care that I'm in Italy. Just about getting my workout in, eating right, and going home thin. Very fucking familiar. Feel good but kind of gross holed up in my musty apartment on the Alterano. Class ends. Supposed to stay alone and travel through Italy for three more weeks. But get fever and think I have lice. Call home, panicking. Whole body is itching. Use shampoo four times. Everything pulsating. I look across the window at the gorgeous Italian man cooking and the clothes hanging on the line. *God, I want him, this Italian prince, to resuscitate me.* I'm having a complete, utter panic attack. There are bugs in my body. I can't get rid of them. Call home. "Mom, Dad, I've gotta come home. Please get me on a plane. Today is too soon, feel too sick to move, Mommy . . . tomorrow, yes." Go to hotel. Skip dinner. Take three baths. Keep applying shampoo and soap all over my body. *Shouldn't this do the trick? Do I need to get another bottle?* Can't sleep all night. Twisting and turning. *I really do wish I could stay here. See the rest of Tuscany. Meet an Italian lover. Buy more Superga sneakers. Maybe a green pair, already have navy and red. But feel too tired. What is wrong with me? I need to go home. Rest. I think something is up besides the lice. Do I even really have lice? I need to chill out. Maybe go up to Connecticut with everyone for the remainder of the summer. Or visit friends in Santa Fe in late August. I have to get out of here.*

Hate flying. Eight-hour ride. Feel calmer. Feel great that my size 8 pants I bought at the beginning of the summer are falling off. Twenty minutes before we land I start talking with a cool black American musician. Starting to feel real safe again. Aah, America. We land. Everyone claps and cheers. Yeah! We're home. Can't wait to see Mom and Dad. Oh, there she is. Mom looks at me proudly. Somehow I am a size 4. She tells me I finally did it. I lost the extra weight. Feel better, both pulsating and bugs stop. But I'm fucking exhausted, already. At meals my parents ask, Are you starving again? Don't do it again. You look perfect now. Never perfect.

I was not safe. All along, my enterocele was growing like the Blob, between my rectum and my vagina. And there was nothing about being home, or with Mommy and Daddy again, that could stop it.

9. Finding a New Home

Here I am, living in Tucson, Arizona, in a very bright, white, and spacious adobe home up in the Foothill Mountains. There are minimal furnishings, just a futon and two blue-and-white Tibetan rugs I have picked up at a local arts and crafts market. The place has huge windows that stare out at the sky and down on a big golf course. It's in one of those overbuilt complexes that has old retired couples from Texas building new homes on it every other day. Granted the construction workers are making a lot of noise, but it still is pretty great to look at the incredible view of Sabino Canyon and all the golf caddies. I just hope that when I stand outside on my deck, a golf ball doesn't hit me. Settling into this town does seem weird, so different, but kind of cool. Finally I have done something that is totally unpredictable and doesn't have any feelings of déjà vu. This place is completely neutral. A blank canvas for me. I don't have awful memories from here, or a connection to any relatives, or many belongings to weigh me down. I can create a new home. A new self.

My first few nights it takes me awhile to fall asleep. I lie in bed composing a pleasant montage of past and future daydreams. It's been three weeks since I left the ranch, and I can't wait to hear about teaching my class. There's still been no news. It reminds me of when I used to go to bed excited about a painting I had done or was going to do, or an event that was coming up that I really was looking forward to. I also lie there thinking of how lucky I am, how much I love this house, how even though I'm alone, there is a cozy comfort. I remember a year ago, the suffering, the fear, my strong disbelief that I would ever be able to think and be again. I am relieved that my mind is still holding on.

I'm pleased that my parents have agreed to this. And glad that they have respite from me, and can relax a little because I am no longer pleading constantly for their help. I also think about B, my art professor, and how I built him up in my head out of complete desperation. I laugh that I once could have thought he was my soul mate. I recently e-mailed him. Of course, he didn't respond.

Then I think of Kyle, and the soft kisses we have shared already. The first time we held each other in a hot tub under an evening, dark sky lit up with sparkling stars, at the small hotel I stayed at the first week after leaving the ranch. He made me feel so sexy. We were both wearing just Fruit of the Loom undershirts, his black, mine white, wet and see-through. He was so strong, but his hands were so gentle. I imagine getting to know him better, hearing what he thinks and feels. I wonder if he's going to come by or call. And then I start to worry that I am obsessing about him and that I will end up making it awkward between us.

But suddenly I hear noises and become afraid and turn on the light. I consider getting a knife from my kitchen to put in the drawer by my bed. Then I realize that I have the power to stop thinking about everything, Kyle, my physical pain, and, instead, just concentrate on believing I am safe. I count sheep and fall asleep. When I wake up warm and cozy, I can see the early blue light of dawn out the window.

10. Sabotage

Kyle and I date for about a month. I know I can fall in love with this man. But being with him is bittersweet. I just can't do it. I watch him play his guitar and see how pensive and moody he gets afterward and it scares me. He seems to have trouble expressing his feelings to me. And I have my own moods to contend with, as well as some major physical healing to do. I don't even know if I will be comfortable making love. We haven't done that yet and I'm scared. One afternoon, when we sit in his beat-up Honda, on a grass lot by a park, we look at each other and we both cry. What are we really crying about? That we know it can't work, or because it actually can, but I don't want to try. I stare at the rubber ducky sitting on the dashboard, which I gave him on one of our first dates, as he tells me he could fall in love with me. All I keep thinking is, *"But no. Not now, when I can't even hold myself up, when I am a different person on Prozac and still in pain. Not when I'm unable to show him the real me."* Yet all I tell him is that we should just be friends.

I also am trying to comprehend why I spent an incredibly constructive time at Canyon Ranch, left feeling excited and hopeful, and within a month have gone back to my postsurgery behavior. I drank a bottle of Corbet Canyon last night. But I know the answer. Life for me can't really be the 100 percent life I'd like it to be. I'm dissuaded because I am not all better and don't know if I ever will be. I constantly want to numb myself, whether it's to relieve the physical or mental pain.

Maybe it's also because I'm still in limbo and I can't stand it. I'm waiting to see if I will be able to teach my art workshop. Also, I went from being around tons of people at the ranch to spending a lot of time alone. At first I thought some solitude might be beneficial because it would force me to start painting. It was a nice idea, but I'm not having success. At least I had found a part-time job at the Jewish Community Center, holding babies and changing their diapers.

I go to see Suzanne, my acupuncturist, in her downtown Tucson office. While I lie there with twenty long paper-thin needles sticking out of my entire body (even my nostrils), feeling like a science experiment and complaining about everything, she asks, "Jenny, are you ready to get well?"

It kind of stuns me, her manner of asking me this. It's as if she is implying that I'm not and that I haven't been doing what I need to do. It also annoys me that Bob, my physical therapist, and Bella, my craniosacralist, have also asked me the same question. As if they are really getting at something deep. As if they're confronting me with the most brilliant life-altering question. As if I haven't asked myself the same thing. *Like I'm that stupid.* Whether they are putting it out there just to rile me, or to insinuate something, or to encourage me that I have the power to get well, it still bugs me. Because I don't know what "getting well" means anymore. *Uh, get well from surgery, digest food better, cure my eating disorder, end my depression? All of it?*

I've been working on this stuff for so long, observing myself and other people, and at this point, I'm not sure what it would mean to be truly well, or *who out there even is*. Do I want to be out of physical pain? Yes, of course. Do I want to be out of emotional pain? Absolutely. Do I want to do all the things that may, and I emphasize *may*, help, like quit drinking coffee, smoking a few cigarettes (which I still did even at the ranch), eating dairy, and sipping wine. No. Not really. I ask myself, *If I take all these things out of my life, then, uh, will I get well?*

Should I be doing more chi gong, tai chi, yoga breathing, and meditation, instead of surfing the Internet or having myself a good ol' writing/drinking/smoking fest or looking for cute boys? Will the attempts at doing and living a so-called clean life do the job? But at what price? Becoming anal again? Maybe I would try harder if I really thought it would pull up my sagging body and undo the botched surgery.

I want to be well, of course. But like this: I want to be running and painting again, and I'd like a boyfriend to eat meals and travel with. A baby or two would be nice. I want to be able to be strong and loving, and rid myself of this fucking eating disorder. I don't want to feel lonely. I'd prefer to live in New York and Santa Fe as I planned, reunite with lost friends, go back to the time before my surgery, and have the strength to push away my depression. I'd like to teach yoga, hang out with Nikki, Edward, and Joan, and date great older artists who I'll meet at dinner parties in those huge kick-ass Noho lofts. And they ask, *Do I want to get well?*

Life changes, life goes on. It is what it is. I know I need to find acceptance, and believe that everything I'm going through is part of a larger puzzle. But sometimes I think I am lying to myself if I pretend any longer that it's truly okay with me that it all happened this way.

◆ ◆ ◆

This morning I stay in bed and imagine running. I close my eyes and put myself back in time, wearing my navy blue leggings and orange Princeton sweatshirt. I think of stretching and then moving around the reservoir in that hungry state, feeling lithe like a cat. At first I can't. I try harder and then I can almost feel what it used to be like to lift myself off the ground. I wonder if I envision it enough if I will be able to. When these yearnings come, they are so powerful. Not to get thinner, really, but how badly I wish I could run again, how much I miss it. The anger at the doctors and the people who disregarded me comes tumbling back. Then I worry, *Shit. I'm going backward.* I thought I felt some forgiveness toward them and was starting to accept my situation. Am I a horrible person if I still feel the anger inside of me and I long for the possibility of having had a different outcome? People say anger is a waste of one's time and energy, but I don't understand how anyone can deny such feelings. I still want to write a letter to the surgeon and to Dr. Worthless telling them how much they *hurt* me. But for what real purpose? What's done is done. But the frustration always comes back when I just want to take off and fly, and when I'm about to get my period.

Later in the day I actually force myself to run two and a half miles around the high-school track by Sabino Canyon. It doesn't feel very good, but I am capable of doing it. I can see my body's shadow on the dirt struggling. I try to fix my posture by manually holding my rib cage in place with one hand and my upper back with the other. Then I switch positions and try to hold my sinking belly up instead. I look strange. I am embarrassed when a few people run past me so I drop my arms and pretend I am running with ease.

As I make my way along I decide that I cannot live without running. I will proceed to keep coming here until my ass becomes alive and well. I must have faith that one day my cells will regenerate and I will come to relate to this new-formed body. And my physical therapist says that my surrounding muscles can compensate for the destroyed connective tissue of my abdomen and rectum. Okay, cool, and maybe even I'm young enough that in years to come my connective tissue will *connect* again.

But at a certain point during my great attempt to fling myself around another loop, I fall down to the ground on my knees and cry on the track. I long for that endorphin high and the sensations of my old body but I just can't get it. I grieve over the loss. When I have enough of a fit, I haul my body up and say in my mind that I will be triumphant over such anguish and not allow myself to be defeated. Then I continue to hobble around.

Of course all this running ends up to have been a horrendous idea. That night I get a fever and have aches and pains for two weeks. I can't turn my neck either. I recall all those *inspirational* Sunday night made-for-TV movies where a paralyzed person gets up and runs just by sheer will. Or the person who breaks his back but ends up finishing the New York Marathon. *Where's my happy ending?* I want to keep pushing, but pushing too hard may be the worst thing for me. Maybe that is what someone up there keeps trying to tell me.

I finally get a call from the ranch. I can start my workshop in January. That means I have two more months to preoccupy myself. I phone Kate and we go out and celebrate. In the meantime I come up with the idea to make Art Feast even bigger. I think about opening my own art space in Tucson. In order to do research, I start hanging out downtown on Fourth Avenue near the college, where most of the eccentric artists live. I meet lots of people of all ages and eventually find my own studio around there and begin painting again. I don't feel great, but the excitement of teaching and the possibility of starting my own business keeps me going. As well as my weekly phone sessions with Dr. P. He tells me he is proud of me that I went after something and got it. He also encourages me to continue with this project on a grand scale. But until I get my plan to work, I still call home to my parents almost every day, not just to say hello or *whine about the pain,* but also so I can ask for money for my continuing health regime. Because besides my three hours working at the Jewish Community Center with kids (for five dollars an hour), my days are filled with physical therapy, acupuncture treatments, and two new modalities I have added to my repertoire: one called jin shin jyutsu, an ancient healing acupressure art form revived in Japan, and one called color therapy, which I get a real kick out of. When I enter Mona's office she asks me to choose from a rainbow of translucent bottles that are lined up on a shelf, and it is mighty hard to repress my giggles as Mona starts chanting and squirting me with the colored perfume that best suits what "I might need that day" to enhance my aura. *Okay, so it may not be Lauren or Romance, but it's worth a shot.* Even though I don't tell my mother the specifics, she still supports me but sometimes she says, "Another treatment? What is that one all about? Don't you think you're doing too much already? How do you know which one is helping or not, or if at all?" Then I can hear my father say in the background, "How does she know they're not taking her for a ride? She falls for this all the time. I hope she's not seeing any astrologers." *He is a very cynical person.* I tell my mother not to worry, I'll cut down on treatments eventually, but I have no other option. And whether or not any of this is working, I am intrigued by the kind people I am meeting. None of them seem like quacks, because they all believe passionately in what they are doing and want to help. I learn that it is all about intention. *Their intention,* and mine, is enough to help get me through an afternoon. I also spend time painting, and sitting at cafés writing in my journal and jotting down ideas for my art space. Not to mention heading to bars at night to visit Kate and some of the new friends I have made, who include an exotic, voluptuous Israeli boutique owner who designs her own jewelry, and a guy with a goatee who dresses like a Sikh, talks about tantric yoga and kundalini releases, and smokes a cigar.

I start my class at CR. It's great to be back there and see everyone. I run into Naomi and we promise to do dinner. I don't mind seeing Kyle, and we exchange warm hugs. When I bump into Tad, he still flirts. I teach two afternoons a week. I have bought tons of supplies that I set up in separate plastic buckets by the pool, and when it becomes too hot or rains we go to the tiny art room. Not a lot of people attend, it varies from three to ten participants at the most, but it's enough. We have fun. I talk to my students about my own experience teaching myself how to paint. I show them books by two of my favorite self-taught artists; Bill Traylor, whose simple lines and figures on cardboard are delightful, and William Hawkins, whose fabulous color sense and creatively drawn animals are bright, whimsical, and explosive. I tell them it's all about the exploration. It doesn't surprise me that after an hour and a half people are still engrossed in their drawings or watercolors and don't want to leave. One week a painting is left for me at the receptionist desk that some of the participants made that reads ART FEAST in colorful painted letters, with personal signed thank-yous. It makes me cry.

But over the next few months, I'm not getting much better physically. To top it off, I've caught strep twice and a horrible ear infection. Supposedly it's from being around the children, and according to the doctor at the clinic, my immune system is just not strong enough. I don't want to quit my job at the JCC but I have to. I can't afford any more ill health.

My great dream of opening my own art place fizzles over time. It turns out that the older British guy who I met a few months earlier at the yoga studio he owns in town, who charmed me with his strong accent and enthusiasm over my concept, who promised he was going to invest with me, isn't actually as serious as I thought—in fact, he now seems to want something else from me. His shady character and my lack of judgment are disappointing, but worst of all, I realize I just can't keep up my stamina. *I'm still a mess. Run my own business? Come on now, Jenny, you're ridiculous.*

I still hold my workshop until my second summer in Tucson begins. And then I really start to get antsy. Two days a week at the ranch is just not cutting it for me. It also gets too damn hot. *It should be illegal to live here in the summer.* When I first came out last July I was too excited to care. I was also very weak and cold half the time. But now I'm driving around in my rented Cherokee during the blazing heat of the day, and all I want to do is rush back to my air-conditioned house.

I've also been dating about five men over the past few months, all of whom know each other, and I think I'm getting myself into trouble. I have turned into an immoral, promiscuous girl (though I still haven't gone all the way with any of them). I will attribute my wanton behavior entirely to a lethal hodgepodge of Prozac, Valium, white wine, heat, boredom, and low self-esteem. I mean, what else would cause me to make out with two male best friends simultaneously in a hotel room at the infamous Club Congress. *Yikes! Who is this girl?*

One hot morning when the temperature has already hit the hundreds, I call up my best girlfriend Mel in Santa Fe and I say, "I think I'm ready to come back. Can I stay with you a few days?"

"Absolutely. When will you be here?"

"Tomorrow."

I hang up, go buy cardboard boxes, blast some music, and start packing up the house. By midnight that evening all my belongings have been either tucked away in taped-up cartons left to be picked up by movers with my furniture, or thrown haphazardly in my car, and I am leaving Tucson, on the road to Santa Fe. For a girl who has trouble holding her body up, I can sure move fast.

11. Getting Lost

At ten o'clock in the morning I park my car on Canyon Road right outside the art gallery where Mel is working for the summer. The bells jingle as I open the door and go inside. Mel comes out from the back looking beautiful as usual, all done up in her cowgirl glam: a long black prairie skirt, black silk blouse, silver-with-turquoise-on-leather conch belt, beaded earrings, black cowboy boots, and all. Her blue eyes are sparkling and her blond hair is longer than ever. She says, "Oh my God. That was quick. Did you get any speeding tickets?"

I laugh and tell her, "Mel, you know when I wanna do something I do it."

She says, "You look a little tired. Do you want to go straight to the house or hang out? Unfortunately, my boss will be here soon." I do look a mess. I am wearing a ratty old brown floral dress that my thighs bulge out of and a white hooded sweatshirt, and my hair is up in a disheveled bun.

I tell her, "I need a cup of coffee. Should I go get us some?"

She says, "Yeah. There's a coffee guy right down the alley."

I am giddy to be back in Santa Fe and dizzy as hell from driving nearly eight hours straight. The ride was also pretty hard physically. I kept propping my bottom up with pillows. Sometimes I had to put a small cushion under one buttock to try to balance, because I've noticed how lopsided my sitz bones are.

The coffee guy is dressed in a Guatemalan blouse with stripes and pants made from hemp, and he is gorgeous. I ask him for two cups.

After I pay him and turn to head back toward the gallery, he says, "I know you."

I look back. "What? Excuse me?"

He says, "I used to live down the street from you. I kind of partied with you."

And I rattle my brain and an image comes to mind of a skinny kid with a long dark braid and glasses, carrying a book.

"Holy shit," I exclaim. "Joab, little Joab? My God!" I head back toward him.

"Yeah, remember me?" he says in a deep voice.

"I sure do. You cut your hair, though. And, um . . . uh, you've really grown up."

"Yeah. How ya been?"

"Oh. Well, okay, I guess."

"Are you back?"

"Uh-huh. I think so. I see you still have a book with you." He's reading Tom Wolfe's *The Electric Kool-Aid Acid Test*. "Any good?"

"Haven't started it yet."

"Well, it's great to see you. Have to get back to my friend."

"See ya around," he says.

I return to Mel and exclaim, "I know the coffee guy! He's so hot."

She agrees, "Yeah, I knew you would think that."

Mel and I sit down on the couch in the gallery and I fill her in on my recent months and explain to her why Art Feast didn't work out. And as I speak to her, I begin to get emotional and start to cry. It feels as if I haven't talked to anyone for ages.

I say, "Mel, It's awful. I'm scared to death. I still function, even date guys, and go through the motions of some kind of life, but I'm not the same. The surgery was a complete disaster. I think it only made things worse. Half the time I'm so tired from using most of my strength to just be. And I panic because I think I'm literally trying to hold all of my internal organs up myself and wonder when it will ever end. Isn't this bizarre?"

She rubs my shoulders and says, "It's going to be all right. You need some good bodywork, Jenny. You should definitely go to see Keifer, my osteopath. He's amazing. He's the one who got my arm working again after I couldn't move it for a year. Remember I told you about him?" I start to get more hopeful.

I'm also very glad Mel has been kind enough not to comment on my weight. I've put on at least ten pounds since I saw her in the winter when she came to visit me in Tucson. It's from drinking too much again and not watching what I eat. I like that I don't obsess about food that much anymore, it's just too bad it has to show. I also quit swimming along with most of the other activities I had done at the ranch, although I did continue physical therapy through the late spring. On my frustrated days, I made attempts to run the track again or do my old Body by Jake routine from a tape cassette an instructor made for me when I was fifteen, but anything like that always left me in agony and tempted me to down the whole bottle of Tylenol. *Oh well*. I'm beginning not to care anyhow. *A few pounds here and there, so what.* I am also starting to learn that it doesn't seem to affect my relationships with men either. Most of the guys seemed to like me in Tucson as is. *At least I think they did.*

I wipe away my tears and tell Mel I can't wait to see Max. I haven't seen him since he was eight. He was at his dad's the last time I visited. He's thirteen now. She gives me the house keys and I grab a newspaper from the machine across the street so I can start looking for a rental. As I drive up the road I still can't believe I'm back. The place feels different. It looks brighter and more crowded. There are more tourists, many new galleries, and a lot more kitsch in the windows.

Later, when I see Max, I feel like crying again, but I don't. I want to be the cool aunt. He has a full head of floppy blond hair and big bright blue eyes like his mother. And tons of freckles. He's friendly, obnoxious, and curious about me all at once. He's a thirteen-year-old, after all. I enjoy the next week, bonding with Mel and Max. Every morning from the couch in the living room I hear Mel's morning moan as she stretches in bed, or her whispers to Max when she goes to wake him. Then I know she's about to come out to the kitchen where she will linger in her pajamas and make coffee for us. I love our kitchen talks, when I sit on the stool at the counter among scattered papers with phone numbers, bills, and invitations to art openings and she hands me a big mug of her strong brew. We begin our day here, and wind down in the late evening, chatting away.

After a week goes by, I am still looking for a place to rent. When Mel goes to work I drive around feeling lost. I stop at some of my old haunts, the galleries where I used to work, the cafés where I used to hang out drinking lattes, writing in my journals, and where I met some of my old flames. I am rather self-conscious. I wonder if people can tell that something is going on with me, that I am different from when I was last living here after college, when I was twenty-three and super thin. I am probably about twenty pounds heavier. Although I'm now twenty-seven, I keep thinking I actually look younger than before, like I have baby fat on me.

One morning, I run into Joab again. He's sitting on a short pink adobe wall, hanging out with another guy in front of a restaurant. He's wearing a white T-shirt and faded jeans, smoking a cigarette and looking real mellow. I stop to say hello. "Where's the coffee cart?" I ask. He tells me he's not working today and introduces me to his friend. I have nothing better to do so I take out my pack of Marlboro Ultras, light one up, and go lean myself right up against the wall and close to Joab.

After an hour of conversing and reliving old memories and filling in his friend on our earlier wild days, I'm starting to notice that I'm in real physical discomfort from standing so long. I suggest we head up the street to the cowboy bar/restaurant and have some brunch. I offer to buy them both mimosas because *God knows I need one.*

We drink one after the other. His friend eventually leaves and it's just Joab and me. He tells me he used to have the biggest crush on me. I think I knew that, but I wonder about now.

We spend the rest of the day together. We get in my car and I let him drive. He takes me to see all his favorite roads and homes around Santa Fe, and the secret places he has found during all his hikes growing up here as a lonely, bored, and inquisitive kid. He drives me up one winding dirt path so can I see the most incredible view of the mesa and horizon from this spot. I am honored that he shares this all with me.

In the late afternoon we grab a bottle of white wine and go to the Cross of the Martyrs, a big park that looks down on the entire city. We sit on a picnic table and watch the sunset. But I'm not that into the view because I can't stop looking at him. His light green eyes are alluring. His lean body is enticing, and I want to run my hand through the soft dirty-blond curls of his hair. And then he farts and I can't stop laughing. I find it adorable. He is so sweet, and so boyish. I must have a thing for younger guys now. *Guess I got over my Electra complex.* He will be twenty-four soon. It's only a few years' difference. We end up kissing, and that, along with the bottle of wine and the high altitude, is an intoxicating combination.

For the next two months, Joab doesn't leave my side. He helps me find a studio rental, cleans it, and puts up the towel racks. And he ends up staying with me in my new home, where we make papier-mâché, draw, smoke some pot together, cook meals, play classical music, watch videos, and make love. And yes, it does hurt sometimes, especially in my stomach, where it stings me in various spots, but more because I actually don't feel that much *down there*. I mostly like just lying together wrapped up in each other's arms.

The only problem is that he quits his job after an argument with his boss and doesn't find a new one. Every morning I circle the possibilities in the want ads of the newspaper for him but he doesn't follow up. I wouldn't mind him not working a nine-to-five, and making art like I'm trying to do, except that I start to pay for everything we do. It gets old fast. Also I need some time to myself. I have to start painting and find a new physical therapist and make some appointments with all the alternative healers Mel suggests I should work with. I'd also like to spend some more time with her, catch up with old friends, and just settle in. I got here and it's as if *we're* settling in. I'm into him but all of this has happened way too fast. I've even blown off my phone sessions with Dr. P. One afternoon I get Joab out of the house to do some errands for us in my car and I finally talk to him. When I tell Dr. P the deal he says, "It sounds great, Jenny, just make sure he gets a job."

A month later, when Joab confides that he might have to go to jail for getting caught with illegal drugs in his car a year ago and because he didn't show up in court for two DWIs, I am *not a happy camper*. I think to myself, *Only you, Jenny, only you. Wait till you explain this one to theparents.* When he finally does go to jail for a few weeks, I bawl for days. But as much as I care for him, I just can't visit. Although I am curious, the thought also makes me cringe with fear as I imagine crowds of leering and hissing caged men in orange. I'm also realizing how unstable Joab really might be. When I receive a letter from him I don't know how to respond, so I don't. And when he calls collect and asks for bail money, I get a little pissed. I tell him it's over. I know I've hurt him, but I'm just so lost, and I know I can't find myself with him around.

I start spending a lot of time with Max. We hang out at Starbucks and he teaches me to play chess. We see lots of movies and we dye our hair together. He comes over one night, and after he assures me that Mel has given him permission, we drive to the drugstore and come back with the goods to make his hair bright red and give me some violet high-lights. After he grins at himself for an hour, I drop him off at home, where Mel screeches with delight. "Max, you look great. I love it." I'm glad I have done such a good job for him, but she says she can barely tell I've done anything to my hair. I return to the drugstore to get some more color options and it turns into an all-night art project for me. I wash and redo my hair four times, because under the poor bathroom lighting my attempts have been useless. I finally go to bed and am horrified in the morning when I look in the mirror with the shining sun coming through the window and see all the mismatched shades of red and purple. It looks terrible. My father was right. "Never touch the hair." I mourn for my black hair until it grows out, but at least I can finally say I *rebelled against him.*

At Max's bar mitzvah I am the proud aunt. I cry when he sings in Hebrew. And even more when I see the tears rolling down Mel's face as she watches her son from the front pew. My parents have sent Max a navy double-breasted blazer, a white oxford shirt, and charcoal flannel pants to wear for this occasion, and in his final speech he doesn't forget to thank me for his great suit. All heads turn toward me and I look down, embarrassed, but very touched by Max's acknowledgment. At the reception I enjoy looking at the centerpieces I created for the ta-bles. I based their design on Max's favorite obsession, Star Wars. Mel and I snuck into his room and stole his box of miniature Star Wars fig-ures so I could wrap them up in Saran Wrap and float them inside huge crystal fish bowls that I covered with Star Wars picture cards. Max tells me they're cool.

At the party that night I chaperone with Mel. It's also Halloween, so I dress as a femme fatale in a short black bob wig, a long fake fur white-and-black-spotted pony overcoat, big jet sunglasses, and bright red lipstick. Mel is an Indian princess and wears a hot pink sari and a transparent veil covered with sequins. She has to sit outside most of the time to monitor the guest list, so I go in to check up on everyone. I try to dance and keep up with the teenage girls, who all have outrageous bodies. I act goofy. I make them laugh with some funky moves.

Although I have yet to see any physical therapist, receive any body-work, or start painting, things are going relatively well. But when I get a few menacing phone calls from Joab and hear he's returned from prison, I decide to move out of that first house because I don't want him creeping around. It also has too much sad energy in it. After all, it was really Joab's and my place. I find a new one-bedroom adobe up the hill next to a nice older couple. Everything goes smoothly until Christmas Eve of '99.

12. The Accident

Nikki comes to visit for the holidays. Since I know she's just had her wisdom teeth pulled I want to give her a relaxing vacation. But she's also never been here, so I want to introduce her to everything and have her fall in love with Santa Fe the way I have. The first day we start by walk-ing around the plaza, going to shops, and then we eat dinner with Mel at my favorite restaurant (where I had my big date with B).

The next afternoon we drive a short ride north toward the Rio Grande so I can show her where I originally stayed with my parents, and the view of the mesa. I'm upset because all the Sangre de Cristo Moun-tains are covered with snow and the sky is gray and foggy. None of the large, open blue sky I have told her about is in sight.

I take her to Santuario de Chimayo, a church in a small village that has an interesting religious history. For years, people have been making pilgrimages there on Easter weekend hoping for miracles. We both go into the room where there are crutches and eyeglasses gathered to the side and religious quotes on the walls. And then we each take our turns bending over the holy dirt, running it through our fingers and praying.

I thank God for bringing me back to Santa Fe, for helping me get stronger, for Nikki's visit, and for being alive. Nikki takes a plastic bag and fills it up with some dirt to take back with her.

On our way home, we stop and get massages at Ten Thousand Waves, a Japanese health spa. Before we go in for our treatments, we sip chai teas and I let her try to relax.

We are both sleepy that night from our bodywork, but we manage to dress up and meet Mel for the Christmas Farolito walk. Although I can't walk for long, I want Nikki to experience the beautiful tradition, when Santa Feans bundle up and stroll through the historic east side neighborhood, which is adorned with millions of glowing candle-lit paper bags, singing Christmas carols and sipping hot apple cider. Afterward we go to a party at a friend's house and have a glass of Mexican Mescal. We start to have fun. I meet a cute guy standing outside by the bonfire who smokes a pipe, and Nikki talks to a woman about UFOs. Then all of the visitors huddle together out in the snow and Nikki and I hold each other's arms while we watch the Persian hostesses fly a few transparent rice-paper kites into the pitch-dark night sky. *God, I love it out here.* Then we grab my cute pipe-smoking new friend and make quick stops at two bars, where we share holiday hugs, cigarettes, and I introduce her to some people I've mentioned in our phone calls. Then we exchange numbers with the pipe-man, say goodnight to all, and exhaustedly head toward home.

When we arrive in front of my house, Nikki is shivering and tired so she rushes to get out of the car to the entrance. I know the altitude has also been getting to her, and I feel bad because I think I pushed her a little too hard. I open the driver's door but still keep my foot on the brake of my car as I search through my bag for my keys. *Where the hell are they? Boy! That guy was handsome. Maybe he'll call me. Shit, I better hurry up and get Nikki inside. Ahh, here they are.*

When I finally find my keys, I turn the ignition off. And then I start to experience a hot flush of fear running through my entire body as the car starts inching backward and I can't get it to stop. I try to jam the gear into Park. But it's already in Park. Isn't it? I don't have time to think that long, I just see a vision of me bumping all around in the car as it flips over the ledge at the bottom of the hill. My only option is to jump out, but as I take a lunge for it, the heavy open door smacks into me, knocking me down. I slide on the ice underneath my Silver Cherokee and brace my head with my arms as the car rolls over me. It and the noise in my head stops. I start laughing. I actually find it hysterically funny that I have managed to stop a four-thousand-pound machine with my 137-pound-or-something-close-to-that-but-who-wants-to-weigh-myself-these-days body.

After I don't show up for a while, Nikki comes back around the corner. She sees me just sitting there in the middle of the driveway on the icy cement in my torn velvet forest green skirt next to the askew car and she starts to yell, "Oh my God. Oh my God."

I say to her, "Um, uh, Nik, I think the car ran over me or something."

She starts to cry and scream for help. Then she says, "You hold on. You just hold on there." She sprints around to my neighbor's house. She's fast. She was on the track team in high school.

Nikki and the nice couple who are in their pajamas and snow boots come rushing out. They are carrying huge blankets that they put around my shoulders and tell me not to move. For a few minutes I lose the vision in my right eye and fear it will vanish in the other one too, but when I hear the sirens and the ambulance comes, I regain it. I actually remain relatively calm, especially when the EMTs put me on a stretcher and load me into the van. I only start to get angry when they keep asking me what my name and age is, and I continue to tell them over and over. I just want them to hurry up and give me those damn painkillers I know so well.

At the hospital, the young male nurse is chubby, has a beard, and is dressed in a green Santa's-elf costume with a floppy hat. He makes me laugh all night in between my naps. At one point he informs me that I have a broken left arm, two cracked ribs, and a small tear on my spleen.

They have to keep me there a while to make sure my spleen doesn't rupture.

"Oh, okay. Can I have some more Percocet?"

At six o'clock in the morning I look down and notice that I am still wearing my long velvet forest green skirt from the night before. They could at least have given me a gown for the occasion.

I ask a nurse if I can please call my parents so I could fill them in. "Please hand me the phone so I can dial it and speak first so they don't get scared," I request. But then I hear, "This is St. Vincent's Hospital and we have your daughter on the line." *Idiots.*

I get on the phone and my mother is already speaking in a very high-pitched tone at the end of the receiver, "What! What happened? Oh my God!"

"Mom. Mom. Calm down. I'm okay. I told them to let me talk first."

"What. What's going on?"

"Well, uh, I had a little accident."

She says all trembly, "You had an accident. What kind of accident?" Then screams, "Jerry, come here!"

"Well, a car accident. But I'm really okay. Truly. Just a few broken bones. I'm alive, though, Mom. It's good news, actually. You shouldn't worry."

She starts to sob.

"Mom, really, I'm all right. It could have been bad. It's a good holiday. I was actually spared."

My dad gets on the phone. "You had an accident, huh." He kind of states this nervously but also matter-of-factly, as if he always knew this might happen.

"Yeah. I did. But I'm all right. Please calm Mom down."

After I tell him most of the story he says, "Well, I guess this is good news, then. You're alive."

"That's right."

My mom gets back on still crying. "We'll be out there as soon as we can."

"No, Mom. You don't have to. No, go to Jamaica. Go to Aunt Ricky and Uncle Ralph's. I don't want to ruin your trip."

Her voice gets even raspier and she just seems to be totally losing it, saying, "No, I need to be with my daughter now."

My dad is still on the line and agrees, "Jenny, we're coming out. We'll be there as soon as we can. Let's get off so we can make arrangements and get on our way."

My mom quickly interjects, "Is Nikki all right?"

"Yeah, she's fine. She wasn't in the car, thank God. She's getting some sleep now."

My mother can barely get her words out. "Okay, Pumpkinface, see you soon."

I wake up after sleeping a few hours. Mel, Max, and Nikki are all standing there. *This reminds me of something. A time before.*

"Heyyyy," I say dreamily, "Hi, guys."

Mel whines, "Jeennnny. Jesus!"

"I know. I know," I say. "Ridiculous."

Max says, "So the car really rolled over you?"

"Max!" Mel reprimands.

"Uh-huh. Pretty amazing."

He says, "Must have been pretty heavy."

I say, "Yeah, but my body can take it. It's a good thing I have some extra meat on my bones."

Nik touches the unbroken arm gently and says, "Furrrr, I'm so sorry. I was cranky. I was rushing you."

"Nik, give me a break. Things just happen. It's nobody's fault. Anyhow, I was distracted thinking about that cute man we met at the party. Now you guys should go get some breakfast. Mel, take Nikki to Pasqual's so she can try their burrito with green chili and red salsa. And give her a big bowl of beans."

I hear a little bit of murmuring still as my eyes start to shut.

In the afternoon, I call Dr. P in New York. He picks up the phone and I blurt out the news. I tell him that I have managed to run myself over with my own car. I say, "I even have the tire marks on my whole left side to prove it. But I'm okay." After he gets over the initial shock, he says, "Jenny, can you please stop trying to impress me," and asks me to promise that I keep him updated on my spleen.

I am watching the television when my parents both walk in wearing sweatpants, sneakers, and their matching navy Polo Sport jackets.

My dad says, "Jenny, you look like you've been run over by a car," and makes me laugh. He doesn't say anything about my weight gain but I know he notices it.

My mom comes to hold my hand and stares down at me lovingly.

I keep telling them that this is the happiest New Year ever.

That we should all be thankful.

The next day Nikki calls. I tell her it's okay, that, yes, she should go home to the city and get some rest. She'll visit again soon, or I'll come back to New York. I know she kind of wants to stay, but she doesn't feel very well herself.

I leave the hospital after four days because my spleen is fine. The rest of the week my parents take me to dinners, and we tour the galleries, even though I walk very slowly with my arm in a sling and my ribs aching. My father buys me a beautiful antique Kiowa doll to add to my collection, a Navajo leather bow guard for my mother to wear as a bracelet, and a rugged turquoise necklace for himself. In the end, I don't think they have such a bad vacation.

But this accident affects my parents more than my surgery did; it is horrific to them. They realize that this time they really could have lost me. When people call my house, my brothers, my aunts and uncles, my cousins, I say that I'm fine. But everyone sounds freaked out.

"You sure you're okay now?" they all ask hesitantly.

"Yep. Really. I'm thanking God."

But what I really want to tell them is, "I've been a wreck for a few years now. This is nothing." But I understand that everyone can relate more to a car accident than the idea of my intestines falling between my legs and my stomach being cut open and put back together to fix it.

So even though I keep telling everyone how lucky I am, and they say, "Wow, this accident must have affected you profoundly," and I respond, "I know, can you believe it, the mere fact that I have been spared!" I'm not altogether being honest. I play it up, and talk about how amazing it is, how this must mean I'm supposed to live, do something important with my life. But who knows anymore?

The truth is I'm just kind of sad. Because I'm not sure that I care that I survived.

13. Living Alternatively

After a year of living in Santa Fe and getting sidetracked by too many parties and distractions, like *a car accident,* I finally go see Keifer, the osteopath Mel has told me about. He is Belgian and wears an ascot and knows a hell of a lot about the body. Although he's not so sure about mine.

I also move into another home down the street from Mel, and force myself to go to my painting studio, a small space I have found on Canyon Road. I put on support hose to help hold my body up and I lock myself in there for two weeks and make thirty paintings. I know that this time *I have to say something.* Making pretty pictures at this point doesn't seem to match the landscape of my life. So I do a whole series of abstract torsos with scars and scrape out a man's face covered with a mask with him floating in the middle, and I paste words from my journals like "I wanted to feel empty" and "lost power" all over them. Shit like that. They are similar to the muddy watercolors I did prior to surgery, and very dark. I use maroons and browns and navy, and they are truly ugly.

And then I take a break from doing anything creative, another long one. And my days fill themselves up more and more with appointments to get well. I see Keifer, as well as a Pilates instructor, an acupuncturist, and a gynecologist who gives me saliva tests to check my hormone levels and who injects vitamin B shots in my ass because it might help my muscles. Most of my days are devoted to these appointments and then resting from these appointments, until I go out and get wasted on the weekends, stay hung over, and then have to recuperate the whole following week with the aid of these appointments.

Yes, I still manage to have fun, and even get myself a tiny black cat and hang out with my artist girlfriend Gena, who's just moved here from New York, and a tall dark-haired gardener/caterer named Ace, from San Francisco.

But Keifer eventually tells me he's done all he can and feels like he's just missing something, so he sends me to Dr. C (for Dr. Cool), another osteopath who works a bit differently.

Dr. C is a Robert Redford look-alike, a family man from Maine who dresses in plaids and polo shirts and drives a jeep, but could at any second probably turn into Brad Pitt's bearded wild man from *Legends of the Fall*. He has said to me, "Jenny, stop being afraid. Maybe you have to go into the wilderness to find your way out. I once spent six months alone in the forest. If I didn't have a wife and three kids to ground me, I'd probably stay there." Dr. C's hands and heart create magic. He is the only one capable of bringing me completely back to life for a few hours, who helps me feel at all connected to myself.

The first time I see him, he says afterward, "Wow. It's like there are no fluids running through your body. You are completely in shock."

He explains that the top part of my frame is not sending messages to my lower half. He says there is a disconnection. He also explains that it's as if there is a short circuit in my system, and everything moves away from my midline. The energy flow in a human being should line up through the center. He is the first person to get what I've been saying all along. He's amazing, because he understands what's happening just by touching me gently, and reading the rhythm of how my cranium, sacrum, muscles, connective tissues, and energy fields all work together. And no doubt about it, he also uses his very special intuitive gift to balance everything and even manipulate my bones. Without any big spinal adjustments or scary cracking sounds like a chiropractor makes.

He says, "I think you'll feel a little different after this, but rest today. Next time we'll really get to things more." I end up seeing him for almost a year, but unfortunately even he can't solve it all for me. When he sends me to a homeopathic doctor I have a horrible reaction to the little pellet he gives me. The back of my head and neck tightens, I can't take a deep breath, and I get a migraine. I rush to see Dr. C, who tells me I have gone into a fight or flight mode, and that it's as if the membranes around my brain just froze. Fortunately he is able to calm my body down, but this tightening starts to happen more frequently and I can go for days in pain until he releases it. No one else can. He says he thinks I am experiencing post–traumatic stress disorder from my surgery and asks if I'm in talk therapy. I tell him I have been for years but I stopped about ten months ago, ever since Dr. P got a contract to write his theories on Biological Relativity (*whatever the hell that is*), and decided to stop seeing patients. Although, when I have visited my parents in New York, I have called him and he has made an exception to have a session with me. Sometimes we e-mail, but I figure that he's busy, so I'm just letting our relationship drift. Anyhow, Santa Fe life is quite different from New York City life and I just don't want to have to talk about everything, especially my exploration of "unconventional" healing treatments that he might balk at. I also want to live in the moment.

Dr. C. suggests I go see Eva, who does something called "soul retrieval," because in cases like mine, having suffered so much trauma, I may also have some "soul loss." Eva is a psychotherapist and a shaman practitioner. She is in her forties, resembles a schoolteacher with her simple dress and modest face, and is as down-to-earth as any doctor

I've ever met. And you would never know that she sits in lotus position on her Navajo blanket, beats her drum, chants, and uses her spirit animal guide to blow lost parts of your soul back into you. I love her! Finally there is someone who melds my own affinity to mythology, storytelling, and interest in the spiritual realm into the context of her psychology practice. She truly speaks my language, and I know I can learn a lot from her.

While all this supposed healing is taking place, I also manage to meet a significant other. The week of 9/11 I notice Grant at a dive where my friend Ace and I are gloomily watching the news. It seems like everyone in the place just wants to connect, and I just can't help noticing his smile. After a few glances and an introduction across the bar and then a second run-in the following night, my first real relationship begins, and I actually do it: I fall in love.

Initially I think God has sent me Grant, an adorable chestnut brown–haired guy from New Hampshire. He dresses in ripped and faded light pink Polo shirts and cut-off khaki shorts covered with paint, and an orange baseball cap, tells me I remind him of the writer Anne Sexton, and that he felt like he was dreaming when we danced together that first night at the bar. I even joke about being a little chunky, and he says, "I like your flab."

On our first date he takes me for a $250 French dinner and tells the waiter to make sure the creme brûlée is real crispy (and even though I cringe a little at that, I think, *Well, he's just assertive*). He wears all white linen and sandals that night and I am dressed in a black kimono, short skirt, and heels, and we go dancing afterward and stay out late and kiss and kiss. It is as if our mouths are made for each other, *as if we are magnets drawn together by inescapable circumstances, by the power of the cosmos, by sheer unrelinquishing lust*. The next date I meet him at a bar and I get goose bumps when I see him sitting on the stool waiting, in a navy blazer. *I have found him*. He matches me in my black equestrian jacket. He takes me to hear "The Four Seasons," but during intermission he urges that we go down the street to get drinks. He gulps them down. I sip.

On the phone a few nights later he sings a song for me that he has written on his guitar, "If you ever leave me . . . I don't know what I will do." I giggle. It's a little mushy, but his voice is beautiful.

On another day, he sends me flowers with a card that reads, "I am crazy about you."

On his birthday, a week later, I throw a small party for him. I invite some of my friends and his brother who lives in town, but no one else at his request, because he doesn't feel that close to anyone. *After all, he's only lived here for a year,* I think. I put streamers up and hang a wreath on the door that says "Happy Birthday Grant" with handmade letters. I cook roasted chicken, potato salad, and corn on the cob and buy a Häagen-Dazs ice cream cake to serve. He shows up at my house in his Hawaiian shirt and jeans with a big buzzed smile on his face. We dance to the *Saturday Night Fever* record and Duran Duran and he dips me and I almost break my back. My friends like him. They think he's fun. Mel finds him very attractive, but also *a bit drunk.* Although I have been starting to drink less and less these days because I'm becoming more conscious of my own behavior and I want to receive the benefits from all my healing sessions, I don't really mind. *Okay. Well, maybe a little.*

After the party winds down, Grant drives me in his pickup truck to where he is housesitting. He takes off his shirt, sits at the edge of the bed, and plays more guitar for me. And then, as we tackle each other and he starts to undress me, I say, "Listen, Grant, there's something I have to tell you. This is the deal. My intestine fell between my legs and I had to have surgery and it probably happened because I had an eating disorder, and I live in pain. So I understand if you don't want to . . ."

He interrupts me. "Shhh. I don't care. Shh. I've been through a lot myself. Shhh."

"Like what?" I say. "Rehab or something?" I take a wild guess.

"Nah. Just stuff. It doesn't matter. Come here."

And we go outside on the deck and make love in the hot tub. Then, again and again, in bed. We fall asleep and wake up holding hands.

For a few weeks he stops drinking and he is silly, playful, and affectionate everywhere we go. We spend an evening shopping at Target for necessities such as Tide and Bounce so he can do his wash at my house.

We also buy pajamas with Mr. Potato Head on them, take snapshot photos, and throw gummy bears at each other.

After I had been dating Grant for about a month, he, Gena, and Ace accompany me on a trip to LA. My brother Greg and a friend have organized a benefit art auction for 9/11, and Gena and I both have a painting in it. When we get there, Grant and I cozy up in the hotel room and make love, eat, and watch *Legally Blonde* in bed. That night, we have sushi with Greg and his girlfriend of a year, Elizabeth. They think he's cool and that *he likes me a lot.* In the ladies' room, Elizabeth giggles and says, "So cute! You guys act so natural together." The following night Grant surprises me with pearl earrings. But then at the event, he drinks a lot and seems to get annoyed when Gena, Ace, and I mingle in the crowd. We invite a large group back to our connecting hotel rooms, and he goes out onto the terrace with a handful of beers and doesn't come back in for an hour. Later, when we go to bed, he rolls over and ignores me. But when I go to give him my hand, he waits a few minutes and then grabs it.

The next morning when my brother comes to meet all of us for breakfast, Grant stares off into the distance. He doesn't say a thing. After we say good-bye to Greg, we all drive around the Hollywood Hills in our rental convertible. By midday, Grant gets really cranky because he wants a hot dog. "Where can we get a goddamn hot dog?" he mutters. Ace and Gena look at me like, *What's his deal?* But I just keep running my hand through his soft wavy hair as we stay curled up together in the backseat.

Before we leave town, Greg calls me on my cell and warns me, "Jenny, I think you better be careful. I've seen this type of guy before. He's moody. Just keep it light. Have fun, but that's all. I don't think he's the one." I tell Greg that I want to give him a chance, but not to worry, I'm not getting married.

When we return to Santa Fe, Grant seems a bit down. We both try to take some time alone for ourselves. But on the days I need my own space and don't call him back immediately or I go out with Mel and my girlfriends, he becomes annoyed. One day he leaves me a note that says, "It was rude of you not to call last night. I am starting to feel like I'm at the end of a rope here."

But . . . it's too late. I have fallen.

Grant is a carpenter, and I help him with an exterior of a house, even though I get very sore and achy. I don't mind, though; I like spending time with him. And he needs the extra hand so he can finish up and find another gig. It is difficult to get jobs here, and after each one he blows all his hard-earned money bingeing on alcohol and buying everyone at the bar drinks. Sometimes when he has change left over, he takes me to dinner, or brings me home a lobster to cook, or a necklace. And I am touched. But I don't care about the money or his gifts. *Or the binges.* I love him and want him to stay with me in my house, because he calls me all the time and says, "Hey, little rascal rabbit, hey, beautiful . . . what's cooking?" in an adorable voice. And because for two weeks we both go into hibernation when he gives up the alcohol (*come on, he only parties a little*) and play together. We go to the movies, stupid and artsy ones, and share popcorn and Nestle's Muncha Crunchas. We laugh at the same jokes or discuss our deep insights, although occasionally when I tell him something he says, "Yeah, so what's your point?" and I get a lump in my throat and just shut up. We eat out at our favorite Italian restaurant and share fried calamari, pasta, and tiramisu with extra whipped cream. We also grab fast food and I take bites of his big juicy hamburgers. We rent videos, and he says, "Leave the dishes, honey, come snuggle with me." He gets upset if I don't come right away. I think that's cute. We share toothbrushes. Afterward he says, "Don't forget to rest it on the other side, honey. I like it right side up." Okay, I promise. We drive around and see the sights. We look at the houses we might want to buy together some day. Sometimes when he's in the driver's seat he plays classical music but then switches the station to heavy metal. I tell him to please turn it down. And then he turns it louder. "Bully!" I call him.

When he comes to live with me, we are like a married couple. It is peaceful and loving. For about a week. But then he starts to act a little strange.

If I get out of the bed early he says, "Where you going? To check your e-mail? Got an e-mail romance going with someone?"

And if I go into the other room to sit at my desk and check my e-mail, he says, "Yeah, I knew it."

If I put makeup on, "Where you going, to meet some guy?"

If I put a skirt on, "Who you dressing up for, Jenny?"

"Uh, um, you, Grant," I say as I stare at him bewildered.

If I smile in the restaurant, "So you got the hots for the waiter, huh?"

I just start looking down.

And I find myself starting to play his game, especially when we go out and he downs ten margaritas and I notice him looking at the bartender's midriff. I have to call him on it; after all, maybe he's been projecting, right?

In the meantime, all his drinking and chain-smoking at night starts to turn me off and I quit smoking. And especially because he says *it is disgusting to smoke during the day* after he has gone hiking, skiing, or biking to sweat out the toxins from the night before. *Hmmm. Reminds me of my own bingeing days.* I also have quit taking Prozac because it gets in the way of my sexual pleasure. *I think.* And because Grant says, "That stuff really fucks you up. You should see my stepmother who doesn't shut up at dinner. She's like a babbling idiot. Don't take that shit anymore, sweetie."

He also uses it as a defense if I bring up, *ahem,* his *illegal* drug use. He says, "Don't start getting on my case, Jenny. How can you tell me that I can't do some lines when you've taken Prozac? How can you rationalize? It's all the same. Cocaine, marijuana, prescription drugs. Don't kid yourself."

I start to wonder if he has a point. Except that I like to think of Prozac as choosing life instead of destroying it.

I do break up with him once, partly because of his drug use, but mostly because he can be really mean, especially when he's coming down. But then three weeks or so later we get back together because I miss the original guy I met and think he'll return. I also hear through the grapevine that he's heartbroken over me. And then I miss him even more. But I still beg him to talk to a therapist, except he is not very gung ho about the idea. His father is a psychiatrist and he likes to steer clear of that world now. After all, he grew up with it his whole life, *why would he need it?* So I try to forget about the drug issue, and after all, *who am I to judge? He only does cocaine occasionally.* I just tell him he's not allowed to use in my house.

By midyear making love is actually really starting to hurt. My pelvis feels cockeyed and so does my lower back. I keep on going to Dr. C but he never tells me to stop trying to enjoy myself. Just suggests I rest a bit more after my treatments.

And when I go for my weekly appointments, Grant seems very bothered.

"Another one, again? You and your Pilates. You and your Dr. C. Ohhhh, Dr. C! I love you, Dr. C. Hey, has he ever made a pass at you?"

But sometimes afterward when I come home from them, he makes me tea and homemade chicken soup and just lies next to me being respectful of my need to rest. *And his need to detox.*

I try to make it up to him on the many other days he calls me from work to ask me if I can bring that pack of drill bits and drop cloth he forgot. I come immediately and also bring him watermelon slices or gazpacho and bottles of water. I stop by to visit him throughout the day, especially when he's working on the ladder at a public space. I am proud of him. I also lend him money so he can get his contracting license and he promises to pay it back. Then he gets angry that I lent him the money.

Some mornings when I am in less pain and plan to meet a friend, he says, "Hanging out at coffee shops again? What do you people do at coffee shops all morning? You're not even painting. What exactly do you do with your days, Jenny?" *I spend them trying to get well and doting on you, jerk.*

The following April I make reservations to fly to Florida to see another very special osteopath who runs his own clinic. Originally I heard him speak at the healing seminar at the Marriott on the benefits of cranio-sacral therapy. He believes that our bodies have a whole physiological mechanism that lives in the spinal cord and the brain and that any disturbance of this can lead to sensory, motor, or neurological dysfunction. Through hands-on practice he has found noninvasive techniques to restore normal circulation in the cerebrospinal fluid to correct ailments in the body. I believe he is the reason I even started receiving this kind of work at Canyon Ranch in the first place, and then here in Santa Fe. I am on a waiting list for four months, and when I get a call that I can see him personally for three treatments, I know it's meant to be. And my headaches and fight-or-flight reactions are getting worse and worse. I often don't tell Grant, because I'm afraid he will get mad if I have to go to another appointment, so either I go for a drive to do "errands" and call Dr. C from my cell, or I just bear it. But I really can't take it anymore. Grant is upset that I have to leave but urges me to go if it will really help me.

After the gargantuan gray-haired sixty-five-year-old doctor with big saggy jowls and huge hands (I'll call him Brutus) reads my operating report and starts to do his own magic on my body, he says, "I hate your surgeon."

"Why?" I say. "He fucked me up, right?"

"Well, have you read your report?"

"Yeah, but it's all a foreign language to me."

He says, "He's got your colon tacked to your sacrum. He did a rectopexy on you, and a lot of other unnecessary things. I can't even believe the guy admitted this in your report. These idiot surgeons. I mean, your whole nervous system is a wreck. It's affected your whole craniosacral rhythm. No wonder you're anxious and can't think half the time. Your sacrum is basically the power energy center of your body, but it's got scar tissue and staples in it. Poor thing."

I feel sick. I feel hot. I want to throw up. This is probably why I've felt so horrible for almost five years since the surgery. And why I can't get my muscles to work that well, or get them very toned. *I am ruined!*

The second session, Brutus puts his hand on my chest and throat for a while and I start to feel as if I'm spinning around the room. I tell him this, and he says, "I know, honey, just hold on. It's from the tube they shoved down your throat during surgery. You've been holding trauma in there and we're going to release it." After an hour I calm down and go back to my hotel feeling very depressed.

The third session, Brutus says, "Your tissues are also very toxic, young lady. From being so constipated. Nothing can regenerate with tissues like this. I want you to go take Epsom salts, magnesium pills, and get a colonic to start cleaning yourself out. There's a great lady who's real gentle who works across the street. God, I hate your surgeon." I start to cry. What good is him fixating on my surgeon going to do now?

I say, "Do you know anybody who could undo this, correct this?"

He says, "I would only let one surgeon touch you, but he passed away five years ago."

Then he continues, "We'll work with what you've got. I think you should stay here for our intensive program for two more weeks. Let's get some of the scar tissue to break up. I can't do it personally, but I've got great people here who will help you."

I call Grant and let him know I'm going to stay for two more weeks. He's not happy about it at all. "Two weeks!" he whines. "But I'll miss you too much." He decides he has to join me.

I go to the mall and find some fresh pretty skirts and some bright colored tops and get tan in between sessions so I will look good for him. I cut down on my eating. I'm not hungry anyway because I have such a shooting headache. It won't go away. I can't wait until he gets here. I know the water and the sun will be good for him. He's been working so hard.

When Grant arrives he barely hugs me hello and just stares at me weirdly. He complains that the hotel is filled with old people. He is angry most of the time and says he resents me for him having to spend his newly earned $700 on this trip. And that he has no desire to meet the doctor and that all this is very depressing. Meanwhile he sleeps, swims, tans, jogs, and rests as I have three people's hands all over me six hours a day trying to give me back full use of my body. *Especially so I can make love to him in some other positions and maybe have his baby one day.* But the reason for his antagonistic behavior is obvious to me. In the last few nights before he left, he must have gone out and gotten high and now feels guilty about it. Because when we spoke just four days ago, he was extremely loving, and said that all he wanted was to get out of there and come be with me.

On the Friday night before Grant is to leave, we drive to West Palm Beach and have some drinks. I really shouldn't but I have one Bellini. He sips his beer and then tells me he wants to marry me. I feel like crying. Nobody's ever told me that. But I choke inside, wondering how I will marry a man who is kind of mean sometimes.

That night I'm tired but he wants to keep partying. He has switched to margaritas. After all, he says, he hasn't had a drink all week. But with all the bodywork I really should rest. And anyhow I'd rather cuddle. When he wants to go to a ghetto to get a little something, I've had enough.

I say firmly, "Get in the car, Grant, now. We're going back to our room."

He says, "No. Just leave me here. I'll get back later."

We are forty-five minutes away from our hotel. I'm about to fall apart but I have to be strong. I cannot enable him, or this, anymore. "Get in the goddamn car now!" I yell.

As I drive he says, "You just want to control me, huh. It feels good, huh. Conquer me like all the rest."

Yeah, that's really it. Sure.

I park at Taco Bell and get him some enchiladas to put in his stomach and he ravishes four of them. Then he gets sleepy and says, "Thank you, Jenny, for stopping me." And my heart breaks. I know he needs help. Yes, I know he *smokes* cocaine. *But I love him.*

The next day we drive to Palm Beach, browse in shops, and he eats one of his infamous hangover hot dogs from a stand. We go for a quick

252 • Jenny Lauren

visit to the Polo Store, where Grant sits on the couch, and I cringe when he notices the beautiful blond saleswoman in a baby yellow collection evening gown. I buy him some shirts. The manager there says, "You're Jerry's daughter. He's so awesome," and I agree. Grant smiles and says, "Yeah, looking forward to meeting him." We go for a nice meal. Everything is calm now. We don't discuss the night before, but decide what movie we'll see later.

But we never make it. That night he starts puking so hard that I have to drive him to the ER. He cries and moans and I'm scared. He tells me I am bad luck. But I hold him and massage his feet as we wait two hours. We find out he has food poisoning from that damn hot dog. After he recuperates for a day, he gathers the strength to return to Santa Fe. I need to stay one more week. I cry when he leaves because I will miss him but more because he says good-bye to me with cold eyes. And I know I'm the one who should have the distant look.

The trip didn't do much to help me. In fact, after having so many hands on my body, it feels like my insides are even more confused. The only good thing has been the colonic. I feel lighter. Afterward, everyone at the clinic says I look different. Maybe it is because it is the first time I have shit in fourteen days.

Grant and I remain living together for the next few months. Although I know that our relationship is doomed, and that I should break it off, I can't bear the thought of saying good-bye. I can't imagine not lying next to him, not smelling his sweet boyish-scented skin, rustling his smooth sandy-brown hair, and never locking our mouths together again.

But the hardest part for me is that Grant doesn't realize that as I lie next to him so fatigued by the constant distress, I feel myself slipping away, from him, and from my health. If I could, I would love him with reckless physical abandonment. *Emotionally I already have.* Losing this freedom is terrifying. How hard I have tried to fight all these years to be normal, to get better, especially so I can share a life with someone else.

I believe some force has pulled us together, and I have become committed to this man. Maybe because I understand his suffering.

But this dream of creating a world together seems less and less credible anyhow, and *absolutely horrific,* when I start finding him in my back bathroom two or three nights a week for hours. I get up from the bed, go into the kitchen, and see the empty Coke cans, the box of baking soda, and the burnt spoons. *Jenny, do you realize you are living with a crack addict? This is bad. REALLY BAD.* I raise my voice, "Grant. Grannntttt? Where are you?" Then I yell louder, "Grant! Grant! I told you not to! Please don't!" No answer. My body stiffens up again, my heart fills with fear, and I am as alone as I've ever been.

Then when he finally enters the living room where I have been sitting and pondering what to do, he says all dreamy-eyed and calmly, "Baby, don't be mad. Please don't. Come here. Come lie with me." I look at him with disdain. One time I finally become really brave and tell him he has to gather his things and get out. He starts whimpering, throws himself down onto the couch, with his body crunched up in a defeated ball and says, "I'll leave. Okay, I promise I'll leave. But where will I live?" For two solid hours I watch him cry. And the sad thing is, I still really don't want him to go.

One day in midsummer, Grant calls me from his job site after I have just had a long conversation with my mother. I tell him I have to fly to New York again for some tests. This will be my third time back home to see a specialist from Cornell who is intrigued by my case and is trying to help me. She had heard about my situation and called my mother up of her own volition. My mother is excited about this doctor. I kind of am too. Who ever heard of a doctor doing this? The contrast to Dr. Worthless and Dr. Fuckhead and the others is unbelievable. How can I not take advantage of this? (This cool lady is Dr. Awesome!) I have to go. I know something is wrong. Very wrong. I am no longer shitting at all on my own. In fact it is so bad that I have been getting colonics once a week for at least two months now. But Grant gets really pissed. He says he hates staying in the house alone and that it's got bad energy. *Well, I wonder why.* He hangs up on me angrily, like he does often.

And then that afternoon, Grant calls me back to inject me with venom and viciously says, "You're just a fat rich Jew bitch. And a very sick girl. You can't even ride a bike. Or take a hike without being in pain. To top it off, you can't even shit. You're going to get cancer. You probably can't even have a baby. You're not the right girl for me. This relationship is over."

Then calls back a few hours later, when I am still crying, and says, "I love you. I miss you. I'm sorry."

14. Coming Home

I give credit to Mel and Eva for helping this thirty-year-old little girl find the strength to go back home to New York. Eva listens to my frantic phone calls and Mel literally puts me on the plane because I can barely stand or see straight. I feel like I'm going to pass out at any moment. I need to be with my mother. But I also want Grant. At this point I don't know who I'd rather have a hug from. *I also need another goddamn colonic. Can I get a good one in New York? Where is my Grant?* I can't breathe. *I'll die without him. Don't think about it, Jenny, just go.*

A car picks me up at the airport to drive me to my parents' apartment, where I will be staying. My parents know all about my situation. Trust me, they know. I have called them hysterical a hundred times. And so have Mel, Ace, and Gena during the past spring because they were starting to worry about me. And maybe I should have listened to Mel when she said, "You're losing your light, Jenny. He's bad news. Even Max is worrying about you." But I couldn't. Greg ended up calling Grant once to warn him to get his act together and, believe it or not, in the last week, so did my mother. (I was mortified when I found out, but also impressed by her gall. *My mother?*)

My mother opens the door and opens her arms to embrace me but when I see her, I suddenly feel very angry and walk right by. I can't look at her. I head straight into her den, plop my things down, sit down on the sofa, and stare up at the wall. She comes in, "Honey, you look drained. Have you been eating?" I laugh to myself as I look at her bony body and gaunt face and say, "Yes. I have been. It's just the colonics. It's about time I got rid of this crap. I was holding extra weight because of it. But I'm not drained, Ma, just thinner. And, yeah, I don't feel so hot. Nothing new." Then I say bitterly, "Mommm. How could you? How could you call him? I was dealing with it. Mommmm. God. I can't take this. I don't want to be here. I miss him. God."

My mother then explains to me that the only reason she called Grant was because she heard he was getting physical. *Huh?* I try to calm down. "Moommmm," I whine. "Mom, that isn't true. Jesus!" Maybe my friends thought something like that was happening because over the past few months I had been losing weight and looking worn out. *Well, okay. So I don't tell my mother this,* but they might have noticed the black-and-blues I had on the backs of my arms where he squeezed me too hard after one of our more extreme fights. But still he never *meant* to hurt me. Well, not *that* way. My mother says the verbal abuse was bad enough, and that if my dad knew the extent of it, there would have been real trouble.

We meet my father at dinner that night after he is finished with work. I can hardly balance at the table or swallow a bite of food, but the first thing my father says is, "I know you're not feeling so well, but I just have to say, you're looking very dramatic these days. Susan, look at her fingers. How long and thin they are." *OH. MY. GOD.*

My father redeems himself with, "Any man would love to love you. But he has to be nice and treat you well. You'll find a good one now that you've got rid of that nightmare. Ecch. What a low-end character. I'm glad you're home."

But then he adds in no uncertain terms, "And Jenny, you are not to ever see or talk to that guy again, do you understand?"

Deep down, I know they are giving me the right advice, but I still put up a fight. *It's my decision, after all.* I beg them to let Grant visit so they can have a chance to understand his good side, but my father says, "Absolutely not. I do not want him stepping foot in my house. But Jenny, are you serious? How could you think of being with a man like him?" It's too late. They would never consider meeting him now. But I keep telling them how much I love him. That they should have sympathy; he has a drug problem. And what's so different? I had an eating disorder. My mother says, "Jenny, you've learned how to live with that, but now you have a physical condition that you need to get help for. It's completely different. If he loves you like he says he does, let him get treatment then. But he'll need years of it. Anyhow, where're *his* parents?"

Later that evening, I sneak into the bathroom to listen to Grant's messages on my cell phone. He cries and says, "Jenny, I don't want to lose you. Jennyyy. I miss you. Please." And I feel like I might just die. But the worst part is that I don't even care anymore about the name-calling. I just wish I were well enough to work through this relationship. I wish I were healthy enough to go back, stand up straight and strong, and make him go to rehab, give him the ultimatum. I know he could get well. But I'm not. In fact I'm getting sicker and sicker and I am too weak to deal with him.

After crying for nearly a week, I just go into a trance. Because besides being grief-stricken, I also take a load of Valium. But I manage to find a good place for a colonic and make it to some appointments with Dr. Awesome.

Dr. Awesome says, "The tacking at the sacrum doesn't appear like a problem, but this does not look like a very healthy colon," as she stares at the lit-up X rays on the screen that are from my barium study. Then she points to one part, "This here almost looks like colitis. I better do a colonoscopy. I want to get in there and check this out." My mom and I look at each other frustratedly, like, *here we go, another one.*

A few days after she drugs me and I have my fourth colonoscopy, she says, "You have a very inflamed and spastic bowel. I've sent out biopsies to all the specialists and nothing is revealing any bacteria or signs of Crohn's or colitis. I don't know what all this is from. But we'll keep on working to figure this out. I promise."

"Dr. A," I say, "Why don't we just do an exploratory surgery?"

"Because I don't think you respond very well to surgery. But maybe you better talk to your original surgeon and see what he has to say."

Fuck.

Two weeks later, when I finally leave my parents' to stay at my 63rd Street apartment in the building I grew up in, my eyes spasm, my lips shiver, my heart aches, and I begin to have what I think might be considered a nervous breakdown. *And I cannot eat at all.*

15. The Return of Fashion

While I am lying in bed with the covers raised high above my head, ruminating over whether to phone Grant or contact my surgeon to schedule an appointment and *why I should even get up,* my mother calls before her midmorning exercise class to remind me that the Ralph Lauren fashion show is this evening. In her message she says she will leave a ticket down in my lobby just in case I decide to attend. I chuckle to myself, like, *yeah, that's the very thing I want to do right now, go see a bunch of gorgeous models.* I don't even remember the last time I went to one of those events. Maybe eight years ago?

When the phone rings again, I screen it, and then pick up because I hear Brad's voice. He informs me that he and Amy are going tonight and the show is at this fabulous new place, the gardens at the Cooper Hewitt Museum uptown, and I ought to come.

I say to my brother, "Are you nuts? I can hardly walk or breathe. Why would I go?"

Brad says, "Because you need to get out of the house. You shouldn't be alone so much. Maybe it will be fun, Jenny. You'll see Andrew, David, Dylan, your cousins, remember those guys?" I wince for a moment, thinking how long it's been since I've seen them.

I tell Brad there is a very slim chance I'll be there.

At 6 P.M. after I have been almost comatose all day, falling in and out of sleep, my mother calls to check in. I start to cry and tell her that I can't believe they actually expect me to go to this in my condition. I tell her I haven't showered, I look a mess, and *what the hell will I wear, anyhow?* She says if it's too much, not to worry and just to rest.

I call her back five minutes later. "Well, can I go with a rugged look? I mean, Dad hates my hair up, but it's curly and it will be awful down. Can I just put it up in a bun?"

My mom says, "Absolutely, honey. Do your bohemian thing."

I say, "Nah. I don't think so. Have a good time."

I continue to lie flat on my bed like I'm dead, for an hour. The darkness is hovering over me, enveloping me like the past, as I stare out the building at all the windows and then back up at the ceiling. My brain is acting like a radio newscast that runs over the same painful headlines and themes. BRUTAL PAIN. EVIL DOCTORS. SHATTERING BREAKUP. I fixate on the fact that I may never get better. *This is your life, kiddo. You're screwed.* I wonder where Grant is at precisely this moment. The next, and the next. *Is he at the Cowgirl Bar? El Farol Restaurant? With a girl? I AM GOING TO BE SICK. GRANTTTTT!!!!* Then after hearing his pleas for me in haunting whispers, I slowly crawl out of my bed, look in the full-length mirror that my parents put on the back of my door while I was away, think, *Well, at least I'm thinner* (on Dr. Awesome's scale I weighed 108 . . . *boy, it dropped off mighty fast*), and say aloud, "Fuck it. I'll go." I'll be damned if I'm going to sit around thinking of him and this bullshit all night. But I have exactly fifteen minutes to make it.

Ten minutes later, I head out the door in a black hooded sweatshirt and huge tan cargo pants that hang low because I still can't wear anything too tight around my waist or crotch or I'll freak out, with my brown sandals (the only pair of shoes I ever wear because I have room to wiggle my toes), and my hair pulled up in a high ponytail, so I resemble *Pebbles. This will just have to do.*

In the cab up to 90th Street I grip the seat trying to find a comfortable position and think to myself, *Okay, Jenny. This is a good thing you're going out. You can function like a normal person.* As I peer out the window there is nobody in sight along the Upper East Side. It seems so dark, so lonely. *Probably just me.* Then I think about my old cab rides on the mornings I was late to class at Barnard. I'd be shaking with anxiety, urging the taxi driver to speed it up. Now I'm just numb.

But when I get out of the cab and two doormen in black tie escort me up the stairwell and into the mansion I start to feel myself waking up a bit.

"Jenny! Wow! Jenny's here!" A man I hardly recognize, who I assume works for my father, pounces at me.

My mouth is frozen. It doesn't seem to want to form the word "Hello," or to kiss his cheek. Not because I'm feeling shy, but because of a combination of two things; I'm out of practice socializing, and because all my muscles in my body are weakened, even in my face.

After managing the first encounter, I walk slowly through the large wooden doors, down the stone stairway to the outdoor garden where there are a huge white tent and millions of gigantic planters of flowers. Suddenly I feel like I'm Cinderella entering the ballroom, except I'm still in my rags, and my so-called prince is in Santa Fe with a *glass pipe.* If anything, I feel more like the pumpkin. The space is filled to the max with white petunias, and roses, and lilies, and mobs of elegantly dressed people, along with cool young hipsters in outfits like mine, and waiters who are walking around serving hors d'oeuvres and champagne. But where is the runway? *Okay. Fashion shows never used to be like this. What is this world coming to?* There are even leather couches all over. This is like the largest party I've ever been to. I am not prepared. *Just walk through, Jenny. Go to your seat.*

I still can't smile or focus on anyone's face but I do see my mom and dad from afar. My mother is holding a wineglass, my father is noshing on pigs-in-blankets, and when I raise my hand, his face lights up with surprise, he nudges my mother, and then motions for me to come over.

After I trip over a few feet and finally reach the area where my parents are, my father says to the couple standing with them, "Do you remember my beautiful daughter? She's fresh in from Santa Fe." I look down, embarrassed that he always has to play me up.

"Jenny, do you remember the Adamsons?"

"Of course I do," I lie. "So nice to see you again."

Then some young woman who used to date one of my cousins and works for the company now comes prancing over to me.

"Jenny, oh my God. You look fabulous. You got so thin!"

Yeah, she should only know I can't digest anything anymore. And I'm sticking a vacuum up my ass to shit.

Then I see my cousins and they all wave to me from across the distance. David gives me a thumbs-up like he's really excited to see me. And it really hurts. Because I wouldn't have let all this time go by between us if I hadn't been so ill. In many ways they used to be my best friends.

The crowds are heading toward the runway, which is finally becoming more visible. Brad and Amy are already in their seats on the huge leather sofas that surround the entire central podium and I join them. My other relatives, aunts and uncles, Janice, my cousins Beth and Susan are in our row. Somehow I forgot it would be a family reunion. Even though I survive the hellos, and everybody tells me I look great (which is amazing because I've never felt worse in my life but *hey, I'm skinny now, so you know*), I don't find much to say except that I left a crazy boyfriend in Santa Fe and I'm in town to see more doctors, and maybe I'm back for good, but who knows. I am relieved when the music starts to blare, and the chattering stops. But it is so loud and the lights are so bright that I can feel my anxiety pulsing, my veins throbbing, and I notice I'm still shaking and shivering.

Then the stick-thin corpses come jutting out, walking hard, moving fiercely, hips and pelvis thrusting forward, with soft spring florals, ripped jean fabrics, and bohemian silks falling loosely on every one of their angles, with their lips formed into crooked pouts and parted smiles. I am in culture shock. I have never seen a single one of these models before. It's a whole new crop of faces *and bodies*. Now they really, really look anorexic to me. *Have I been dead for a few years? Do people still care about fashion? Clothing? Makeup? Their weight?* And, heck, the only place in Santa Fe where you can get anything decent, besides commercial western clothes, is Target, and I only bought white T-shirts there. I guess I thought when I stopped caring *that much,* the whole world did too.

When the tall dark-haired girls with the light green or blue eyes and the thick eyebrows saunter by I feel dizzy. I remember the first fashion show I was in. My uncle's smile, his admiration. I start to laugh inside at the mere irony of all this, that I have put myself in this position, coming here, and that I am privy to a life that doesn't do a thing for me anymore. All I want is my body to hold me up, to be back in Santa Fe with Grant, cuddling in bed or at a movie, or driving with him, looking at the sunset with my hand overlapping his as he changes the gear. The clothing is incredible as always, but who needs it? I used to dress this way, the ripped jeans, the short blazers, the sparkling beads, but who gives a rat's ass anymore? For what? I'm not going anywhere special, I have no one to look cool for (although *he* sure didn't care that I wore the same outfit day after day), and I don't feel well. I want to go home. *Wherever that is.*

After the show, it is too crowded to stand on line to say hello to my uncle, so we wait and hang around by the tables of food, and everyone is sipping pink champagne and munching (except for me). My father says, "Amazing, huh? Just amazing. He did it again. Jenny, we need to get you some of these clothes. Susan, she should have some of these things. She'll look great in it. Take her to the store or the showroom this week, okay?"

I whisper to my mom, "The girls are really skinny. I can't fit into that shit."

She says, "Yeah, and so are you, Jenny. You can wear it all. And you better not lose any more weight."

"I don't care about any of it, Mom. The clothes. Being thin. I just want to get well. None of it matters without your health. Absolutely none of it."

She doesn't speak.

My cousins drift over and we exchange hugs. I ask Andrew about the new movie he's producing and joke with Dylan that I'm afraid to go into the candy store she just opened and will have to wear handcuffs. I am really excited to see David, and he tells me he is so happy I'm back in town and that he's heard I've had a rough time. I nod my head yes but don't even know where to begin. He says maybe we could do dinner and chat, and I could check out his new apartment downtown if I'm up to it. I give a noncommittal response, "Yeah, uh-huh, sure, maybe. Sounds great." I really would love to, but I don't know if I have the energy.

Then when I finally see my uncle in a jean jacket, tweed pants, and motorcycle boots and my aunt in a white lace blouse and brown leather pants, both making their way through the crowds toward us, I feel a warm and safe feeling, because the image of them is almost as familiar to me as my own parents. They represent so much of my childhood, my origins. My father stares at my uncle, then points to me, and I notice tears forming in my uncle's eyes. Mine start to water too. He has to look away for a second to compose himself. When both my aunt and uncle arrive next to us, I kiss them hello and say to my uncle, "Well, I made it after all these years. It's a beautiful line. Very artsy. Very cool. Can I have some of it?" Uncle Ralph gives me a huge grin. Then suddenly, and just like in the past, I become shy, turn toward my parents, tell them I'm ready to go, and I blaze through the crowds and I'm out the door.

16. My Asshole Surgeon

My mom, dad, and I sit in the surgeon's office in September 2002, five years since my surgery. My surgeon says, "Well, it's been tough, huh?"

And surprisingly enough, I'm not as angry as I thought I would be. He is gentle, soft-spoken, the way he was when I first met him and he agreed to do the surgery. But I also notice how dumpy and round his body is. He actually resembles the Pillsbury Dough Boy. I don't think he's ever lifted a muscle in his life, just *somebody else's*. I think to myself, *How could this man know about the body, when he doesn't even respect his own enough to get some exercise.* I didn't notice this before. I was too distracted.

This time I do all the talking. (I don't need my parents to say a thing. And I've requested that they don't.) I speak in a reserved, slow and mature tone without getting accusatory, as my dad has warned me not to.

I say, "Yes, it's been quite difficult. I understand you had the best intentions, and I came to you in a dire situation in 'ninety-seven, but can you please explain some things? Um, first off, what part of my colon exactly is tacked to my sacrum?"

"Your rectum and your enterocele, which is part of your sigmoid, Jenny."

I gulp. *It is true.*

"And where is it? Is it on my vertebrae?"

"No, not really" he says, "but it is sewn to the thin bone tissues surrounding your sacrum. Near your S1."

I try to take a deep breath.

"I see. So it's not stapled, though?"

"No. It was sewn with a one-centimeter permanent suture made of indissoluble thread. But you do have a few nonreactive titanium staples where I reconnected your colon after resecting part of it."

"Oh. Uh-huh. I probably have a lot of scar tissue, right? Do I have any on my sacrum?"

"Yes, Jenny. That, in fact, was my mission. I purposely tried to create scar tissue to help keep the colon tacked up there."

"So basically my colon stays up with a thread and scar tissue. If I didn't have it like that it would fall between my legs again?"

He doesn't speak for a second, and then nods his head sympathetically, "Yes, Jenny, I'm afraid so."

I say, "There wasn't any other way of doing this, like creating some kind of artificial pelvic floor with fascia or mesh?" *I have looked this all up on the Internet by now.*

He explains, "Jenny, it's not great to put a foreign material in your body like mesh because it can cause infection. And if we used fascia we would have had to take it from another part of your body, like your knee, and that's a whole other operation."

"Um, oh, I see." *Focus, Jenny, focus.*

"Now I have an important question, though. If my colon is spastic, wouldn't I feel it tugging on my whole spinal cord?"

He says, "Perhaps."

"And couldn't I feel it even with natural peristalsis? I mean, the colon needs to move no matter what."

"Well, you shouldn't."

"And couldn't it pull out my natural alignment?"

"Well, your vertebrae are stronger than your colon. So it shouldn't."

"But couldn't it cause pain in the neck, and my headaches."

"Maybe."

This is all just too much to believe.

And my parents are just watching this interaction like, what is my daughter talking about?

But I have done my research. Not just on the Internet. My body tells me enough.

I try to remember everything I want to ask. *Oh yeah, how can I forget?* "Well, could you explain to me why I can't defecate?"

"I'm not sure about that, Jenny. But I think I should examine you and see what's going on now. Will you come with me and the nurse for a second?"

I grit my teeth and agree.

In the room as he does his thing, he says, "God, someone would kill for that tone. Boy, I did a good job."

And then I remember why I *really* hate him.

When we return to his office, I look at my parents with a sour expression.

As the surgeon sits down behind his desk, he says, "Well, it is possible that during the surgery I did damage to some of the nerves of your colon. I'm sorry. It happens."

I start to cry. *I'm so exhausted. I need to go sleep. I miss Grant.*

My mother then asks, "Okay, Doctor, so what does she do? Do you think these colonics Jenny's getting are healthy?"

He says, "Well, she has to do what she has to do. I think she needs a good physical therapist too."

And then there's really nothing more to say. He can't do a thing to help.

We all stand up and my parents both shake his hand and say, "Thank you, Doctor."

I say nothing. I don't smile, I don't frown, I just let the tears roll.

As we head toward the door my surgeon says to me, "Jenny, by the way, thank you for that beautiful card you sent me. It really touched me."

What? What card? What is he talking about?

And then I remember I sent him a Christmas card the winter following my surgery for at least trying to help me.

17. Searching

My hour-long talks with Rosie, my new colonic lady, are *very cathartic*. They are better than therapy. I call them Colonic Talk, instead of Coffee Talk *(very big whoop)*, and I have now told Rosie about my entire life, which includes crying to her about missing Grant and complaining about my ill-fated health situation. She in turn tells me about her boyfriend, her healing rituals, and her take on my physical dilemma. Rosie is convinced that the positioning of my colon to my sacrum is the problem, that I would have healthy peristalsis and function more normally if my asshole surgeon hadn't done it this way. What was he thinking, she keeps on asking, shaking her head. "But maybe your body can adapt." She suggests I see a very special doctor who saved her life as a teenager, when she was diagnosed with epilepsy. He got her off medications and aided her to wellness through nutrition. She hasn't had a seizure in over fifteen years. "He knows everything," she says, and then whispers, "He's psychic." And even though he has a six-month waiting list she is able to get me an appointment immediately.

The psychic turns out to be a very knowledgeable seventy-year-old Indian man who wears a suit and tie and does not have a crystal ball.

But he looks at me when I meet him and says, "Oh boy."

I tell him my medical history and about just leaving Grant.

First he tells me, "You cannot go back to that man."

"I know. But why not?" I ask, "I love him."

He says, "You know love isn't necessarily what you need. It can be very dangerous. You can't go back because it won't bring you harmony. Here. I will give you a Bach flower remedy to help you with your emotions."

Then he takes my pulse, looks at my tongue, and tells me that most of my physical condition, the muscle ache, the weakness, and even the very original problem, *and possibly the eating disorder,* is from parasites. I am riddled with them, he says. *What a pretty thought.* And here we go, *back to the very beginning.* He explains, "Anybody with a twitch like you had has to have parasites. I hear about this from a lot of my patients." *You do? Other people get the twitch?*

He also says my C1 and C2 vertebrae are being affected by the surgery. Then he exclaims, "It must be horrendous living with such Chinese torture. Sheesh, having your colon tacked to your sacrum. What is wrong with modern medicine? I wish you had come to me before." And I become so sad and angry at myself when I think of how impatient I was five years ago, when I basically handed my own body over to the meat cutter.

He gives me a whole plan of attack. I must quit coffee, sugar, wheat, alcohol, and *anything else that has taste.* Okay, I will, I promise. This time it's no joke. He prescribes homeopathic remedies, herbs, and writes down the address of a place to go to have a parasite test and receive his special vitamin drip formula. I rush to the health store near his office, where he is thought of as Dr. God, and I spend $500 on the goods. I am grateful, though. I will do anything. I will finally heal myself as naturally as I can.

I start eating beautifully, absolutely perfectly. Cooked white fish (no sushi . . . it causes parasites, Dr. God warns), grains without any gluten, and steamed vegetables. And within a month, my skin clears and my hair and nails grow long, but I am getting more and more depressed and have an awful stomachache all the time.

The test shows I do have parasites, little amoebic ones, and I take antibiotics for a month. Dr. God says to keep going with the colonics because I *must kill off these parasites, flush them out.* Unfortunately I think I am also flushing the healthy bacteria out, although I take acidophilus. I leave Vera and Colonic Talk like a total zombie, dizzy and bent over. By October, besides being "too" skinny, I also look crippled. But I don't notice anybody checking me out anymore. I don't give a shit anyway. Even if they might, I avoid their eyes. I am invisible.

As winter nears, I am freezing all the time, I can barely walk and I feel paralyzed between my legs. It reminds me of right after my surgery. I also continue to have these horrific reactions to homeopathics and end up choking all night. My neck and head tighten up so much that I start to wonder if I have a brain tumor. But worst of all, and to top it off, I have the original twitch. I call up Dr. God and he says it's called a healing crisis when all the original symptoms show up. "Just try and get through it," he says.

I spend my days struggling as I hail a taxi to go for my hour-long vitamin drips, cook my meals, go for my colonics, and in between I remain curled up on my bed in agony. I also spend every minute hating my parents. I don't want to see them ever. It's as if suddenly, I'm trapped back in my nightmare, in a tunnel with nowhere to run. I am right where I was all my years growing up, literally and metaphorically. I am lying in the bed in the same building I grew up in, the apartment I stayed in during most of college, where the twitch started, and continues, five years later. I actually wonder if I am dying from complete physical deterioration or from the anger. I resent my parents all over again. I can feel it in my cell memory, the emotion of sheer terror welling up throughout my body, from the year before my surgery; not being heard by them or anyone else, then immediately afterward, none of them understanding the maddening physical pain. And now I have had to leave a life I was starting in Santa Fe behind *even if it did get messy,* because *they let that man cut me open and tack my colon to my sacrum.* When one of them calls, I yell, "Leave me alone, it's all your fault, you never heard me! How could you let them do this to me?" But then I hang up and sob from the most abysmal grief. Because I know I'm hurting them and none of it is really their fault. It's just circumstances. The truth is I hate myself. I hate myself because I let that surgeon cut me open and *I can't even blame him.* I hate myself because I was so self-destructive and capable of ingesting poisonous ipecac, of sticking my hands down my throat, of wearing my body down, of treating myself without respect. And now *just another thing,* because I got myself in a toxic relationship that I have had to flee from. I hate myself, because I am tired of falling apart.

I feel as if I have no choice but to be back here in New York City where I can *maybe* get help physically, because I wasn't necessarily finding it in Santa Fe, because I can barely stand, and because I have to keep away from Grant. Yet, I don't want to be here. I don't want to play the role of the troubled daughter anymore. I want a life; to heal, to get well. In order to do that, I vow to be vigilant about my new regime. I choose to stay by myself and focus. Away from my parents, away from everyone and anything that will be an obstacle this time to getting the right answers and to getting better. I cannot afford to get frustrated by their shticks or have them get frustrated by mine. But here it goes: My mom keeps sending food over, steamed, plain, no salt, no sugar, no fruit. She follows my diet for me strictly. She tries very hard. My dad leaves messages on my machine asking if I would think about talking to the rabbi, or at least to Dr. Hannibal again. But I don't go to their house. I don't answer their check-ins. It's almost as hard as resisting Grant's calls, even though I still dream of him every night and wake up startled, wondering where he is.

I make a few attempts to hang out with my brother Brad and his wife, Amy, especially because they are expecting a baby in the spring and I am very excited by that, at least. And when Greg and his *now* *fiancée*, Elizabeth, come into town I do force myself to meet them at their hotel and Greg says, "Wow. You're looking very detoxed. But don't get any thinner." No one seems to get it, though, that *now it physically hurts* to eat.

At this point the only person I will gladly see is Nikki, who comes over every week, gives me healing gems from the jewelry she is making, and introduces me to her psychic-energy worker named Cassandra. *And thank God for this woman.* She is an ex-hippie, with short hair, and wears bright colored sweats without a bra, and exotic dangling earrings. I can tell immediately she doesn't seem to give a shit what anyone thinks. As soon as she comes over she says, "Wow. Cool trucks," referring to my parents' Buddy L toys that now line the shelf. While I was away they redid the place to house some of their folk art collection. It is very white and airy now, with sleek lacquered open shelves for their antiques, brown leather chairs, glass tables, and nickel lamps. I am relieved, because otherwise being back here in the setting identical to college and the one before surgery would really blow my mind. Then Cassandra goes straight to the beaded American Indian gloves and says, "Someone really powerful wore these." "Good powerful, or bad?" I ask. "Oh, good. Very good."

She sits down on the white couch next to me, closes her eyes, and begins to tell me what she sees. She starts to laugh. "Whoa, boy, have you gone off course. Somehow you lost the memo to have fun, Jenny. You were supposed to be an entertainer, a dancer, an actress, onstage. Something happened, I don't know what, and you got steered in the wrong direction. But this is not your life forever. You are not going to be in pain for eternity." She tells me it will take some time, probably at least two years though. "You have to get rid of the pattern. The eating-disorder pattern, and get some chi in that colon. Cut out those colonics, they're bringing everything right back up. All these symptoms, though, the choking, the twitch, the bearing down, it's related to a cellular pattern, and it started young, or maybe even in a past life. That's what you need to work on with tai chi or chi gong." She also tells me I have the Epstein-Barr virus and eating well and doing energy work are the best things I can do to get rid of this. She says people don't understand this virus yet. Then I tell her Grant's birthday and she says, "What a difficult man. Yikes. You don't want to go back to him. He is a narcissist. And a parasite. He is feeding off you even now." *Hmmm, is that why I lost all the weight?* "You have a soul connection but it was about learning what you don't want. Forget him. Now back to your health, I think everything's too cramped in there, something with your uterus." *Hmmm. Another theory.*

I say, "But tell me more about Grant."

"More about the Psycho Loo Loo? What. What do you want to know?" and I laugh for the very first time in a long time.

When I have a test for Epstein-Barr it turns out I test positive for it. But of course even Dr. Awesome downplays it. "Not a big deal." Except when I call Dr. God again, he says, "Oh, boy. Well, don't worry, the vitamin drips will address that because they're helping your immune system."

And after I tell Dr. God about Cassandra, he says I must talk to Sean, the best Vedic astrologer (who studies from the ancient belief system in India) in the States. So I call him up in California, where he lives, give him my birth information, and he does my chart for me. It turns out that I have a seventeen-year cycle in *one planet* that conjuncts *some other planet* and is in *the house* of physical debilitation (*oh, Jesus*) that started in 1996 (*holy . . .*) but it is a *neechabhunga,* which means it is actually a blessing in disguise. He says this year is about friends and health, and that I will undergo a major transformation. He tells me that my personality has an inner conflict because I crave independence, but also flourish in partnerships, and that I will need to find a healthy balance of the two. He asks, "Are you very close to your mother? Does she worry a lot?" *Yes.* "Is your father very critical?" *YES.* Then he says my chart shows a weakness in the area of digestion and the muscles of the body, and suggests that yoga and meditation would be very grounding for me. He provides me with what he calls a prescriptive reading the following day and tells me what mantras to say, and what gemstones to wear to influence my karmic pattern and change my aura. He says, "Do not wear any black or blue gems or clothing of that color." I say, "No turquoise? I used to wear a turquoise ring on every finger." He says, "When?" "Most of my teenage years." "Well, don't wear it anymore. Wear coral. And wear diamonds. That would be good for you." Then I say, "What about navy? I wore navy overcoats my whole life. And jean jackets? And lots of black." He says, "I would wear some lighter colors, Jenny. Blue is too Saturn for you. Call me again if you have any questions." So I start wearing white in the dead of winter, check out the Tiffany windows, and start playing my *Om Vreem Mangalaya Namah* tape over and over all day even when I'm not there. I light candles and try to sit up enough to chant in the morning, evening, and whenever I'm in utter pain. So I chant the entire day. I have to come all the way back to New York City from Santa Fe, New Mexico, New-Ager la-la land to turn into one myself.

Meanwhile, I'm not happy with the seventeen-year-cycle thing, so Vera tells me about Diana, who does good old-fashioned western astrology. I call her up and she tells me this year is about repatterning, healing, and that I will be feeling much better in all ways by the summer. I keep calling her.

At my third visit with Dr. God, he suggests I start going for neural injections, a form of therapy founded in Europe that involves shooting procaine into scar tissue to break it up. Dr. God thinks my physiological mechanisms are all going haywire because of my scars. I receive these new treatments three times a week from an osteopath who forcefully cracks and manipulates my body instead of the gentle coaxing I've obtained in the past. He's rude and reminds me of Freddy Krueger, especially when he's bending over me with those shots. I continue seeing him only because he's got the license to practice neural therapy and there are not that many doctors in the city who do.

And, as if all this isn't enough, Dr. God thinks rolfing, a massage technique that goes deep into your tissues and is supposed to correct all kinds of body issues, might help too. So I have the shit kneaded out of me by the nicest woman ever. I sign up for the fifteen sessions that are supposed to transform my whole body. I complete all fifteen, but my rolfer eventually tells me she really thinks my problem is internal. The tacking is something she has never dealt with, although she has successfully treated people with rods in their back. She says, "Things are not right inside. I think you oughta do an exploratory."

In November, Dr. God takes my pulse and tells me he thinks it's my appendix. "That's it!" he exclaims, "I knew there was a missing link." He says it has been chronic appendicitis all along. The parasites have been eating away at my appendix. He says it would help to have it removed but if it doesn't show up in an exam, he doesn't know who will do the surgery.

I am so desperate once again, because now it is nearly impossible to eat without experiencing excruciating pain on my entire right side. If it really is my appendix, I want it out. NOW.

I call Dr. Awesome and she sets up the examination, although she says the likelihood of all this being caused by my appendix is very minimal. Still I have an abdominal and pelvic ultrasound and a CT scan. The ultrasound results read a "fluid-filled inflamed appendix" (*well, whadda ya know*) but after I throw up the radioactive iodine (which they inject you with to highlight your organs on the screen), the CT scan doesn't reveal anything. Dr. God says, "Appendixes usually don't even show up in ultrasounds, which means we're really getting at something. It doesn't matter about the CT scan. Let's just pray someone will agree to get rid of it."

When I call Dr. Awesome she is hesitant because she really doesn't want to see me have to undergo any unnecessary surgery, but she agrees to send me to one of her laparoscopic surgeons to discuss my results. And in December, when I meet the new, young, and hip surgeon, regardless of what my parents or anybody else says, or my own relentless fear, I beg for surgery again.

18. Camp Letters

While my mother was cleaning out her closets the other day, she came across an envelope of camp letters that she had saved from the summer I was ten. She asked me if I wanted to see them. At first I was hesitant, because I didn't want to seem too interested in what she had to say, and also because I wasn't so sure I could bear to reunite with the past. But my curiosity was piqued, so I asked her to drop them off.

Dear Mommy and Daddy   *July 20, 1982*

Hi! I just wanted to talk to you on the phone. I'm so happy I got to talk with both of you. It was so nice hearing your voice. Thank you for telling me about eating. It's just that I feel so fat. I don't know why. And I'm afraid that I look fat. Don't be mad at me though. It's just Oh I don't know. I wish I was with you. I don't want to gain weight, that's all and everyone else eats so much and they're even skinnier than me. I don't eat hardly as near as much as everyone else and I'm even fatter than them. It's not fair. But don't worry because I'm eating. It's just the junky stuff I don't eat like the bread and desserts and all that. So don't worry. Oh I love you so much. I can't wait to see you. I love you more than anything in the whole world. I love you. I miss you so much I wish I was home with you. I read a book called Anastia Krupnik (and then I read another book called Bridge to Teribitha. It was kind of sad. And then I started a book called The Trumpet of the Swan. I'm on page 124 . . . I miss you so much I'll see you soon. I love you so much. I love you more than anything.

I love you, Love, Jenny

As I read tears start to form and I can't help but go down memory lane. I begin to dream of my favorite sweatshirts, soft and loose, hanging gently on my body, a faded gray, a faded Harvard burgundy, and then images flow into movement . . . dancing, flowing, jumping. I am back there in ballet camp, staring at the Adirondack walls of the dance studio and then peering down at the pink elastic band around my waist that reminds me to hold in my stomach, then I am looking in the mirror, and as I point my toe, tears run down my face because I miss my mother. My homesickness feels like death.

My parents rush me home from camp and Daddy is crying in angst, wondering if I will eat. I see the melting pralines and cream ice cream cone. It's creamy and gloppy and sugary sweet, and Daddy holds my hand as I lick it. *Don't cry, Daddy. . . . Don't cry. . . . I'll eat. . . .* DADDYYYY! MOMMMMYYY!!! ILOVEYOU!!! DON'TLEAVEME!!! UGGH. I CAN'T TAKE THIS.

Dear Greg,   *July 17, 1982*

Hi! I miss you so much. How is everything? I miss you so much.
Tomorrow our bunk is going to Friendly's. You see every bunk gets
to go once a summer so we picked tomorrow. We're also probably
going to sneak it and go to McDonald's too. I'll probably get a cone
or a scoop in a dish or something easy. Everyone else is going to get
junk like Reese's Pieces sundaes and all that junk. Please don't tell
Mommy and Daddy but the other day at a campfire everyone was
eating S'mores. S'mores are graham crackers, Hershey Bar and a
marshmallow made into a sandwich. I didn't want one. Then
Nancy comes up to me and goes, "I want you to at least eat a
graham cracker. You look too thin." She started giving me this
lecture that I had to eat more. She almost put me at her table. She
puts the girls who don't eat at her table and makes them eat
everything. But my counselor told her to let me handle eating for a
week and if I didn't eat enough she would put me at her table. I
can't stand it! I eat but I just don't eat the junky stuff and the
bread. After dinner they always serve something like brownies and
stuff and I don't eat that. But before that they always serve some
kind of fruit. I sometimes have that. Don't worry I'm eating. So at
Friendly's I'll just get something easy and I won't have dinner at
camp. Instead I'll have chicken McNuggets at McDonald's. I don't
care what Nancy thinks because I'm eating and she thinks it is her
problem. You don't know how much I wish we were all together at
home and we could be eating Mommy's delicious cooking with
Mommy and Daddy there to tell us what to eat. See you soon.
Can't wait. 35 more days until we're together. I love you so much
and miss you.

Love, Jenny

Suddenly I am at our house in Connecticut in the freezing cold winter, running from Greg, who is chasing me around the red barn in

mountains of deep snow. He catches me and throws me down like a football and looks at Brad, who is filming us, and screams, "Touchdown!" I keep getting up and he throws me down until we've had enough laughing and I have eaten enough of the cold snow . . . GREGGIEE! BRADDDDD!!!

And as I continue reading more of these notes, I start to convulse with violent tears. All I want is to be young again and playing with my brothers . . . swimming in Florida, building sand castles on the beach with them, or drinking lemonade and watching the toy sailboats in the pond at Central Park. *Where has the time gone? How old am I? What's happened since?* The realization that it will never be like that ever again is devastating. Especially because I had a healthy body then.

I don't think I needed so many therapists through the years to analyze me to death and tell me about my problems. The pain is revealed in these letters. There were thirty of them, all similar. Each one showed how lonely I was, how much I wanted to please my parents, and how food had come to represent security, togetherness, and home to me. I feel so bad for that little girl. *And for the big one.*

I finally have to put them down because I can't afford to experience the aching that my memories bring. And trying to figure out how I got here, over and over, is not going to help anymore. I decide to go chant in the living room. I close my eyes and try to forget. I think about moving on, away from the past. And getting well.

19. The Full Moon

On December 19, 2002, although I'm a little worried about the full moon because my astrologer Diana says you can bleed more at this time of the month, I go in for my second surgery.

When I arrive, my new surgeon commends me for coming in, because I had called panicking about it a few days earlier. I actually told him, "I'm not so sure I should come in on the full moon. But Mercury will be in retrograde after the holidays. This day is the best of all evils but . . ." He interrupted me as he chuckled and said, "I do a lot of surgeries on the full moon, Jenny, and never heard that."

I said defensively, "Well, some of us *more spiritual* people believe in these kinds of things." But then I laughed at myself. I would like to think that after the disaster of my first surgery, I might listen to my astrologer, but I still don't. I'm not waiting two months for this. Uh-uh. And after all, I have free will, right?

I tell my parents they better go on their winter vacation to South Africa as planned. In fact, I don't want them around when I have surgery. I don't want the fussing, the worrying. I don't want it to be anything like before.

Brad and my "aunt" Madeline (my mother's best and lifelong friend) take me in for my one-day procedure. Although I'd rather be alone, it is a hospital policy that someone needs to accompany me. I give my good luck gems from Nikki to Brad to hold and I head in.

Cut. Chop. Snip. Close. Done.

Brad and my Aunt Madeline tell me afterward that my new surgeon is ecstatic. That he had to leave, but he had come to them with a huge smile on his face, good news, and a drawing of what he found inside. I am told the surgery has been a total success.

Apparently he saw tons of adhesions, and something was wrong with my uterus. It turns out that my appendix looked fine, but he took it out anyway, *but Dr. God said . . . oh, who cares! Tell me more!*

When I go to see the surgeon for a checkup a few days later, he explains it all to me. He says, "Wow, Jenny, you must have suffered from a lot of pain during your sexual relations, because basically your uterus, in other words, your vagina, was adhered down to your pelvic region and was caught and pulling on your sacrum. It must have been like that since your first surgery. You also had adhesions on your fallopian tube and I lanced some others I found. There was a big one on your secal valve. And some of your bowel was also adhered down, so I freed it up.

I didn't touch where your colon is sutured to your sacrum area, though, because I didn't think that would be a good idea, at least for now. I don't think your colon is strong enough and it would probably fall again. Anyhow, give it some months to see if any of this makes a difference overall in how you feel."

Okay. So the fact that I was right all along does not amaze me. It pisses me off! My uterus wasn't sewn too close to my rectum like I thought, just stuck! Same thing! For five fucking years!

"Will I start going to the bathroom, Doctor?"

"I don't think this will solve that. But I promise I will continue to help you. Let's take it one step at a time." *For every hundred assholes, there's always a prince.*

But even though I am happy about the finds from his archeological dig and *his autographed drawing,* I'm in a hell of a lot of pain. I am so bloated (they fill you up with air for the surgery) that I'm afraid I'm going to literally propel off the ground. And that's exactly what I do. I am unable to relax or let myself heal. Within a week I find myself out on the winter streets trying to rush around. I don't know where I am. And then, as if I'm fifteen all over again, I regress to my old behaviors. I start to binge. Sugar, sugar. Carbs. Salt. Chocolate. Ice cream. Aggh! On Christmas and New Year's Day, Grant calls me. I can't talk! I don't pick up! I am going into fight-or-flight. I don't know where I am.

20. Running from Myself

When my parents return from South Africa with photos of zebras, baboons, and elephants, I still have no desire to see them. I'm too tired to go over to their apartment. I wish I could, but I'm in no shape to enjoy the zoo or converse with them about the surgery when I don't even know if it's truly helped yet. But as my mood gets worse and I find myself spinning and shaking from sugar and fear, and more dissociation, *Did I just have surgery again? Holy Fuck! Who am I?* I know I can't do this alone anymore. I phone them and tell them I need help. I'm just too exhausted. My dad begs me to call Dr. Hannibal.

I will. I surrender. I must.

I haven't seen Hannibal in five years.

Fine, I'll see shrink and shrink and shrink. I still speak to Eva on the phone in Santa Fe but I don't consider her *one of them*. Eva is my spiritual guide, shaman, and friend. But even *she* thinks I should go see Hannibal. She says I need a vacation from the pain, from the suffering, from my mind. She tells me I should probably take something, a pill. "It's all right, Jenny, you can stop being so hard on yourself. You'll still find the answers." And I totally agree. Fuck homeopathy, fuck herbs, and fuck being a martyr. Give me the goddamn Prozac *now!*

Dr. Hannibal has moved offices and is working on the same floor at Mount Sinai, where I went into the psycho ward after my surgery. *This is all just getting too weird.* When I wait outside for my session I notice the familiar moving cart with the stack of hospital food trays being rolled down the hallway toward the locked unit. I remember the Danishes. The cereal and milk I couldn't get down. I'm tempted to ask for a breakfast tray for myself, now that I have broken Dr. God's diet. I also have broken ties with him. I should have known that setting up a bulimic like that was a catastrophe waiting to happen. Following his rigid diet has only emphasized past feelings of deprivation and triggered more fear again around food. Not only was it *physiologically* dangerous for me not to ingest any sugar at all (he even suggested no fruit), but it was also a total *mental* hazard. And I don't really trust him anymore, because there was probably nothing wrong with my appendix.

Dr. Hannibal is aware of what's been going on. My father no longer sees him regularly but went in a few times to discuss his worries about me. Hannibal knows about Grant, my semi-nervous breakdown, my quick weight loss, and the surgery. He immediately wants to get down to business.

"Jenny, you've been through a lot. I'm sorry for you. You have never been comfortable in this body since you were young, and you still have to endure more agony. It just won't give you a break. But we need to get you functioning again. You're an artist, a creative person. I remember your Christmas cards (*yes, my infamous ones, it seems*), and the pictures you showed me of your paintings. Lovely. The colors. The sensitivity. We need to get you up and at 'em again. There is life beyond that body. Do you know who Stephen Hawking is?"

"No." I start to remember Hannibal is a great storyteller.

"He has ALS, Lou Gehrig's disease, but he studies the black hole with all his passion. He can't use a muscle in his body, and is completely debilitated, but his mind is as sharp as a nail and he doesn't let it stop him. And Chris Reeve, look at him. And Frida Kahlo . . ."

"I know, I know all about her, Doctor. I get it."

But then he quickly shifts, "So describe more about the second surgery and what they found and the physical pain now."

I give him the lowdown. Without emotion or upset, just the details.

Then he says, "Tell me about the guy."

"Uh, you mean Grant."

"Yeah, tell me about Grant."

Tears start to well up, and I can barely speak, but I continue and tell him about my love affair.

Afterward he says, "You know, Jenny, you didn't cry when you told me about your surgery and the physical pain. But you cry when you talk about the guy. Do you realize that? You loved him. You really did, didn't you?"

"Yeah, I did. I do. But it can't work."

He says, "No, it sounds like you made the right decision. It's just too bad he had to be so screwed up. You must be very disappointed. But you haven't done the emotional grieving yet. You need to."

And how the hell do you really do that?

He continues, "Jenny, the good news is you're capable of loving someone and letting someone love you."

I get angry at that comment. Of course I'm capable.

Hannibal gives me a prescription for Prozac and suggests I try Neurotin (a pill for epileptics, but nerve pain as well). *Him and his pills.* As soon as I pop the Prozac I feel immediately calmer, possibly from placebo effect, but I also think my body is hungry for the seratonin, and it remembers instantly. The Neurotin, though, is BAD stuff. I don't choke on my tongue this time, but I get tremors and wild hallucinations. My face swells and turns bright red too, and now I really don't know where I am. *Oh yes, I am in the pharmacy buying large boxes of caramels, butterscotch sucking candies, chocolate kisses, and thirty packs of gum to chew on all day.* I cannot be alone with myself.

I start to get more and more panicked. I am spiraling out of control.

As I stuff piece of candy after piece of candy into my mouth, I lie in bed wondering what the hell I am going to do. I try to brainstorm. Finally, I stop chewing, look through my phonebook, and decide to call a healer I went to see in Sacramento about eight months ago. I had flown there literally for the day from Santa Fe. At the time, I thought he had done some profound energy work on me, but obviously it didn't help all that much. Still, I have nothing to lose. His wife answers, and she remembers me. She says, "You're the girl with the big blue eyes, right? You don't sound too good. Unfortunately, Zane is booked all month, but can I help you? I do energy work too." I tell her about the surgery, and that it's really serious. I actually confide to her that I'm afraid I could be dying. She says in a softer voice, "Yes, I sense tremendous suffering." Then she says she's heard about this amazing place in Brazil where a healer named John of God works. A friend of hers was very ill and went down there to receive psychic surgery from him. *Psychic surgery? HUH?* The woman stayed down there for three months to recuperate because they provide a hospital setting as well as emotional and spiritual support. She gives me a website where I can inquire about the place. I thank her profusely. She says, "God bless you."

I get on the Internet immediately to find out what this is all about. But I already know I'm going. I just don't know when or how. Then, as I see a picture of John of God, a man with light, soulful, aqua-colored eyes and a compassionate smile, and read that he doesn't charge a thing for healing, and that it has been his mission for the past forty-five years to help the suffering, I am even more convinced that I have to make the trip. I order a book about him called *The Miracle Man* by Robert Pellegrino-Estrich, so I can get all the details. When I receive it a few days later, I find out that surgery can be done without cutting, without knives, blood, or too much pain for the most common as well as mysterious ailments, and it's called invisible surgery. From then on, I keep *The Miracle Man* under my pillow like the Bible.

But within the next few weeks, I am becoming more and more hysterical. I can't stop shaking. I decide to call Cassandra, the cool psychic who prophesized that something was happening with my uterus. *She obviously knows her stuff.* When I reach her and she hears my trembling voice, she tells me she'll be right over to do some hands-on energy work. This time as soon as she enters she says, "Whoa. You weren't supposed to get this weak. Shit. Okay. Let's go."

I lie down on a bunch of blankets and she starts to move her hands around on my organs and at my chakras to try to balance them. I don't shut up. I keep talking to her, babbling. I'm on overdrive. She tries to soothe me, makes me laugh.

I tell her about John of God. I give her the CliffsNotes version of the book, telling her that he built a sanctuary called La Casa in a small town in Brazil on top of a quartz mine where people from all over the world go to meditate, pray together, and get well. And you have to wear all white when you go there.

Cassandra hasn't heard of him, but before she leaves, she riffles through the pages of the book and puts it in her bag. As she heads out the door, she says, "Jenny, you hang in there. Your colon will not drop out of your body again. I promise."

The next day she e-mails me that he is the real deal. And then, during a phone session with Eva, I find out she's actually been down to work with John of God herself. I ask her if she thinks I should go and if she has witnessed any miracles firsthand. Eva says that no matter what, it would be a profound experience and she happens to know a lovely woman who takes small groups of people there. But then in a worried tone, she asks if I am really strong enough to travel yet.

When Cassandra comes back the following weekend for a session, she is not her usual relaxed self. When I lie there and try to receive the help from her hands and her divine gift, she tells me that I am so out of my body it's horrifying. She says, "There is only so much I can do, Jenny. You're fragmented all over the place. Even when I try to work, your adrenals go into overdrive." She says, "We need to get you to Brazil. *Pronto!*"

21. Psychic Surgery

I tell my parents that I am going to Brazil for a healing retreat for yoga and meditation. Somehow I don't think they'll be that into "psychic surgery." Within two weeks I use all the strength I can marshal to get my passport renewed, a visa, and plan my trip with Heather, who will be the guide for me and fifteen others in her group. My parents are not remotely happy about this idea and want to know all the particulars and *have I told Dr. Hannibal, and what does he think, and I should be recovering here,* and SHUT UP! I'M GOING NO MATTER WHAT! I'M GOING TO SAVE MY LIFE! During a week of back and forth phone calls, I tell my mother that I am going, and there are no "ifs, ands, or, buts" about it. I have never been more certain about anything I've wanted to do, and it feels empowering to stand up to them. I even manage to meet them at Ginos for dinner, where I clasp the table trying to support myself and attempt to keep my eyes focusing on them while they're spazzing all over in different directions. I try to swallow my food, and then tell them in a calm manner that I truly believe that this trip might help me. I play up the yoga part. *As if I really could do yoga now.* I may be lying to my parents for the very first time but I am doing this because I absolutely have to. Although my parents both keep telling me how worried they are because I'm so thin, it still amazes me that they just don't get it, how sick I am. But my father is in a relatively good mood that evening, his day at the office must have gone well, so he says, "Go, have a good time, maybe it's not a bad idea. Susan, I think she should." And I can't believe that it's still as if I have to get permission from them, when I have spent nearly six years searching for my own answers. I know I will be borrowing their money, which I vow to pay back, but it is actually far less expensive than they imagined, and at this point I can't waste any more time feeling guilty about the money situation anyhow. We're on completely different wavelengths, and I have been and will continue to be experiencing a personal journey that I don't think they will ever comprehend. I don't even know if I care anymore that they don't. I just have to save myself. Modern medicine hasn't helped much; I don't even think the second surgery necessarily has. I have absolutely nothing to lose at this point—except my life.

Meanwhile, after I have packed my white clothes, my bottles of Prozac and Valium, and my Smooth Move tea, and I am sitting waiting for the car to take me to the airport, my parents both come over to my apartment. And then suddenly I realize how much I have missed them. I've only seen them about five times in five months. *Jenny, now is not the time to get sentimental.*

"You sure now, honey, you're okay to do this?" my mom asks.

"Yes, I need to. I have to."

My hand starts trembling.

My dad sees and says, "What is that Jenny? I never saw that. When did that start happening?"

"Uh, I know Dad. That's why I'm going. I need to relax."

I'm very worried about the fucking tremors, the choking, the not shitting, and the panic attacks. It's endless. I'm also worried about not having a colonic for two weeks, but I figure it doesn't matter at this point. Hopefully, John of God will help with that.

As soon as I get on the plane, swallow ten milligrams of Valium, and start talking to the twenty-five-year-old guy who is going on a fishing trip in the Amazon, I feel better immediately. Just getting out of New York, out of that apartment I've been in for five months straight, and lifting up and away is a relief.

When I arrive in Abadiânia, Brazil, it reminds me immediately of New Mexico. It has a huge blue sky, rugged homes and roads, but it has more greenery, colorful exotic flowers, and a lot of cackling roosters and mooing cows. The *pousada* I stay in is across the street from a gigantic lot of open land where you can hear all the farm animals roaming through the night, along with the gusty winds of the rainy season, as well as the entity spirits doing their work when the doors keep slamming during the night. *Holy shit!*

Suddenly I have gone from gray New York hell to a rural, tropical, and mystical setting. I wake to the strong aroma of exotic coffee, fresh papaya, and warm air, and find myself engaging not only in conversation with the others from the group but also, in bits of Portuguese I pick up, with the family who runs the place. I instantly feel a very strong connection to our guide, Heather. She was born in Brazil near La Casa but also has a place in New England, where she practices Reiki and soul retrieval, like Eva. She is a beautiful, strong, blond fifty-year-old who confides to me that she happened to have an eating disorder that nearly killed her when she was a teen. She says that, through the years, she was able to heal herself of anorexia, but *then proudly* states that John of God was able to get rid of her ovarian cyst after one of her first visits.

The first afternoon, Heather takes us over to La Casa and shows us around. The sanctuary is all white with blue touches and is surrounded by gardens full of colorful flowers. The place is maintained by friendly volunteers and people who have received healings of all kinds here. Inside, there are benches for prayers, and the walls are covered with photos of all the "spritual entities" that pass through the medium, John of

God. Supposedly John of God is a normal man, kind, humble, and even awkward, but when he is working, he enters into a trance and acts as a vessel for great spirits of past healers, doctors, scientists, surgeons, and religious prophets to move through to cure and heal. He doesn't remember anything afterward. *Oh God, please let him be able to help me. This is too wild. Am I crazy? What am I doing? But I have no other choice, do I? Maybe there is something here, though. Show me that life and this universe are bigger than I ever imagined. Help me transform. Save me. Rock my world.*

Heather continues to run us through the procedures that we will follow when we return to the house on the last three days of the week, when John of God will be receiving visitors. There are two "current rooms," and when we stand before him, he will tell us which room to sit in, then we will close our eyes and meditate and create a "current," a healing energy to help the entities do their work. After that we may have psychic surgery if he recommends it. We can have physical (with cutting or laying on hands) or invisible, depending on what we choose. And numerous surgeries can be done to various people at once and address issues both physical and emotional. *My God! Will I get stronger? Will my colon be healed? Invisible this time, absolutely!*

Heather also explains that the divine spirits are working on you during your whole stay and back home for at least 120 days. She also says that there are not always instant miracles, that John of God/the entity may prescribe herbs, and that sometimes it takes time to change cellular patterns. If we get herbs we must follow a simple diet, which means staying away from spicy hot peppers, gassed bananas, pork, and alcohol. I haven't had a drink in eight months at least, so that's not a problem, but gassed bananas, maybe, *whatever those are.* And often people have to come back.

Within the next few days, I become friendly with everybody in my group. I bond with a mother and daughter from Seattle who are here because the girl has just had brain surgery and still suffers from grand mal seizures. She reads poetry and draws in her journal, and we often end up sitting together analyzing her work and talking about what we are experiencing. Then there is another mother with a young boy in a wheelchair who can't see or speak. He was healthy as a baby. This breaks my heart. I try to chant *"Namyo ho renge kyo"* (her chosen Buddhist mantra) with her when she gets upset. I also converse with a masseuse who has fibroids, and a couple with various ailments who are involved in the healing profession. And sometimes I hang out with a young teenager who believes he was bitten by a vampire.

Not everybody knows what they're doing here, but somehow we all seem to agree we were led to this magical place. *Somehow we are meant to be here, right?* We reassure each other. I keep saying, "You think this is all possible? That we really can get better?" Sometimes in the midst of people with such horrible circumstances I feel guilty, like my problems aren't severe enough. But I also know that despite the facade that I have been keeping, I am not doing too well. And when I gag and choke after eating and I'm unable to hold my chest up straight, my body bent and doubled over, I am certain that I do fit in with this group of fifteen people from all over the States and of different ages, mainly because we are all looking for similar things: guidance, direction, and some peace.

The entire village is steeped in religion and faith of all kinds. There are people dressed in white all over La Casa and they are French, Italian, Israeli, etc. You name it. There are Buddhists, Catholics, and Kabbalists. But I swear it could be St. Bart's for holiday vacation. Although many people look sickly or are in wheelchairs, there are also many who are tan, chat vivaciously to one another, smoke Gitanes, and look gorgeous in the ethereal setting with their crystals and their beads. *I can't help but notice.* Just seeing the trails of people walking before me toward the sanctuary is enough to keep me trying to use my legs, following along so I can be with everyone. Sometimes, though, I take a taxi for the short ride with a sweet guy who has MS and tells me dirty jokes. He is a Jewish periodontist from New York. In the mix of those conversations we discuss the notions of mysticism and Kardec's theories on spiritism, on which so many in Brazil base their belief systems.

And it's amazing, because I'm in a little town far away from anything that I think I know, and my anxiety seems to be dissipating. My moods are still volatile, but somehow I manage to start eating the meals. When the cook at the *pousada* serves us chicken and okra and rice, although it hurts to get it down, I realize just how ravenous I am. Heather blesses my Smooth Move tea for me, and my Prozac, and *even my Valium,* asking that it help me cleanse and heal my body and mind and do what it's supposed to do.

When we return to La Casa for the first big day that the medium is present and I stand in line listening to the soothing music that plays throughout the house, I have goose bumps. And when I go before John of God "in entity" and he looks into my eyes and scans my body, I sense that he sees the pain I feel, the root cause, and my outcome in one flash. I look at him with desperation, admiration, and gratitude already. He writes a scrip for herbs I will get from the La Casa pharmacy afterward. He hands it to me and smiles softly. "Surgery, Friday," he tells Heather in Portuguese. And sends me off to meditate.

As I sit, I close my eyes like Heather has told us to do. (Because otherwise you can pick up negative spirits detaching themselves.) I am surrounded by at least sixty people. I peek through one eye and immediately notice a few cute guys, as well as the people in blatant agony, and I force myself to try and keep my lids closed. I attempt to let my mind relax, do whatever it needs to do. For a few minutes I just keep thinking how unbelievable all this is, hearing cynical thoughts, but I shove them away and feel that even if none of this works, this ceremony is based on the most touching, beautiful concept. Then I let myself swirl. I start to think of my family, of my parents, of Brad and Greg. The days growing up. The love. The pain. The fortune. The LOVE. *I would never trade my family in for another.* I start to pray for my mother to worry less and my father to stop being so hard on himself. A vision comes to mind that Brad and Amy will have a baby boy. A boy! I can't wait. I see a happy wedding for Greg and Elizabeth. Greg finally found his soul mate. Yeah! I think of Nikki and of Mel, two of the most incredible friends a girl could have. I think of Edward, of Joan, and of so many of the other people who have been part of my life through the years. I think of all the people who have been helping me this year and in years before. Santa Fe. Tucson. The men. I think of Grant. I ask God to help him, and to help me disconnect, but from a place of love and not of anger or hurt. I ask for help physically, emotionally, and spiritually. I ask for help with my root problem and the pattern. I ask to be free, as long as that is what I need.

After the three-hour morning session, everyone stands on line to receive the homemade holy soup cooked by the kitchen staff volunteers and then sits at the outdoor tables to eat. It is delicious. We also drink bottled holy water (it's been blessed) that we pick up at the gift shop. In addition, I purchase special herbs, crystal rosaries, and a citrine ring. Then I go back to my room and sleep for hours, letting the entities continue to work on me until I go back to La Casa for the afternoon, where I will meditate some more.

Two days later I have my invisible surgery. I am led to a small room where a group of at least forty people have been assigned for our procedures. I sit on a pew between a woman and a man and I nod softly to each, wishing them well. Then we are all instructed to rest our hands where we believe the work needs to be done. If there are multiple issues or if the roots of the problem are unknown, then we are told to put our hand on our heart. What feels like a common desperate-yet-hopeful silence fills the room as we all close our eyes. I lay my hand on my heart, asking to be healed, and I wait for something big to happen. Within a few minutes I hear John of God's voice as he enters, blessing us all in Portuguese and then saying, "By the grace of God, you are all healed." I open my eyes and everyone is already getting up and being led out the door, as some people just look down and others stare at each other in disbelief. I notice some crying, others holding their sides in pain, but the majority just appear stunned. I don't know what to make of any of it. Then, within five minutes, I find myself heading toward the infirmary room so I can lie down on a cot. Suddenly, I am so tired. So fatigued. I feel drugged. I am heavy. I notice buzzing pain all over, but I've had that before, from the second surgery and the Valium. Or is it a different feeling? A woman with a limp covers me with a blanket, feeds me a cup of holy water, smiles, and whispers, "Rest." I pass out for an hour. When I awake I groggily thank the woman who has been watching over me and the others and I walk outside in a daze and run into my nineteen-year-old friend, who has just had physical surgery and also seems to be floating around aimlessly. The entity (medium John) put clamps in her nose and twisted her nostrils. Supposedly this kind of procedure can start to help many different ailments all at once. She said it hurt, but she's okay. I tell her we should head back. We are supposed to rest afterward, just return to our *pousada* and take it slow. I feel depressed because I have no clue if anything happened or not.

After conking out for the entire afternoon, I awake at dinnertime and realize it would be a good idea to call my parents and let them know I'm okay. When my mother answers, she says she's so happy to hear from me and that she knew I must have been very involved for the past week and assumed that's why I hadn't called. Then she says, "So, any miracles yet?"

I say, "What? You know where I am?"

Then my mother says, "Jenny, do you think we'd let you go anywhere without doing research? You gave us your itinerary and you told Greg where you were going. And you won't believe this, but I was on the phone with your cousin Janice and she asked, 'Oh, is Jenny down there to see John of God?' It turns out one of her friends is very sick and went there three times. She has cancer."

"Wow. Was she healed?"

My mom says softly, "I don't think so."

Shit. Stay positive, Jenny. I ask, "But you're okay, then, with me being here?"

"Maybe it can help. Hopefully it will."

"Well then, can I show your photo? I brought it with me. The medium can do distant healing if I ask your permission and if he senses that there is any physical, emotional, or spiritual issue that needs to be dealt with in your life."

"Mine?" She giggles nervously. "Well, all right. I guess we can all use some healing." This feels like a breakthrough. Every so often my mother surprises me.

My dad grabs the phone, "So. Are you healed?"

"Well, not yet. I know you think it's weird."

"No, Jenny, if it can make you feel better."

"I mean, Dad, you believe in God, right?"

"I do."

"So then maybe . . ."

"Absolutely. Just don't want you to be disappointed if it doesn't work."

"That's okay, Dad, because I'm learning a lot."

"Jenny, um . . . uh . . ." I can hear my father start to choke up and begin to sob.

I immediately feel like crying myself and say shakily, "What, Dad? What is it? . . . What's wrong?"

"Jenny, I'm sorry you've had to go through all this. I'm so, so sorry. You were blessed with so many wonderful things, but you also got a raw deal. I know you suffer. I wish I could take it away for you."

All of a sudden, I feel stronger and more positive than I have in a long time. I say reassuringly, "Dad, Dad, it's okay. I'll be okay. Don't you worry about me. I'm going to get better. I promise. I love you, Dad."

And I hang up, stunned at my father's very first real acknowledgment of what I've been going through.

Although I feel a bit woozy, I force myself to get on the bus for the weekend trip to a large cathedral, where there is a labyrinth to walk. We also stop at a crafts market. The colors, the festivity, and the handmade items from the huge fair are like candy. The bus almost leaves without me when I get caught up buying indigenous jewelry, accessories, and white lace baby clothes to bring home.

At the beginning of my second week there, Heather takes our group into La Casa. We sit on the pews and try to connect to the entities. We meditate in silence for half an hour, and at one point my eyes open, and so have Heather's. She comes over to me and guides me to the entity's chair, where he usually sits. *Me? Why me? What are you doing?* She gently whispers, "Kneel down and put your hands on the entity's chair." Then she holds my back and says, "Now ask for help to open yourself up for healing. Ask to be able to open your channel. You are bright light, Jenny. They've told me. You just don't see it. You are loved. You deserve to get well. Ask for help, Jenny."

22. *Family Ties*

When I land back in New York City at 6 A.M. on Sunday morning, I decide to go directly to my parents' apartment bearing gifts: crystals from La Casa, beads and woven bags from the flea market, and I want to show them the outfits for the baby. I also want to tell them about John of God.

When my mom opens the door, she smiles adoringly at me, hugs me, and says, "Hi, Monkey Face."

My dad comes out in his navy sweatshirt and sweat pants, in his socks, with his black-gray hair all full and disheveled, wearing his huge tortoise-shell spectacles, and holding the newspaper.

"It's my Brazilian princess! I was afraid you might end up joining a cult there, or getting married. I'm glad my daughter-key is back."

I hug him affectionately.

Then he says, "You have a glow, Jenny. I don't know what they do there, but I think it did you well." And he looks for wood to knock.

I tell him it's the little bit of tan I managed to get in between meditations.

"Come, let me show you our new weathervane. Susan, has she seen it yet? Did you tell her we found a dog one and gave back the horse?"

I laugh because I haven't cared about their collection in ages. But I want to care.

He brings me into the living room, where he has placed it on a stand by the window that looks out to a huge cathedral on Park Avenue. "I love it, Dad. The patina on this one is really gorgeous, and the shape of his tail with the deep ridges."

"You know. You always know. Such taste. I wonder where she gets it from."

Then my mom starts in, "Are you drinking coffee these days? Can I get you a cup—oh, you like mugs right? And maybe some oatmeal? You should eat something."

I take my mom aside and whisper, "Can you tell I'm not as thin? I need to start watching it. Ate like a horse in Brazil!" I am half kidding and half serious. It's habitual.

My mom says, "Where, Jenny? I don't see a thing. You're very thin. My daughter is a sicky. . . ." she teases.

My dad overhears and says, "I hope my daughter's not getting a little anorexic here. . . . You look beautiful. And not as drained. But you need to eat. Come on, Jenny," my dad says, "have a little coffee with me, it'll give you a lift."

We sit down at the round glass table in the dining room, which is covered with the Sunday *Times,* the *Post,* and *Antique Digest.* My dad says, "Snooze, I need more Sweet'N Low for mine. And get Jenny a cup."

"So. Tell me," he says.

My mom comes back with a huge mug, a soft-boiled egg, and oatmeal. I'm too excited to eat yet. Filled with happy excitement! I just feel different. Hopeful. High. Safe. Loved.

I want to tell them everything and give them their gifts. I get out all my stuff and my mother's herbs. My mother says that maybe she'll take the herbs, *as long as she can have one glass of wine at dinner.*

We start to talk about God.

Then my brother Brad calls. Amy is having contractions.

My mom says, looking elated, "Okay, guys, I guess this means we should go. Jerry, will you dial Greg?"

As my parents get dressed, I gather up my crystals for the baby, grab my bag, put on my new Clint Eastwood meets Pocahontas yellow-and-blue-striped poncho and then take a moment to breathe and hold this moment. I have returned just in time.

We hail a cab to the hospital, and as soon as I see Brad I hand him quartz triangles to go give Amy. My parents and I stay in the family visitor's room all day waiting. It's nice to be on the other side—this time I join them while we eat the pretzels and licorice, and drink Diet Cokes. Then I fall asleep on the couch for a few hours. The jet lag is finally getting to me. And when my brother Brad comes to wake me up, I cry out of joy because my beautiful nephew Benjamin Alexander Lauren has been born.

Later, as I lie on my parents' pullout sofa in the den, I'm still in physical pain. I didn't experience any miraculous physical healing that I know of *yet,* although the Smooth Move tea is *really* starting to work. But I don't go back to my own apartment until two weeks later because I am just too happy bonding with my family and visiting baby Benjamin. I've never seen anything more precious in my life. His tiny fingers, his little nose, his mushy face. When I gaze at my brother and my sister-in-law holding him, I think how lucky we all are and how, if he were *my* son, I would never let him out of my arms.

Acknowledgments

There would be no book without the incredible talents, compassion, and devotion of two women: my agent, Betsy Lerner, and my editor, Greer Hendricks. Both these women recognized this story from the first time they read bits and pieces of the manuscript, and took this project and *me* on with gusto. I couldn't have been more fortunate to be granted the opportunity to work with them both. I am grateful not only for their amazing technical skills but for their constant patience, enthusiasm, and friendship. Thank you with all my heart.

It is amazing how many people's efforts are put into one project: Thank you to the entire team at Atria Books, especially Judith Curr for wanting this book in the first place! And the whole gang: Suzanne O'Neill, Tracy Behar, Karen Mender, Shannon McKenna, Seale Ballenger, and Anne Harris, and also Erin Hosier at the Gernert Co.

I cannot fail to mention how wonderful it was to work with my very first editor, Cynthia Green, in New Mexico, who believed in my writing and me. Thank you, Cinny!

And if I keep working backward, I find that there is always another person who got me here (besides my parents). I give a huge thank-you to my close friend and mentor Joan Snitzer, who made my Barnard College days happier and who read my college thesis on painting and said, "You know, you can actually write." When I showed her hundreds of pages after my surgery, she said, "Hmmm, who should we call?" Thank you so much to Adam Bellow for that lengthy conversation we had on the phone and for suggesting Betsy. Wow. In terms of the Joan connection, thank you so so much to Rachel Felder for remembering and caring that I was writing a book.

I believe that if I had not been fortunate to have a loving support team, this book would not have been completed. Thank you to my angel—my mother, Susan; my other angel—my father, Jerry; and my other best friends—Brad, Amy, Greg, Elizabeth, Nikki Geula, and Melanie Beck for all inspiring me, checking up on me, and always being there. And I cannot forget to thank my aunt Madeline Moses and my cousin Steven Buchbinder, both whose kindness and light always give me hope. I must also thank Julia Martinho, who is a second mother to me and one of the most generous and thoughtful people on the planet. And thank you beyond words to my nephew Ben, whose birth and bright face has brought life force and happiness back to my soul.

I would like to acknowledge those whose friendships through the years, and the memories of them, have kept my heart warm: Rachel Zabar, Jessica Aufiero, Sara Botstein, Tracee Ross, Cathy, Michael and Robbie Moses, all my cousins (there are too many to list), Shelley Goodyear, William G., Arthur Fort, Kaiija Knorr, Jennifer Nehrbass, Arie Atlas, Max Beck, and Roberta Franzheim.

I am also extremely grateful for the best pen pals a girl could have during the process of writing. In the early days: Mark Feuerstein, who helped loosen my writing voice in a committed and meaty e-mail relationship, encouraged me to write, and best of all, made me laugh. And in the most recent days: Angelo Rene Jacques for his devoted letters and inspiring words of wisdom and prayer.

There is a long list of people whose intention and compassion to help others is remarkable and I have been blessed to meet them on this long crazy journey toward finding health of mind, body and spirit: Thank you to all of you: Dr. Stephen Curtin, Ellena Vera, Dr. James J. Strain, Dr. Richard M. Pico, Dr. Ellen Scherl, Dr. Jeffrey Milsom, Frederick Verjswiwer, Celeste Skartis, Kenneth Leacock, Prudence at M.S., Beth Franzese, Stephen J. Weiss, Marion Hochberg, Dr. Valdez, Karen Fox, Dr. Kenny Cahill, Tera Judell, Marilyn Freedman, the entire

Canyon Ranch staff in Arizona, Jane Kester, Jim S, Sabin and Robert in New Mexico, Terry Lawton, Michael and Raphaelle Tamura, James Kelleher, Leda Serey, Ron Navarre and J. P. Farrell.

And last but definitely not least, my deepest gratitude goes to Lille O'Brien and Anne Scholder for keeping me alive, and to Heather Cumming and John of God, for saving my life.